# IT HAPPENED TO ME

Series Editor: Arlene Hirschfelder

Books in the It Happened to Me series are designed for inquisitive teens digging for answers about certain illnesses, social issues, or lifestyle interests. Whether you are deep into your teen years or just entering them, these books are gold mines of up-to-date information, riveting teen views, and great visuals to help you figure out stuff. Besides special boxes highlighting singular facts, each book is enhanced with the latest reading lists, websites, and an index. Perfect for browsing, there are loads of expert information by acclaimed writers to help parents, guardians, and librarians understand teen illness, tough situations, and lifestyle choices.

1. *Epilepsy: The Ultimate Teen Guide,* by Kathlyn Gay and Sean McGarrahan, 2002.
2. *Stress Relief: The Ultimate Teen Guide,* by Mark Powell, 2002.
3. *Learning Disabilities: The Ultimate Teen Guide,* by Penny Hutchins Paquette and Cheryl Gerson Tuttle, 2003.
4. *Making Sexual Decisions: The Ultimate Teen Guide,* by L. Kris Gowen, 2003.
5. *Asthma: The Ultimate Teen Guide,* by Penny Hutchins Paquette, 2003.
6. *Cultural Diversity—Conflicts and Challenges: The Ultimate Teen Guide,* by Kathlyn Gay, 2003.
7. *Diabetes: The Ultimate Teen Guide,* by Katherine J. Moran, 2004.
8. *When Will I Stop Hurting? Teens, Loss, and Grief: The Ultimate Teen Guide to Dealing with Grief,* by Ed Myers, 2004.
9. *Volunteering: The Ultimate Teen Guide,* by Kathlyn Gay, 2004.
10. *Organ Transplants—A Survival Guide for the Entire Family: The Ultimate Teen Guide,* by Tina P. Schwartz, 2005.
11. *Medications: The Ultimate Teen Guide,* by Cheryl Gerson Tuttle, 2005.
12. *Image and Identity—Becoming the Person You Are: The Ultimate Teen Guide,* by L. Kris Gowen and Molly C. McKenna, 2005.
13. *Apprenticeship: The Ultimate Teen Guide,* by Penny Hutchins Paquette, 2005.
14. *Cystic Fibrosis: The Ultimate Teen Guide,* by Melanie Ann Apel, 2006.
15. *Religion and Spirituality in America: The Ultimate Teen Guide,* by Kathlyn Gay, 2006.
16. *Gender Identity: The Ultimate Teen Guide,* by Cynthia L. Winfield, 2007.

# SHYNESS

## THE ULTIMATE TEEN GUIDE

**BERNARDO J. CARDUCCI, PhD,
AND LISA KAISER**

IT HAPPENED TO ME, NO. 44

ROWMAN & LITTLEFIELD
*Lanham • Boulder • New York • London*

Published by Rowman & Littlefield
A wholly owned subsidiary of The Rowman & Littlefield Publishing Group, Inc.
4501 Forbes Boulevard, Suite 200, Lanham, Maryland 20706
www.rowman.com

Unit A, Whitacre Mews, 26-34 Stannary Street, London SE11 4AB

British Library Cataloguing in Publication Information Available

**Library of Congress Cataloging-in-Publication Data**
Carducci, Bernardo J.
    Shyness : the ultimate teen guide / Bernardo J. Carducci, Ph.D, and Lisa Kaiser.
       pages cm. — (It happened to me ; no. 44)
    Includes bibliographical references and index.
    ISBN 978-1-4422-3046-0 (hardback : alk. paper) — ISBN 978-1-4422-3047-7 (ebook)
  1. Bashfulness in adolescence—Juvenile literature. I. Kaiser, Lisa. II. Title.
    BF724.3.B36C367 2015
    155.5'18232—dc23
                                                                    2014049609

∞™ The paper used in this publication meets the minimum requirements of American
National Standard for Information Sciences—Permanence of Paper for Printed Library
Materials, ANSI/NISO Z39.48-1992.

Printed in the United States of America

*To Caiden, my granddaughter; Rozana, my only child;*
*and Seth, the best son-in-law a father-in-law could ask for.*
*Thank you all for bringing me so much joy and happiness.*

—Bernardo J. Carducci

*To the adventurous spirit of John Larsen Kaiser.*

—Lisa Kaiser

# Contents

# Acknowledgments

There are plenty of individuals who helped make *Shyness: The Ultimate Teen Guide* possible. First of all, we want to thank Tina P. Schwartz, our literary agent, for suggesting the possibility of this book and finding just the right publisher. The right publisher for this book was Rowman & Littlefield. At Rowman & Littlefield, we offer much gratitude to Arlene Hirschfelder, our editor. Arlene provided the right combination of editorial supervision and creative freedom that authors can only dream of in an editor. We would also like to thank graphic designer David Zylstra for his contributions to this book. Finally, we must express our gratitude to those shy people who shared the candid and enlightening stories about their experiences with shyness that you will read about throughout this book. Such stories helped to add a highly personal touch to the pages of *Shyness: The Ultimate Teen Guide.*

## Some Words of Thanks from Bernardo J. Carducci

First and foremost, I wish to acknowledge the support I received from Lisa Kaiser, my coauthor, research associate, and longtime friend. Lisa makes the difficult process of writing a book so much fun. Through our many collaborative efforts over the last fifteen years, I have come to count on Lisa and trusted her to help me craft my message to help shy individuals of all ages and around the world deal more effectively with their shyness than I ever would have been able to do alone. At Indiana University Southeast, I am grateful to Gabrielle Carr, Melanie Hughes, Bonita Mason, Maria Accardi, Kate Moore, Marty Rosen, and Jacqueline Johnson for being the type of reference librarians who were always there to help me find the many references and resources necessary to write this book, even when I gave them almost no time to do so. I would like to express my gratitude to M. Justin Miller for his efforts as a research assistant to do what needed to be done in a timely and conscientious manner when asked to do so. Finally, I must acknowledge the special friendship provided to me by Kathleen Bailey. While writing this book, Kathleen was always there to keep me on track, make me laugh, and provide me with encouragement when writer's block seemed to get the better of me.

## Some Words of Thanks from Lisa Kaiser

Although writing is a rather solitary activity, I must acknowledge the support of a very special community of individuals. As always, I acknowledge the support of the Kaiser family, who have always encouraged me to follow my dream to become a writer, even when that dream seemed impossible. I also want to acknowledge my "literary family" of individuals in the Bay View writers' group for their support and insights: Paul Gurda, Kristine Hansen, Sheila Julson, Neill Kleven, Leon Lynn, Elke Sommers, Danielle Switalski, and Michael Timm. Bernardo Carducci has been a steady friend and partner for many years on collaborations that will help shy people reach their full potential. Steven Salmon shared many laughs about the writing life as I worked on this manuscript. I thank Tina P. Schwartz of the Purcell Agency for discovering me and deciding to take on this project while we attended the invaluable University of Wisconsin Writers' Institute. Editor Arlene Hirschfelder provided a helpful critique that made *Shyness: The Ultimate Teen Guide* a better book. And Joseph Ohm deserves my gratitude for his kindness and humor before, during, and after the creation of this book.

# Introduction

## It Happened to Me: I Was Shy

Shyness is one of the most fascinating personality traits—and one of the most misunderstood. You can find shy people in any country or culture, at any time in the life span, and in any social encounter. Yet most people, including shy people themselves, don't understand their thoughts, feelings, and impulses when they're feeling shy. I hope that this book helps you understand your own shyness, as well as the shyness in others. Shyness is part of the universal human condition—and it keeps us apart.

I should know. I was a shy teenager.

Not many people who knew me back then would have considered me to be shy. If you weren't looking too closely, you would have missed all of the classic signs of being shy that I was experiencing. On the surface at least, I didn't fit the stereotype of a shy person. I had strong friendships with guys I knew from school and my after-school job at a fast-food joint. I participated in class and in extracurricular activities and I got good grades. I even had a few girlfriends in high school.

So why do I say I was shy back then?

Because I couldn't do what I considered to be important: I couldn't talk to attractive girls who I didn't really know. In fact, I couldn't even approach them and introduce myself. And isn't that what a strong, confident, all-American teenage guy is supposed to do?

Not this all-American guy.

When I'd see a girl I wanted to meet, I'd get very nervous. I could feel my heart race. My palms would get sweaty. My mouth would get dry and I just didn't feel comfortable. I was on edge. Jumpy. Jittery. I was sure that everyone could see those physical reactions, too, and it made me feel self-conscious and embarrassed.

While all of this physical stuff was going on, my mind would race. Not only would I think about my nerves and sweaty palms and discomfort, but I'd try to think up something clever to say to the object of my affection. I'd think, "What's that great joke I heard the other day? What's that line that worked for my friend? Would I sound stupid if I talked about the weather?" Not surprisingly, I'd get so caught up in these jumbled, negative thoughts that I'd let the moment pass me by.

After a few of these experiences, I doubted my ability to talk to a pretty girl so much that I never was able to work up the courage to do it. I'd see my friends approach young women with some success, but I didn't think that I was as clever as they were. And that made the little bit of confidence that I did have melt away until it was nothing.

But, as I said, I did have a few girlfriends during high school, despite my shyness. I was a typical shy guy, though. I dated later than my peers. I was a late bloomer who was slow to warm up to dating. Plus, I didn't meet my girlfriends by approaching them when they were total strangers. I asked them out after we knew each other for a while so that when I did take the risk of asking them out, it was a calculated risk. Although I was nervous about doing it, I thought that I had a good chance of not getting rejected. And I was right.

## Why I Study Shyness

My teenage experiences with shyness were so profound that when I was a college student I read everything I could find about shyness. While there wasn't a lot of research about shy people at the time, I learned more about what makes shy people (including myself) tick, as well as what can be done to help people become less shy.

The topic was so fascinating to me that I decided to focus on shyness during my career as a psychology professor. A big part of my research is simply listening to shy people. They tell me their secrets, their hopes, their fears, and their frustrations. In return, I analyze what they have in common and how they can become what I call "successfully shy."

I don't want shy people to become extroverts and completely change their personalities. I want shy people to be aware of their shyness and be in control of it. I've found that there are some simple steps that shy people can take to become successfully shy. It may take some effort and they may feel uncomfortable at times, but I have found that once shy people learn how to break down challenges into easily managed steps, they will be able to minimize the risk of connecting with other people and be successfully shy.

That's exactly what I did when I asked out girls who were already familiar to me, instead of total strangers. I knew that I liked them and they liked me, at least a little bit, and that we had something in common and could have fun together without a lot of uncomfortable silences. As a result, I was able to ask them out, be myself with them, and not feel held back by my shyness.

That's exactly what I want shy people to be able to do, too.

## If You Are Shy

If you picked up this book, either you are shy, you are close to someone who is shy, or you're interested in learning more about this fascinating personality trait.

If you are shy, you are not alone although it may feel that way at times. As I'll explain throughout this book, being shy is incredibly common and a normal reaction to unfamiliar people, places, and activities. According to one of my studies in which more than 1,100 people over the course of eight years responded to my shyness survey, almost half of all people say that they are shy, and almost every individual says that he has felt shy at times in his life—perhaps in the childhood or teen years, when getting to know a new person or when transitioning to a new, unfamiliar situation, such as starting a new school.[1]

Throughout this book I'll provide "shy stories" from people who are shy or who were shy, especially during their teen years. These stories were provided by the thousands of people across the globe who responded to my survey. We don't often ask shy people about what it's like to be shy, which is why these stories are so fascinating. If you are shy, I hope that you will relate to these shy stories and consider sharing your own story with those who are close to you. If you do share your own shy experiences, you will feel less isolated and probably discover that many other people share your thoughts, feelings, and behaviors when they're feeling shy.

## If Your Friend Is Shy

If you picked up this book because you are close to someone who is shy and you want to understand him or her a little bit better, you'll learn about what shy people experience. There's a lot going on under the surface. While shy people may appear to be calm or perhaps even cold during social situations, underneath their skin their minds are wired, adrenaline is pumping through their veins, and their emotions are boiling. That's a lot to deal with when you're trying to talk to another person, which is why a shy person typically clams up or avoids social situations altogether.

And that's why telling a shy person to "get over it" doesn't work. What does work is a deeper understanding of what I call the shy body, mind, and self and then working through some simple steps that help a shy person expand what I call the comfort zone—the situations in which a shy person is free of his or her shyness. As a friend of a shy person, you can help to expand your pal's comfort zone and perhaps learn more about yourself, too.

## If You Are Interested in Shy People

If you picked up this book because you are interested in shyness, you are in good company. So many prominent and talented researchers have delved into shyness from varying perspectives. Biologists are looking at whether shyness is genetic and whether shy people are wired differently than more outgoing people. Psychologists are examining why shyness appears and what shy people have in common with other shy people. Sociologists are discovering how shyness and culture intersect, especially how shy people interact with social media and technology.

## How to Use This Book

Throughout this book, with the help of my writing colleague, Lisa Kaiser, I'll present cutting-edge findings from researchers working today, as well as classic research that has stood the test of time. I will also present my own research and shy stories so that you can understand how the academic findings relate to real life. I will also offer points to reflect upon and activities that you can work through so that you can discover how shyness affects your life, too.

—Bernardo J. Carducci

# GETTING TO KNOW
# SHY TEENS

# WHAT DO SHY
# TEENS LOOK LIKE?

Shyness is one of the most common personality traits—and one of the most misunderstood.

To learn more about the experiences of shy people, I developed a comprehensive survey about shyness, which has received more than 1,100 responses.[1] The results show that shyness is very widespread. According to that survey, over 40 percent said that they are shy. That means that even if you are not shy, it's likely that the person who's sitting next to you is shy. And in a survey with over 1,500 responses, approximately 90 percent of the respondents said they've felt shy during certain times in their lives, indicating that even people who don't label themselves "shy" know how it feels to be nervous, self-conscious, and tongue-tied in social situations.[2]

Shyness doesn't discriminate, either. Both men and women are shy, and it appears in early childhood all through the life span. Shy people were among our early ancestors and will still exist in the next century and beyond. Shy people live in all cultures across the globe, although how those cultures view shyness varies. And poor people and rich people are shy, too, and they work in all sorts of occupations and are immersed in a wide variety of interests.[3]

Although shyness is very common and almost everyone understands in some way what it feels like, it's very misunderstood. That's because few of us ask shy people what it actually feels like to be shy. Therefore, we never get to hear about the frustration, anxiety, pain, and triumphs in the life of a shy person. These experiences remain hidden, and shy people may feel that nobody wants to know what's going on in their heart, mind, and soul. Their silence isolates them.

Because shy people don't talk about their private experiences, they believe that they are the only people who feel shy and therefore something is wrong with them. That's a shame, since shy people have so much to share with the world. Think about all of the unique insights and observations they have that their friends and the world at large never get to hear.

The best-kept secret, though, is that there's nothing wrong with feeling shy. Shyness is not a character flaw that needs to be "cured" or "overcome" or simply

"I often find that I can express myself with no problem on paper, but if I try to say it, it is more difficult for me. I think this is because I focus on myself entirely too much. Also, I know that I expect perfection from myself a lot."
—sixteen-year-old high school student

"I get really stressed out when I talk to someone, even if it is just small talk. After I talk to them I realize I have broken out into a sweat and I start to go over everything I've said, in my mind, to see if I have said anything the person wouldn't like. If I think I did say something wrong, I start to feel bad. I have terrible trouble listening to people because I'm thinking about something good to say to keep their interest."—twenty-two-year-old administrative assistant

"It is difficult for me to answer questions in the classroom even though I am certain my answers are correct. I have also cried when called on to read in elementary school. It was difficult for me to make friends in school and my problem prevented me from enjoying activities with my peers through school."—twenty-one-year-old college student[a]

grown out of during adolescence and young adulthood. Shy people don't need to remake their personality and suddenly become extroverted. Instead, I encourage shy people to become successfully shy—still shy at times, but in control of their shyness. Throughout this book, I'll explain how this can be done by changing some thoughts, feelings, and behaviors that hold shy people back from reaching their true potential.

In this chapter, I'll explain what shyness really is, what adolescence is all about, how teens experience shyness in their own way, and what shy teens look like. You'll also hear from people who are revealing what it feels like to be shy.

## You Are Not Alone

I speak to groups about shyness very often, because so many people are interested in understanding their own shy feelings and the experiences of their shy friends and colleagues. But one audience member's reaction stands out in my mind. After one of my speeches, an eighty-year-old woman came up to me with tears streaming down her face. She said to me, "I wish I would have heard this lecture sixty years ago. I wasted my whole life feeling shy. I had no idea that other people felt the same way as me."

I hope that you take this woman's advice early in life and realize that if you are shy, you are not alone. The next time you are feeling shy, take a look at the people around you. That stranger you are about to meet, the class clown who makes everyone laugh, and the witty celebrity on the TV talk show are likely to feel just as shy as you at times.

## What Is Shyness?

The funny thing about shyness is that people think they understand what it is but they have a difficult time defining it. The definition that I like most is the one that comes from shy people themselves: You are shy if you think that you are shy.[4]

But becoming successfully shy requires a greater understanding and appreciation for the depth and complexities of shyness. This goes beyond just "knowing what it feels like to be shy." You must understand how shyness operates so you will be able to deal with it more effectively.[5]

To get a clear understanding of shyness, let's break it down into its basic elements:

- Shyness involves anxious reactions (beating heart, dry mouth, racing mind), excessive self-consciousness (feeling that you are the center of attention), and negative self-evaluation (believing that you are failing to connect with another person). For example, if you're feeling shy when walking through the hallway between classes, you feel nervous and jittery, blush, fail to make eye contact, and have sweaty palms and a dry mouth—these are your anxious reactions. You think that everyone is watching you—that's excessive self-consciousness. And you think that everyone notices that you have a zit on your chin, are unattractive, sat home alone last Friday night, and will never be part of the popular crowd—classic signs of negative self-evaluation. Not surprisingly, it's really hard to feel relaxed, chatty, and receptive to other people when you're feeling tense, self-conscious, and negative about yourself.
- Shyness affects an individual's physical reactions, thoughts, and behavior, which is why it can feel so overwhelming at times. Typical physical reactions include anxiety, high levels of adrenaline, muscle tension, increased heart rate, upset stomach, sweating, dry mouth, and trembling hands and

knees. The excessive self-consciousness that shy people feel ("Everybody is staring at me") leads them to judge themselves negatively ("What I said was so stupid") and create an irrational belief system ("Nobody at school thinks I'm interesting"). Shy behavior includes avoiding other people, not speaking to others, and failing to approach others despite wanting to make friends and be accepted by other people.

- These signs of shyness appear in response to real or imagined social interactions in which shy people feel that they are being judged negatively by others. Shy teens can feel anxious about having to talk to others while walking through a crowded hallway, whether they will have to do so or not. They imagine these conversations, which makes them feel more nervous about having to talk. This shyness-created anxiety can appear during the social encounter—while being surrounded by classmates in the hallway—or it can crop up earlier. For example, shy teens may start feeling nervous ten minutes before class ends or even when they're at home, thinking about what they have to do to get through the next day at school, when they believe that all eyes will be focused on them.

- Shy reactions are so uncomfortable that they interfere with and inhibit a shy person's ability to perform well in social situations and prevent that person from fulfilling his or her personal and professional goals. Shy teens try to avoid other students, especially during unstructured, rowdy times of the school day such as the time between classes or during lunch or extracurricular activities. Because they are isolating themselves and are disconnected from their peers, they will have difficulty forming new friendships, asking questions in class, joining after-school clubs, developing their interests, dating, and creating a well-rounded social life. Outside of school, they may not feel confident enough to apply for jobs or volunteer work, activities that will help them build a life after high school. All of these obstacles will hold shy teens back from developing their true potential. It's not that shy people cannot be successful. It's that by shutting people out of their world they put more barriers in the way of their success.[6]

As you can see, shyness is more complex than simply being quiet in social situations and preferring to be alone. Shy people want to be with others and feel accepted by them, but they anticipate being judged negatively by the very people they want to impress. Shyness is feeling like you want to make a connection with another person but doubting your ability to do so.

That's right—shy people actually want to be with others. They are not satisfied with being alone or having a small circle of friends. But shy people feel anxiety and discomfort when they are trying to make a connection in a new situation or with new people. Their palms sweat, their mouth gets dry, their heart races, adrenaline flows, and their voice is strained or sometimes they stammer.

Think about that shy teen who feels anxious about facing other students in the hallway. That teen is actually feeling anxious about being evaluated by others negatively when she wants to make a good impression. The anxiety this creates makes it difficult—but not impossible—for a shy person to express herself fully.

The reality, of course, is that shy people are not always the center of attention. The hundreds of students in the hallway are focused on getting to class on time with the right materials, connecting with their friends, and dealing with their own issues. That nervous, shy student doesn't even cross their minds. And even if they do notice that shy student, they probably aren't making harsh judgments. Shy people are truly their own worst critics. Other people are far more forgiving of their shortcomings than shy people are.

## Shyness Is Dynamic, Not Static

A common, but incorrect view of shyness is that it's a static personality trait. You are either shy or you are outgoing, and you either magically grow out of it or the shy label will be affixed to you for life.

But this common view of shyness has it all wrong. Shyness is a dynamic personality trait that appears during times of transition or uncertainty, whether you identify as a shy person or not. Remember—roughly 90 percent of my survey respondents said they have felt shy at times, far more than the 40 percent who identify themselves as being shy. That shows that shy thoughts, feelings, and behaviors can appear whether you are a "shy person" or not.[7]

And although some individuals may feel that they are shy, they can also think of themselves as "experiencing shyness" or "feeling shy." This change in perception can help a shy person think of himself as a unique individual who experiences specific thoughts, feelings, and behaviors during certain social situations. This will help the person identify when he feels shy, how he feels during these times, and what he can do to make himself feel less anxious and more confident about expressing himself.

So what is this dynamic shy experience all about? This new view reveals shyness to be an active process in which an individual experiences specific thoughts, feelings, and behaviors that result in social avoidance or withdrawal. It isn't simply clamming up and steering clear of others.[8]

The "shy process" works like this:

- The shy process is triggered during times of social uncertainty, most likely during times of transition. Common shy triggers are meeting a stranger,

About 40 percent of teens say that they're shy. But almost everyone has felt shy at some time, even if his or her shyness isn't visible to others.

being in a group of unfamiliar faces, speaking in public, starting a new school or moving to a new neighborhood, asking another person for a date, or beginning a new phase in life, such as being single again after a breakup or beginning a new job. Some people even feel shy when they're composing a text or a message on social media, showing that you don't need to be with other people to feel inhibited.

- Shy people get caught in an approach-avoidance conflict. They want to be with other people, but at the same time their physical discomfort and shy thoughts make them want to avoid others so that they can feel more comfortable. This conflict lengthens the time it takes for an individual to warm up to her new encounter, whether it's shopping at a new store or making a larger life transition, such as starting a new school.

- The approach-avoidance conflict makes shy people feel excessively self-conscious, and they feel that everyone else notices their discomfort and is judging them for it. Think about the shy teen in the school hallway who wants to be friendly with other kids but is so nervous about having a conversation she can't do it.

- Shyness disappears within an individual's comfort zone, made up of familiar people (a small circle of friends and relatives), places (typically at home or in specific hang-out spots), and behaviors (playing computer games, reading, doing activities at which that person excels, for example). Shy thoughts, feelings, and behaviors are triggered when an individual is outside of his comfort zone and confronted with uncertainty. Perhaps the person is surrounded by kids he doesn't know, is enrolled in a new school, or gets called on in class when he doesn't know the answer. Being in the "discomfort zone" then allows the shy process to kick in, with all of its self-consciousness, negative self-evaluation, and antisocial behavior.

Now, both outgoing people and shy people feel a little nervous during times of uncertainty and feel the shy process at a certain level. But more outgoing people—and successfully shy people—use social skills to get them through these tough encounters outside of their comfort zone. They know how to introduce themselves with confidence, calm their nerves, seek out social support networks, refuse to believe their negative self-talk, and shrug off rejection or social stumbles without feeling like a total failure.

Shy people, on the other hand, typically don't have these social skills. Instead, they focus on themselves in a negative way while believing that everyone else is effortlessly relaxed and talkative. "I'm not outgoing like that," they tell themselves. "And I will never be like that."

This is an example of what psychologists call social saliency, which means that people focus their attention on the qualities that are important to them and what they feel they are missing.[9] What gets their attention is what they want. When shy people look at a room full of people, they pay attention to the most bubbly,

## Time for Reflection

Take out a notebook or pull out a tablet or your phone, whatever medium you use to record your thoughts. Now, think about the last time you felt uncertain in a social situation. How did you figure out how to fit in? Did you look at other people? If so, who? And why? How did that make you feel?

If you focused on the most assertive or outgoing person in that situation, it may be because you feel that you do not have the social abilities that person has, which is a typical shy response. Throughout this book we'll explore how you can feel more comfortable in unfamiliar social situations without feeling that you lack any positive qualities.

## Adam's Story

Adam is one of those men who is comfortable in any situation—a party full of strangers, a bar filled with jocks, a formal business meeting, or on a romantic dinner date. He has no problem introducing himself or finding topics of conversation that engage his companion, whomever that may be. And he has a slew of friends, both old and new, who speak highly of him.

Few of the people who meet Adam realize that he struggled with shyness throughout his childhood and teen years.

"I was tense and lonely at times," Adam said. "I would get apprehensive when I was around other people. I was always second-guessing myself."

Adam said he had few friends during those years, just his brother and a neighbor. He kept to himself at school and didn't feel accepted by his peers. He was happiest when he was by himself and didn't have to deal with anyone else.

"I don't think that I was born shy," Adam said. "But I lived a very protected childhood. I wasn't allowed to go out and explore the world. I had to be in the house and my parents always had to know where I was all the time and didn't really encourage me to participate in any programs. I think I got my first real friend when I was eleven years old, a neighbor kid from across the street."

It didn't help that Adam transferred schools in the fourth grade and left his established routine and classmates behind in public school. In his new school, a parochial one, he was teased and shunned for being a newcomer and a convert to that religion.

"I was ostracized because I was the new kid and all of the other kids had been together for a few years," Adam said. "The other kids said that I wasn't a real member of their religion because I had converted, and they picked on me. I was getting into fights with them all the time."

Adam didn't know anybody when he entered the public high school as a freshman, and he couldn't find ways to break into any other kids' circles. He thought the other kids were always judging him, noticing his imperfections.

"I was most comfortable when I was alone," Adam said. "When I was in the classroom I felt like everyone was judging me. I sweated a lot."

Naturally athletic, he tried out for football, but was sidelined for a year with a heart murmur. The following year he tried out again and performed so well that the coach would ask the team to watch him demonstrate some moves every once in a while. Unfortunately, that created some resentment among his teammates.

"They didn't like that I was better than them," Adam said. "It was like, 'Who is this new guy?' They'd pick on me. I started getting into fights. After a few weeks, I said, 'It's not worth it.' I wasn't having fun so I quit."

Adam had slightly better luck with girls. He couldn't talk to them, of course, because that made him too uncomfortable. Finally, though, he decided to ask out a girl he thought was cute but had never spoken to—ever. She rejected him on the spot.

"She was like, 'I don't even know who you are.' So of course she said no," Adam said.

That setback didn't last long. A girl he worked with asked him out and they stayed together for a few years.

"She was very outgoing, but she appreciated me," Adam said. "Once I really got to know her I was able to relax and be my true self."

Eventually, Adam began relying on alcohol to relax when he was out. Having a few beers made him loosen up and reduce his anxiety so he could crack jokes and talk to people he didn't know. But that spurred a major insight.

"I realized that there are a lot of people who feel the same way that I do," Adam said. "I'd always been intimidated by other people. I thought they were smarter than me. I thought they were better than me. But once I got to know people I realized that I was just as smart as they were."

Adam said he still feels a little tense and shy when he's in new situations. When he feels this way, he gives himself a little time to get used to his new environment, looks for some friendly faces, and has the confidence and social skills to introduce himself and generate a conversation—strategies that are often used by successfully shy individuals.

He had some words of advice for shy teens who are trying to reach out to others: "Don't worry so much. Be yourself. You're going to make mistakes but that's part of life. That's part of becoming an adult. And you can't grow unless you make mistakes, so you can't let other people's opinions of you hold you back."[b]

outgoing people there because being extroverted is important to shy people. They don't notice the quieter people on the edges of the crowd who are less confident and comfortable. This frequent focus on extroverts then makes shy people feel even more alone because they believe that they will never be outgoing, relaxed, and confident around other people.

## What Is Adolescence?

Like shyness, adolescence is also misunderstood. Most people think of it as those "in-between" years that span from childhood and adulthood. This is supposed to be a carefree time when teens have some independence but don't have adult responsibilities of full-time work, parenting, and being in a committed, intimate relationship. And, of course, this is when teens have to cope with a lot of physical changes, from growth spurts to raging hormones.

All of those things are true, but psychologists know that adolescence is serious business. In fact, far from being a carefree time in life, adolescence has a very specific purpose.[10]

Although many psychologists have studied adolescence, the researcher who focused on its purpose was Erik Erikson, who identified stages in life and the purpose of each phase. According to Erikson, the task or purpose of each stage has to be mastered before an individual can move on—psychologically, at least—to the next phase in life.[11]

For example, infants must learn how to trust their primary caretaker, typically their mother or father. When they see their parent come near, infants need to learn that their basic needs will be met, that they will be fed, get their diapers changed, and be safe from harm. If babies never learn to trust their caretakers, they will have a difficult time forming relationships with others in the future, whether it's other members of their family or friends outside of the home.

According to Erikson, the purpose of adolescence is to build a unique identity.[12] The questions that teens need to answer are, Who am I? Which groups do I belong to? What am I good at? What do I want to do with my life?

For Erikson, adolescence begins around age twelve and lasts until age eighteen or twenty, which is roughly the years that span junior high to high school graduation or the first few years after graduation. During this time, adolescents begin to experiment with their identity. Teens seem to change constantly. In fact, that's what they're supposed to do. Adolescents are supposed to try new activities and develop new interests, perhaps by trying out for an athletic team or hanging out at a variety of places on the weekend with different circles of friends. They change the style of their clothing and hair so that they look different than they did when they were younger—or even just a few weeks ago. They try out more adult

> "I think my shyness stems from being brought up to be 'nice,' to be quiet, to not draw attention to myself."—twenty-six-year-old executive assistant
>
> "I have tried several things to overcome my shyness. I have forced myself to go to clubs and parties, but I always chicken out when it comes to actually having to approach anyone. I psych myself up to talk to people in my class, but I always chicken out there, too. I want to be more open, but it's hard."
> —twenty-two-year-old college student[c]

behaviors, such as driving, dating, working at a part-time job, volunteering, and becoming more independent of their parents.

What's more, adolescents usually experiment with what Erikson calls a negative identity, which is an identity that is unlike what others expect.[13] This is commonly known as teenage rebellion. For example, a straight-A student could fail a class; a shy teen may drink alcohol to become the life of the party; an overweight teen could develop an eating disorder to lose weight. In moderation, flirting with a negative identity isn't a bad thing and is part of the process of growing up, but when taken to the extreme, the teen could fall into some self-defeating behaviors and alienate friends and family.

As teens grow toward adulthood, they get closer to finding the identity that fits them the best. By experimenting with new behaviors and relationships, older teens will find out that they like to do certain activities, have a better sense of what they want to do for a career, and are drawn to people who are like them but don't pressure them to act in a specific way.

## The Slow-to-Warm-Up Teen

All adolescents, including shy adolescents, have to experiment with different behaviors and identities to figure out who they truly are. But I believe that it takes shy teens a little longer to develop their identity because they have a difficult time experimenting and adjusting to the people, places, and behaviors that are outside of their narrow comfort zone.

I think of shy people who take a little bit longer to adapt to new situations outside of their comfort zone as being slow to warm up. Everybody has to warm up to new people or new activities. But shy people typically need more time to warm up during new social situations than more outgoing people.[14]

**Try This**

Everybody needs time to warm up to new people, situations, and activities. When you are feeling uncomfortable in a new situation, remember that you may need more time to warm up to it. Take a deep breath, look around for a familiar face, or simply allow yourself to be quiet as you warm up. Do not assume that because you feel nervous or anxious that you do not belong there or that you will never feel comfortable. Eventually, you will warm up and feel comfortable and confident.

For example, I was slow to warm up to dating. Back when I was a teenager, I watched my guy friends ask out girls and go out on dates, but I was too shy to do so when my friends started dating. I eventually did work up the courage to ask a girl out on a date, but by that time my guy friends had already dated for quite a while, had girlfriends and gone through breakups, and were thoroughly comfortable with dating and rejection.

My experience is pretty typical of shy teenage boys, but teens can be slow to warm up to any new activity, whether it's getting used to high school, developing new friendships, applying for jobs, getting involved in extracurricular activities, or exploring career or college options. Shy teens can be just as successful as their outgoing peers, but it just takes them a little bit longer to get there.

## Shyness during Adolescence

Teens experience shyness at about the same rate as adults.[15] But teens experience shyness in a unique way simply because they're going through a unique time in life. So, yes, shy teens are different than shy children and adults—and non-shy teenagers.

Adolescence is a time of lots of uncertainty, when teens are unsure of their identity and how they fit into their social networks and society at large. And what happens during times of uncertainty? People look to others for cues on how to behave so that they feel more confident in their own behavior. But shy teens like Adam get stuck in their own self-consciousness or self-focused thoughts, and that prevents them from reaching out to others and limits their self-expression.

Here's an example of how this works in real life. Let's say it's the first day of high school. There's a lot of new stuff being thrown at the incoming freshmen. Not only do they have to learn the layout of the school and meet new teachers and classmates, but they've got to deal with more demanding classes and a different school culture.

The first day of freshman year can be seen as the beginning of a transition into being a full-fledged high school student. Some students will sail through this transition quickly and easily, while some students may take a longer time to adapt during this period of change.

During this transition, all of the new freshmen will be looking to each other—and the older students—for cues on how to behave, how to dress, whom to hang out with, and how to cope with teachers and other authority figures. The more socially adept students will be able to pick up on these cues and act on them fairly easily. They'll fit in with at least a few friends and feel comfortable in class because they have figured out how to behave.

But shy students will need more time to feel comfortable during the beginning of the school year. When they look to others for cues, they may look to the most outgoing people in the classroom—that's perceptual saliency, the tendency for people to focus their attention on the qualities that others possess that they feel they lack. And then these shy students will feel that they will never be as outgoing, witty, or just plain cool as the person they admire. Of course, shy people can focus on any kind of quality in another person and feel self-conscious, whether it's athletic ability, attractiveness, or wealth. What's key is that these shy teens feel that they lack a positive quality that others have, which inhibits their social behavior.

## The Personal Fable

Not only are adolescents going through a unique phase in life with unique interpersonal challenges, but teens tend to have a unique way of viewing themselves and the world.

### Try This

The next time you are in an unfamiliar situation, focus on people who display behaviors that you admire, such as politeness, friendliness, maturity, and helpfulness. Then model their behavior so that you will be noticed for qualities that you feel are worthy of possessing.

Adolescents, shy or not, tend to have a strong belief in what's called the personal fable, or the belief that they are special, unique, and invulnerable. In doing so, they become very egocentric, meaning that they only think about themselves and aren't concerned with anything that doesn't involve them. Because they are so self-involved, they also believe that the whole world is focusing on them, too, what psychologists call the imaginary audience.[16]

How does this work in the real world? Well, it sounds like the stereotypical teen. Think of a teenager who gets upset when she has to leave the house in clothes she doesn't like; she believes that the entire world notices that she is wearing off-brand jeans that aren't cool. Think, too, of reckless teens joyriding, risking their safety, convinced that they won't get in trouble or cause harm to themselves or others. And think of the teen who wails that "nobody understands me," with problems so unusual and terrible that she cannot fathom that anyone else has ever felt her pain.

All teens go through a phase where they believe their personal fable and are convinced that they are the center of the universe. But shy teens' personal fables are more intense and a bit more skewed. Shy teens, as well as shy adults and shy kids, constantly feel like they have an imaginary audience watching them. That imagined scrutiny makes them feel more self-focused and self-conscious. Under these circumstances, it's no wonder that they have a hard time feeling comfortable and confident enough to get through difficult social encounters.

Shy people feel that they have an imaginary audience watching them, which makes them feel more self-focused and self-conscious.

In addition, shy teens often feel that no one understands them. They feel that nobody else has ever felt shy, awkward, and tense in social situations. They look around the room and see people who they assume are having fun, are completely in control, and never make a flub. But we all know that assumption is wrong. Just about half of us are shy, and 90 percent say that they have felt shy at some point

## Can You Spot a Shy Teen?

Throughout this book I'll keep reminding you that almost half of all teens say that they're shy. That may be hard to believe, since you don't see half of all teens as stereotypical wallflowers who shun social interactions. In fact, there are many kinds of shy teens, which may be why they are so hard to spot. Here are some types of shy teens you may be overlooking:

- The Shy Absentee: This type of teen disappears. He is so withdrawn and uncertain of his social skills that he doesn't attend school, doesn't go to social events, and doesn't extend himself outside of his small circle of friends.
- The Shy Conformist: This teen disappears, too, but by looking and acting just like her friends, who she depends on for guidance in social situations.
- The Shy Scholar: This straight-A student feels comfortable within the confines of school and academia, but withdraws from social interaction. His "good kid" persona masks his worries and anxiety about his social performance.
- The Shy Rebel: This shy teen overcompensates for her social insecurities by acting out and breaking the rules. She is often a class clown and troublemaker who likes to shock others with her outrageous behavior.
- The Shy Cynic: This teen is "too cool" to get involved in social activities. He is often angry and feels that he is better than other teens and the world at large. The shy cynic is often a target for bullies and keeps away from other people out of fear and a sense of rejection.[d]

in their lives. Chances are that a room full of people has a number of shy people in it.

What's more, shy teens' belief that they have unique problems is holding them back from making social connections. This belief hinders their willingness to share themselves with others, including those who share those same shy-related feelings.

In addition to shy teens' personal fables being more intense, they're also skewed. Instead of believing that they are invulnerable and no harm will come

Successfully shy teens still feel shy at times, but they are in control of their shyness and don't let it hold them back from developing their talents and living a full life.

to them, they believe that they are very vulnerable and don't have control over their own actions or the social situation they're in.[17] For example, a shy teen may believe that he can't have fun at parties or dances, just like his peers do, because he doesn't know how to act, doesn't like to make small talk, or doesn't have a date. The reality is that shy teens can possess all of these social skills if they are truly interested in learning how to develop them.

## The Successfully Shy Teen

Although shy teens often feel a lot of pain and frustration because of their shyness, the answer to their problems is not to become a total extrovert.

I believe that shy teens should strive to become what I call successfully shy, which means that they are still shy but in control of their shyness.[18] Successfully shy teens understand how shyness affects their body, mind, and spirit and make a few changes in their thoughts and behaviors so that shyness doesn't hold them back from living a full life. Successfully shy teens understand which social situations trigger their shyness and create a plan for getting through those situations. Adam, for example, became successfully shy when he reached adulthood and realized that he was just as smart and interesting as everyone he met, and that he wasn't being judged harshly.

This book will offer a deeper understanding of shyness during adolescence, as well as tips for becoming successfully shy. The next chapter will dispel some of the myths and misinformation about shyness and reveal the surprising truth about shy people and the shy process.

### It Happened to Me Shyness Inventory

Take out a notebook or pull out a tablet or your phone, whatever medium you use to record your thoughts, as you reflect on the items in the It Happened to Me Shyness Inventory.

How shy are you? For each item, record the number of the answer that best fits you.

How often do you experience the feelings of shyness?

1. Once a month or less
2. Nearly every other day
3. Constantly—several times a day!

Compared to your peers, how shy are you?

1. Much less shy
2. About as shy
3. Much more shy

"Shyness makes me feel symptoms such as a racing heart and sweaty palms." This description is

1. Not like me
2. Somewhat like me
3. A lot like me

"Shyness makes me think others are reacting negatively to what I do and say." This description is

1. Not like me
2. Somewhat like me
3. A lot like me

"Shyness keeps me from acting appropriately in social settings—for example, introducing myself or making conversation." This description is

1. Not like me
2. Somewhat like me
3. A lot like me

"Shyness appears when I interact with someone I'm attracted to." This description is

1. Not like me
2. Somewhat like me
3. A lot like me

"Shyness appears when I'm interacting with someone in a position of authority." This description is

1. Not like me
2. Somewhat like me
3. A lot like me

Scoring: Add the numbers that correspond to your responses.

7–12: Any shyness you feel is normal. Normally you are not a very shy person.

13–18: You experience a lot of shyness in your life. This book will help you when you encounter these situations.

19–21: You are a very shy person. With this book and some hard work, you can learn to deal effectively with your shyness.

How do you express your shyness? Record your answers to the following items as completely as you can.

Describe factors you believe have contributed to your shyness.

Describe how your shyness is expressed.

Describe the problems your shyness has created in your life.

Describe what you have done to overcome shyness.

Is there anything regarding your shyness that you want to know more about?

As you read this book, you might refer back to your responses to these items to help you focus on those aspects of your shyness that you feel deserve special attention and effort in your quest to become successfully shy.[e]

# BUSTING MYTHS ABOUT SHYNESS

The first step when solving a problem is getting the facts. You can't help yourself if you don't understand what's really going on.

To "solve" the riddle of shyness, it's best to bust the many myths about it. Unfortunately, even though shy people may deal with shyness every day and should be experts on the topic, they, too, believe the many myths and misinformation about it. So it's no wonder that many of them struggle so much with their shyness. They don't have the information they need to truly understand it and start controlling it.

Let's take the first step to becoming successfully shy and debunk the myths about shyness that shy people believe.

## Common Myths about Shyness

Bai's story (see page 24) is a common one that many shy teens can relate to. It also includes many facts—not just the myths—about shyness.

### Myth: *Shyness Is a Complicated Personality Trait That Is Difficult to Diagnose*

### Fact: *You Are Shy If You Believe You Are Shy*

As explained in chapter 1, I like this definition of shyness because it comes directly from shy people like Bai. Although every shy person is unique with his or her own personality traits, there are some common threads that run through all shy experiences.

The definition of shyness that researchers use is *exaggerated anxiety, self-consciousness, and self-critical feelings triggered by social encounters*. Like Bai, most shy people feel low-level unease—or anxiety—before, during, and after difficult

## Bai's Story

Bai is one of the more than a thousand shy people who has shared her personal story with me in her response to my shyness survey. Bai is a young college graduate who works for a law firm. But her experiences as a shy teenager are never far from her mind. She said that she believes that her shyness came from being socially rejected as a teen. Although she had many friends in school, she said that she never really fit in and was not accepted by the popular crowd, who were very critical of her—especially her physical appearance.

"There are a few different ways that I express my shyness," Bai wrote to me.

In social situations, I may look at the floor or concentrate on something else in the room while speaking to someone who I do not know very well. I also find myself repeating the same phrases over and over again when I run out of things to say. For example, I notice that I say, "I don't know" or "We'll see" at the end of some of my sentences. At other times, I become nervous when I think that I am going to run out of things to say. I'll just blurt out anything to try and keep the conversation going.

Then I look at the conversation in hindsight and regret what I have said, because I usually feel like it made me look completely incompetent or just plain stupid. Sometimes in my mind, while I am talking, I just keep thinking, "Shut up! You're embarrassing yourself!"

I also fidget when I am feeling shy. I shift around or play with my hair—anything that involves keeping my hands busy. I also tend to giggle or laugh when I am extremely nervous.

When I am out in public, whether I'm at a party or another social situation, or just at the grocery store, I avoid eye contact with the people around me—except for the people I'm with. If I know that someone is looking at me, I will intentionally make it a point not to look at them.

I'm sure you can understand how this does not help me to meet people.[a]

social situations. Bai gets fidgety, doesn't make eye contact, giggles or laughs inappropriately, and isn't in full control of her speech. Some additional classic signs of anxiety are a wildly beating heart, sweaty palms, dry mouth, quavering voice, trembling hands, and difficulty staying in the moment.

That anxiety turns into intense self-consciousness. During uncomfortable social situations, shy people like Bai cannot focus on anything but themselves. Bai may be blurting out all of the wrong things because she isn't truly in the flow of the conversation. That's because she isn't even listening to anyone—she's only listening to her own internal dialogue. It's like she's wearing headphones and listening to a recording of herself while trying to make conversation with someone else. And that's impossible to do. In addition, Bai believes that everyone is focused on her, too, boosting her self-consciousness and anxiety.

One thing to notice about a shy individual's thoughts: the negativity of their thinking about themselves. Shy people are held back by their self-critical feelings.[1] Instead of thinking that feeling nervous is a normal reaction to going to a party, Bai thinks that she's "stupid" and embarrassing herself. She's so down on herself that she won't even make eye contact with other people. And she assumes that others are judging her harshly, too.

Remember that these are perfectly normal feelings to have when feeling shy, and millions of people feel the same way from time to time. But when they begin holding you back from living a full life and developing friendships, these feelings can be problematic.

## Myth: *Shyness Is All in Your Mind*

## Fact: *Shyness Involves Your Body, Mind, and Self*

Some people who have never felt hindered by shyness just assume that shyness is "all in your head." They think that all you have to do is change your thoughts and you can act confidently in any social encounter. Simple, right?

Well, that belief is truly a myth. If shyness really was all in your head, it would be easy to change and shy people wouldn't feel so isolated and frustrated. If shyness was just an intellectual challenge, becoming not-shy would simply require an individual to change his thoughts and learn to repeat those thoughts when necessary. It would be like learning a foreign language by memorizing new grammar and vocabulary, and wouldn't involve changing one's behavior or emotional and physical responses.

The truth is that shyness is more complex because it involves your body, mind, and self. And that's why shy people feel so overwhelmed by it at times.

- Body: These are the physical reactions that shy people feel in difficult social situations. These anxiety-based stress reactions include sweaty palms, dry mouth, quavering voice, racing heart, trembling hands, and stammering.
- Mind: During new or difficult social encounters, shy people's thoughts are self-focused and self-critical. Instead of concentrating on a conversation, shy people are preoccupied by their self-focused thoughts about their social performance and physical reactions. They judge themselves and assume that everyone else is judging them, too.
- Self: Shy people's self-focused thoughts affect their feelings about themselves and their identity. These feelings are negative and are so powerful that they can lower a shy person's self-esteem. Instead of thinking about the interesting people that they met at a party, shy people focus on what they did wrong during that party. For example, Bai, like most shy people, replays conversations in her mind long after they're over. Bai says that she regrets what she says—and can't let go of that disappointment. When this negative self-talk occurs repeatedly, it will lead Bai to think negatively not only about her social abilities, but about her whole self. Eventually, "I can't talk to strangers" turns into "I'm a failure at life."

This negative self-focus affects how shy people think about themselves before, during, and after their next social encounter. These shy beliefs become more intense, powerful, and negative as the cycle repeats itself.

Shyness's grip on a person's body, mind, and self is very powerful. In section 2 of this book, you'll learn more about peeling these layers away from each other so that you can identify how they affect you and what you can do to lessen their impact.

> "I avoid social situations almost totally. I become tongue tied around others, and very quiet. If the situation is intense, my hands will sweat and I feel nauseated."—twenty-six-year-old editor
>
> "My shyness is expressed by not making eye contact. I feel like fleeing and start feeling anxious. I worry about what to say even before I need to say anything."—twenty-four-year-old salesperson[b]

## Myth: *Shyness Is a Bad Thing*

## Fact: *Shy People Have Many Valuable Qualities*

We may have a negative view of shyness because shy people have negative views of themselves. But this is just a matter of perception, not fact. Think about Bai. Although she may think of herself as being socially awkward at parties and "stupid," she's actually quite intelligent and articulate. She has a good job, a solid relationship, and many friends.

That said, we do live in a society that values extroverts. We like upbeat, outgoing, witty, socially skilled, assertive people who are in charge of their lives. We even reward people who are willing to reveal every part of their lives on reality TV shows.

But is this really a good thing? I, for one, don't think so.

Although our culture values qualities we usually don't associate with shy people, these aren't the only qualities that are worth having. For example, our culture values hard workers, people with personal integrity, good communicators, supportive friends, and creative and inventive thinkers. None of these positive qualities have anything to do with being shy or outgoing. Shy people can succeed in whatever they set their mind to do as long as they work diligently toward their goal, whether it's finding a life partner or becoming a celebrated community leader.

In addition, shy people themselves have a lot of great qualities that our society needs more of. When they're not in the midst of a bout of anxiety, shy people are great listeners, good friends, and quite perceptive. And our society needs shy people. After all, what would our world be like if it was full of rowdy, aggressive, loud, attention seekers?

The fact is that our society needs both shy people and extroverts. In fact, I believe that our society needs more successfully shy people, not more extroverts, because successfully shy people are self-aware, confident, and don't need to constantly act out to get attention.

### Time for Reflection

Think about your own beliefs about shy people and outgoing people. Imagine that your school was only filled with extroverted people. What would it be like? Would you want to attend that school? Now imagine that same school full of shy students. What would that be like? Would you want to attend it?

## Myth: *Shy Teens Were Born That Way*

## Fact: *Shyness Isn't Destiny*

Shyness has a very powerful physical component, which is why many people believe that shy people were born shy or they inherited shyness from a parent. Now, it is true that some people are wired to react strongly to things that irritate them, whether it's loud noises, an itchy sweater, or a roomful of strangers. That physical discomfort, in social settings outside of one's comfort zone, can set the stage for shyness.[2] As will be explained in depth in chapter 4, shy people are highly sensitive and have extremely uncomfortable reactions to new or difficult social situations, which they try to cope with by clamming up or withdrawing from the irritating encounter.

Shy teens often feel uncomfortable in loud, unpredictable, crowded settings. But avoiding these situations reinforces their discomfort.

**Time for Reflection**

Think about some social situations that you find to be physically or emotionally irritating. Do they make you feel uncomfortable and shy? Do you avoid those situations because you know that you will feel uncomfortable? Do you think that you could become less uncomfortable if you spent more time in that situation?

But this sensitivity doesn't doom a shy individual to a life of shyness. In fact, a shy person can override her "wiring" and decrease her sensitivity by exposing herself to that difficult, irritating situation so that it becomes so familiar that the shy person doesn't even notice it.[3]

For example, shy teens commonly avoid attending after-school activities such as football or basketball games. These events are full of hundreds of loud students, the game is fast moving, and social cliques can make the environment seem unfriendly. The first game a shy teen attends may seem horrible. In fact, the teen may feel so physically uncomfortable that he leaves early and promises never to go to another game. But that reaction, although common, will only reinforce that teen's shy wiring, which is telling him to avoid that uncomfortable situation. A more successfully shy reaction is to attend another game but to be prepared for the noise and activity by taking time to warm up, finding some friendly faces, and focusing on the game, not one's discomfort. This may not seem easy at first, but it will get easier and in the long run it's a very smart strategy.

## Myth: *Shy Teens Don't Want to Be with Other People*

## Fact: *Shy Teens Truly Want to Be with Other People*

Many people assume that shy teens don't want to be with other people because they act like they prefer to be alone. Like Bai, they signal that intention by avoiding eye contact with strangers and doing everything they can to avoid everyone except their longtime friends who exist in their comfort zone. That's why so many teens are labeled "snobs" or accused of being aloof or standoffish—or worse.

But the fact is that shy individuals' withdrawn behavior doesn't match their intentions. Shy teens desperately want to be with other people. In fact, they are so concerned about making a good impression and being accepted by other people that they feel anxious about their social performance. That anxiety triggers a shy episode, complete with self-consciousness and self-doubt.[4] Think about it: If Bai didn't care so much about making a connection with someone else, she wouldn't replay old conversations in her mind and critique her performance. Bai is constantly evaluating herself because she believes that an imaginary audience is evaluating her, too, and she desperately wants their approval.

In contrast to shy people like Bai, introverts don't want to be with other people. Introverts are happy when they're alone and feel little need to mix and mingle with other people. When introverts are out in public they tend to be quiet and avoid excessive amounts of social stimulation, such as loud noises and large groups of people. That stimulation—not the sense of evaluation—is the source of their heightened feelings of anxiety.[5]

To clarify this distinction, consider this example of how a shy teen and an introverted teen cope with attending a party. At the event, small groups of kids cluster, their voices get louder, and the music cranks as some teens start dancing and acting out. Amid this noise and low-level chaos, the shy teen will stand by himself and look uncomfortable. "I wish I had the nerve to talk to someone," he says to himself as his heart races and he sweats and blushes. "I wish someone would talk to me. I wish I could dance without looking like an idiot. But I know that everyone will be watching me make a fool of myself."

The introverted teen, on the other hand, is also standing by herself, so she looks shy. But her internal dialogue is very different. "Don't bother me," she says to herself as the room fills up with more dancers, who bump up against her as she presses against the wall. "I'm happy standing here on the edges, just watching the action."

As you can see, the shy partygoer and the introverted teen look like they are experiencing the same thoughts, feelings, and behaviors. But the shy teen is on the edges of the room because he feels like he has no other choice. He can't dance, can't talk to others, and can't imagine relaxing enough to actually become part of the party. The introverted teen, by contrast, is on the sidelines because she prefers to be there. She doesn't feel like she needs to join the action. She's happy as an observer.

## ? Time for Reflection

Are you shy or an introvert? Think about the last time you didn't feel like hanging out with other people. Is it because you cared about how you acted around them? Or were you simply happy alone? If you were more concerned about your social performance, you felt shy. If you didn't care about being with others, you were acting like an introvert.

## Myth: *Shy Teens Are All Alike*

## Fact: *Shy Teens Share Similar Traits but Each Teen Is Unique*

Although we can make some generalizations about shy teens, the fact is that every shy person is different. Each shy person has a specific personal history and experiences and unique coping strategies.

That said, there are some types of shy teens who can be grouped together based on what triggers their shyness.[6]

- The Publicly Shy: This is the stereotypical shy teenager who is quiet, keeps his distance from others, and avoids social contact. This teen is pretty easy to spot, because he is so uncomfortable in public. Think about Bai refusing to make eye contact with strangers and you've got a good picture of a publicly shy person.
- The Chronically Shy: This is a shy individual who has been shy for her entire life and can't imagine being outgoing and relaxed with other people. The chronically shy person feels that she is more shy than other people and says that she has more problems because of her shyness. She believes that she is less capable of conquering her shyness.
- The Privately Shy: This shy person is difficult to identify in public because although she may feel anxious and self-conscious, she is able to perform well in social encounters. She hides her shyness so well that friends may be surprised to find out that she is shy. In fact, I think that Bai is privately shy. After all, she can talk to others, even if she is self-conscious. I think that she's being too hard on herself. The people she's talking to probably don't even notice that she's "blurting" out things or repeating herself.
- The Shy Extrovert: This individual feels very anxious and self-conscious, but he conceals it in social settings by, quite literally, masking his shyness by being very outgoing. This person is so uncomfortable with his true, shy self that he has to present a false front in public. The shy extrovert often resorts to drugs or alcohol to get through social situations—a terrible coping mechanism, but a common one.
- The Transitionally Shy: This person feels shy during new phases of life that are outside of her comfort zone, such as starting a new school year, moving to a new city, or beginning a new job. Once she "warms up" to these new situations, she is not held back by her shyness.
- The Shy Rebel: This shy person overcompensates for his social insecurities by acting out and breaking the rules. As a teen, the shy rebel is often the class clown and troublemaker who likes to shock others with his outrageous behavior.

Not every shy teen is introverted and quiet. Some are shy extroverts who act out to cover up their shyness.

- The Situationally Shy: Specific situations bring out this teen's shyness, such as talking to an attractive person, being called on in class, or dancing.
- The Successfully Shy: This person is self-aware, is in control of her shyness, and has a positive, confident attitude about herself and her abilities. My goal is to help all shy people become successfully shy.

## Myth: *Shy Teens Will Eventually "Grow Out of It"*

## Fact: *Shy Teens Can Take Control of Their Shyness*

One of the biggest misperceptions that people have about shyness is that shy children or teens will simply grow out of their shyness, with no help from parents,

### Time for Reflection

Can you identify with one or more types of shy people described on pages 31–32? If so, which ones? And why?

## Shy Celebrities

Think that all shy people are uncomfortable in the spotlight? Think again. These celebrities have become successful even though they say that they were shy during their childhood or adolescence:

Jim Carrey

Johnny Depp

Lady Gaga

Vanessa Hudgens

Kim Kardashian

Keira Knightley

Blake Lively

Robert Pattinson

Amanda Seyfried

Jessica Simpson

Britney Spears

Kristen Stewart

Justin Timberlake

The lesson we can draw from this is that all of these celebrities developed their talents despite their shyness. They took lessons, survived rejection, performed in public, and competed against their peers in highly challenging professions. Instead of withdrawing from these challenges because they felt shy and anxious, they went to their strengths and focused on their talent, whether it was making music, dancing, or acting. When they concentrated on their talents, their shyness disappeared.

Although we can't all be famous actors or musicians, all of us have talents and strengths that we can develop. And when we concentrate on these abilities, we are not hung up on our social anxiety and self-consciousness. It's one step each of us can take toward becoming successfully shy and a well-rounded person.[c]

friends, or teachers. This hands-off approach to coping with shyness doesn't work. And, even worse, shy people who believe this myth are doing themselves a disservice. They keep waiting to wake up one morning to discover that, magically, they are extroverts who dive into crowds, can flirt up a storm, and are admired by all. But waiting and hoping to grow out of shyness only makes shy people feel helpless, as if they have no control over their thoughts, feelings, and actions. Unfortunately, passively waiting to grow out of a personality trait only makes a teen's shyness more intense.

The reality is that shy kids and teens need to learn more about their own shyness and actively put into practice some simple strategies that will get them through difficult social encounters. I'm going to provide tips and techniques throughout this book to enable shy teens to become successfully shy—still themselves, but firmly in control of their shyness.

## Myth: *Shyness Is a Personality Disorder That Needs to Be Cured*

## Fact: *Shyness Is a Common Personality Trait*

We live in a society that likes to diagnose and label personality traits and offer a pill for many uncomfortable feelings. But shyness shouldn't be one of those things. Shyness is an utterly normal response to difficult social encounters. It is utterly common, too, since almost half of us claim to be shy. It is well within the normal range of behavior.

Shyness cannot be "cured" with a pill because it is not a disease or a disorder. The physical component of shyness includes anxiety and, yes, sometimes that anxiety feels overwhelming, bordering on panic. Some shy people may feel so full of fear and anxiety that they feel that there's something wrong with them, something that can only be solved with medication.

Shy people also say that they feel depressed about themselves and their life circumstances. This is understandable because shyness serves to isolate people

> "I get a pounding heart, high, more nasal voice, noticeably nervous to others, occasional stutter, stumbling of words, perspiring (especially palms). Overall, my shyness is expressed in an awkward way—uncontrollably anxious and nervous and unbearably self-conscious. Being shy has caused heartache and missed opportunities."—twenty-one-year-old supermarket clerk[d]

> **! Remember This**
>
> • Shy people often ask if they need medication to reduce their social anxiety. While this can help them become more relaxed in social situations, medication, like alcohol, is a seemingly easy solution to shyness. Some shy people are curious about taking medication to relieve their anxiety because they don't know what else to do in social situations. They lack social skills and get caught up in the overwhelming symptoms of shyness. But they can reduce their anxiety and become successfully shy without medication—or alcohol—if they learn how to break down their shyness into easily understood segments and then use their social skills to put those small segments into action.

and make them feel negatively about themselves. Shy people often have the same thought patterns as people who suffer from depression—thought patterns that will be explained in depth in chapter 5.[7] For now, it's important to note that while some shy people may be clinically depressed, not all shy people are.

There are pills that can reduce one's anxiety, including social anxiety, as well as depression. But most shy people don't need medication to cope with their anxiety. Rather, self-awareness and some time-tested anxiety-reducing strategies can help them feel more comfortable and sociable.

## Self-Knowledge Is Your Best Asset

As you can see, shyness is far more complex than simply being quiet around other people. Shy people are bursting with energy and things to say if they could only control their shyness. That's why a complete understanding of shyness and one's own unique personality is so important. You cannot change your thoughts, feelings, and behavior if you don't understand what you need to do. Self-knowledge truly is your best asset when you decide you want to become successfully shy.

In the next chapter, shy people will explain why they believe they are shy. Although they point to some general causes, the roots of a teen's shyness are as varied as each person's unique life history. Once again, shy people themselves will help us truly appreciate the complexity of shyness.

# 3

# WHY ARE YOU SHY?

O ne of the most common questions shy people ask is, Why am I shy?
The truth is that shyness researchers cannot explain why an individual is shy. Only shy people themselves can explain it. Some shy people offer a number of reasons that worked together to cause their shyness; others can pinpoint one uncomfortable experience in their childhood that still causes pain so many years later.

Despite all of these notions about what caused their own shyness, shy people still want a definitive answer. It's likely that they ask because they want to be assured that they don't have some sort of personality disorder. They also want to tell their own stories and share their own personal histories, complete with all of the factors that contributed to their own shyness, in an effort to be truly understood.

Although each shy person has a unique story and history, the underlying dynamics of their shyness are all the same. Each shy person feels a conflict between approaching and avoiding a social situation, and then feels lots of anxiety and self-consciousness and copes with this discomfort by withdrawing from others—the classic shy pattern. And even though the causes of shyness may vary, the steps to becoming successfully shy are more or less the same.

In this chapter we'll explore why people are shy, including some evidence that some people may be born "shy." I'll also present studies on how family dynamics, early childhood experiences, and culture can impact shyness. What we'll find is that shyness is caused by a mix of nature and nurture, inborn biology and life experiences.

## Remember This

No matter what "caused" someone's shyness, the underlying dynamics are the same: The shy person feels a conflict about a social situation outside of his or her comfort zone, has anxiety, and feels self-conscious.

### Cristina's Story

Cristina, one of my survey respondents, is a smart, perceptive college junior who wants to become a fashion designer. She feels that she is more shy than other people, but she says she feels free to be herself when she is with her close friends or alone. She isn't sure that she can overcome her shyness, but she has had some success when she has broken down some of her social difficulties into small, bite-size steps that she can handle.

She explained why she thinks she is shy.

"I have often asked myself why I am so shy," Cristina began. "I think life experiences can make a person shy, but I strongly believe that shyness is something I was born with. I believe that certain experiences added to the intensity of my shyness. What I'm trying to say is that I was born a truly shy person, but my shyness either increased or was lessened by how I reacted to certain life experiences."

Some of those life experiences are shared by many shy teens.

"I think having over-protective parents had a lot to do with my shyness as a child," she explained.

Being shy as a child wasn't as bad as it was later in my life. My peers in junior and senior high school were pretty cruel so I never developed a positive image of myself. Even to this day, I also think that my father's death shortly after I graduated from high school contributed more to my shyness through my college years. I guess I was too shy to share my feelings because I wanted people to see me as fun and not sad. But today I look back not on the bad things, but the ones I can smile about.[a]

## Shy People Are Experts on the Causes of Their Shyness

Shy people think about the causes of their shyness a lot (see Cristina's story above), and some can put their finger on when, exactly, they "became" shy—for example, when they were embarrassed in front of a group of people. Other shy people offer up a mix of reasons for their shyness.

Cristina, for example, thinks that she was "born shy," but her life experiences—including having overprotective parents, feeling rejected by her peers, and feeling isolated after her father's death—made her even more shy and withdrawn. As articulate and insightful as Cristina is, even she can't identify the precise cause of her shyness and she acknowledges that the causes have changed during the course of her life. Shy people like Cristina show the impact and interaction of both nature and nurture, biology and environment, on their self-expression.

Although no one else has lived Cristina's life, some common themes are echoed by other shy people when they tell me what caused their shyness. According to an analysis of responses to my shyness survey, 59 percent of shy people claimed that factors within their family contributed to their shyness, while 17 percent cited interpersonal difficulties such as being teased. Intrapersonal factors such as low self-esteem, physical features, and a lack of social skills were named 12 percent

Almost 60 percent of shy people say that factors within their family contributed to their shyness.

**Time for Reflection**

What do you think caused your shyness? Is it something you think about a lot? Do you feel the cause, or causes, of your shyness are more important than what you can do about it? Why?

of the time. Just 5 percent said problems at school caused their shyness, while less than 2 percent said abuse caused it.[1]

Not all families are alike, of course, so I looked into the family variables that shy people claim caused their shyness. Almost two-thirds of them—63 percent—said that family factors such as sibling birth order, parents with low self-esteem, nonverbal family, or some other family dysfunction contributed to their shyness. About 37 percent said their mother or father's parenting style made them shy—things like being overprotective, verbally or emotionally negative, or being abusive or too strict.[2]

## Are People Born Shy?

Many people—including Cristina—feel that they were born shy. They've been shy ever since they can remember. Their relatives always called them the "shy one" and dismissed their behavior because "she's just shy." Their physical reactions in difficult social situations are so overwhelming that they feel they must be signs of an inborn trait that cannot be changed. Many of their family members are shy, so they assume that they must have inherited it via a "shy gene."

Jerome Kagan and a team of researchers at Harvard University have looked into this question and have come up with some answers. It's impossible to test an adult for being born shy, so Kagan and his team looked at the temperament of babies, before they can be overly influenced by their parents, siblings, friends, or culture. All of us are born with a temperament, which is a biological tendency to act in certain ways. Examples of temperament types include aggressive, impulsive, sensation seeking, hostile, anxious, excitable, and quiet or reserved.

Temperament isn't biological destiny, but it is a cluster of behaviors that feel natural to that person and form their dominant response when in stressful situations. You can think of your dominant response as how you react during highly charged emotional situations. Depending on the perceived nature of the threat, some common dominant responses are physical or verbal aggression, being silent, running away, or feeling anxious.

Temperament is most prominent when we're infants, because babies are primarily driven by their physical reactions to their surroundings, the nature side

"I believe I was born shy and there is much shyness in my family, especially my mother and my sisters. Two of my nieces are very shy and two of my daughters are shy. It limits me and my possibilities."
—twenty-six-year-old nurse

"I think my shyness is brought on by not having self-confidence."
—nineteen-year-old warehouse worker[b]

of the nature/nurture formula. Babies aren't intellectually capable of making decisions to change their behavior. But as we grow older, beginning as soon as age two, our temperament isn't as pronounced, because we become influenced by our family dynamics, life experiences, and desire to change certain behaviors. Or, as Christina put it, "I was born a truly shy person, but my shyness either increased or was lessened by how I reacted to certain life experiences." These are the elements that make up the nurture side of the equation.

During their research, Kagan and his team tested babies' physical reactions to new stimulants. They would present infants with new and potentially uncomfortable things, such as a cotton swab dipped in something foul smelling, loud noises, and new people. They found that about 40 percent of babies they tested didn't have a strong reaction to the stimulation. But 20 percent of all of the babies they looked at had a highly reactive temperament, sometimes known as an inhibited temperament. These infants were highly sensitive to stimulation because they have very sensitive nervous systems. During the tests, these highly reactive infants were more likely to have high heart rates, dilated pupils, and tense muscles in their larynx and vocal cords than the calmer children. The highly reactive infants kicked and fussed and cried and had difficulty adapting to new situations.[3]

These are all signs of stress in new or social situations. In fact, these stress reactions were even present while these highly reactive babies were in the womb.[4] One theory links this to the season of their conception. A study by Steven Gortmaker of the Harvard School of Public Health and his colleagues found that these highly reactive babies were more likely to be conceived in August or September, with the midpoint of the mother's pregnancies being during the months of December and January, than calmer babies.[5] During the midpoint of these pregnancies, the amount of daylight is reduced and the temperature decreases. One possible explanation for this relationship is that such weather conditions place additional stress on the mother's body, which results in the production of certain hormones that excite the activity of the mother's nervous system. The

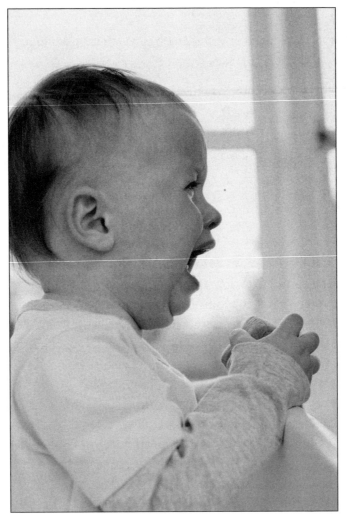

Highly reactive babies have difficulty adapting to new situations.

mother then passes this increased level of hormones to the developing fetus's nervous system.

Notice that none of these extreme reactions seems like the behavior of a shy person. That's because babies are only able to express themselves physically. They cannot tell someone to back off, walk away and hide, or refuse to talk when they're in a challenging situation.[6] All they can do at this age is cry and squirm.[7] These stress reactions are going on under the skin of a shy person during a stressful social situation. They blush, stammer, and have sweaty palms, a racing heart, and lots of adrenaline.

Kagan followed up with these kids as they grew up. He found that the highly reactive children at two months were still highly reactive at twenty-one months. But instead of fussing and kicking when presented with a new toy or person, the two-year-olds showed withdrawing behavior—what's typically labeled "shy."

## Temperament versus Personality

Although the two terms are related, temperament doesn't equal an individual's personality. Temperament is a person's inborn, biological tendency to act and react in a certain way. Personality, on the other hand, is how an individual expresses himself. Part of one's personality is biological or temperamental, while some of it is rooted in environmental factors or life experiences.

Someone with a highly reactive temperament may feel stressed out or anxious in a difficult social situation. But he doesn't have to avoid people or display a shy personality, especially if his parents helped him to make friends and exposed him to new social situations as a child—environmental influences that impacted his biological temperament. On the other hand, if that individual had been raised by shy parents with a limited social life, he'd be more likely to have a shy personality that builds on his temperament.

That said, after about two years of age, it's far more difficult to predict temperament-related behavior. Kagan found that only the infants who'd had extremely strong reactions to new situations were more likely to be influenced by their temperament as they grew up.[8] Some of the highly reactive kids became calmer as they grew up because environmental factors—such as a parent's or caretaker's guidance—impacted their behavior.

In addition, note the difference between the percentage of highly reactive infants, 20 percent, and adults who say that they're shy, roughly 40 percent.[9] That indicates that not all shy people were born with a highly reactive temperament. Their life experiences—the nurture side of the equation—led them to think of themselves as shy.

A different team of researchers—Stella Chess, MD, and Alexander Thomas, MD, at New York University—looked at temperament of children to see how they acclimate to new situations, such as meeting new kids, playing with new toys, and coping with life challenges like attending day care or becoming toilet trained. In contrast to Kagan at Harvard, who looked at the biological roots of temperament, Chess and Thomas looked at children's early social behavior.

Chess and Thomas found that about 15 percent of the kids they studied had a slow-to-warm-up temperament. These slow-to-warm-up kids took their time to adjust to new situations and people. They didn't reject them outright, nor did they rush into them with open arms. Sound familiar? The same behavior, repeated over time, is labeled "shy." Notice, too, that these slow-to-warm-up kids were able to play with other children. It just took them a little longer to figure out how and when to do so, probably because they were anxious about playing with the kids or didn't know how to approach them.[10]

## Signs of a Shy Temperament

While I don't like to label people, especially babies or children, I do find that it is worthwhile to notice if a child has a highly reactive or slow-to-warm-up temperament because it allows parents or teachers to provide that child with enough time to warm up to new situations and people. Some signs of a shy temperament in an infant or child are

- Becomes agitated in noisy environments
- Withdraws from new toys or situations
- Is quiet with new people, at least initially
- Doesn't like to try new foods
- Has sensitive skin or allergies and is bothered by new clothes because they're scratchy
- Likes to have a routine or set schedule
- Is overly sensitive to criticism
- Shows interest in other children but is reluctant to join them

If you displayed most or all of these characteristics when you were a child, that doesn't mean that you are destined to become a shy teen or adult. Rather, it means that your childhood temperament may have caused you to react strongly to new stimulation. But, as you grow up and participate more in the wider world and develop your intellectual abilities, you can learn how to moderate your reactions to new situations.[11]

## Is There a Shy Gene?

Since shyness often runs in families, with many relatives being shy or withdrawn, shy people often wonder if there is a shy gene, some biological trait that has been passed on from generation to generation, like eye color or body type.

There is some evidence that shyness is inherited—but not always. No specific shy gene has been identified, but researchers have looked at twins and other family members to determine whether shyness runs in the family.

At Harvard, Lisabeth Fisher Di Lalla, Jerome Kagan, and J. Steven Reznick found that infants who have a highly reactive temperament with very intense reactions to novelty were more likely to have inherited that temperament. Those who have more moderate reactions were less likely to have inherited a tendency to be shy.[12]

These researchers also found that identical twins were more likely to have intense inhibition than fraternal twins, but they didn't find definitive evidence that this was due to genetics (nature) or their family environment and life experiences (nurture).

So, there seems to be no real evidence that a shy gene exists, although there is an indication that shyness runs in families—whether that's due to nature or nurture is still up in the air.

## Other Genetic Links

Since shyness has such a strong physical component and seems to run in families, a number of researchers looked into whether there is a shy body type or specific physical features that cause shyness. The evidence is mixed.

As discussed earlier, highly reactive infants were more likely to be conceived during August and September than calmer babies, most likely because their mothers had to produce more stress-related hormones in response to the changing weather conditions.[13] Highly reactive infants also tend to have narrower faces than calm infants,[14] possibly leading them to have more difficulty breathing when they are stressed out. That may be why shy or socially anxious people often feel that they need to leave a stressful situation to "get some air." They also seem to have

> ### ! Remember This
>
> ● Whether it's about shyness or another physical or psychological phenomenon, research on genetics and behavior is based on estimates generated from large groups of people. Research based on large samples does not predict the behavior of any one individual and their findings shouldn't be applied to any specific person. For example, saying that identical twins are more likely to have a highly reactive temperament doesn't mean that your identical twin cousins have a highly reactive temperament and are shy. It's more accurate to say that out of all of your relatives, your identical twin cousins are the ones who are most likely to have a highly reactive temperament.

more allergies.[15] Inhibited Caucasian children are more likely to be thin and have blue eyes than their more outgoing peers.[16]

But that's not all. There's some evidence that there's a "shy brain," at least during childhood. Research measuring activity in the two sides of the brain found that inhibited children had more active right hemispheres than the more outgoing children.[17] But these assorted differences do not necessarily exist in shy or outgoing adults, indicating that shyness is a mix of nature and nurture, biology and life experiences.[18]

## Your Family Is Your First Social Circle

Now that we've covered the nature side of shyness, let's look at the nurture factors that influence one's temperament. Perhaps the most powerful influence is one's family. In fact, about 58 percent of the shy people in my study said that family factors caused their shyness. More than half of them said that the way that their parents dealt with them was the cause, for example, by being overprotective or critical of them. Cristina, for example, says she thinks her overprotective parents had "a lot" to do with her shyness when she was a child. So did Adam, who shared his story in Chapter 1. About a third of shy people said that family characteristics—divorce, birth order, or parents with low self-esteem—were the cause.[19]

Cristina and Adam are correct about the power of overprotective parents on a temperamentally inhibited child. A wide range of studies have shown that parents of shy kids are more likely to be highly protective or very controlling of their children.[20] These parents tend to dominate their kids, don't allow them to make their own decisions, and don't foster a sense of independence.

It's easy to see how a child would become fearful of new or unpredictable social situations and highly self-conscious if her parents were always hovering in the background, offering nothing but criticism and second-guessing. For example, imagine a birthday party where a domineering mom is constantly nudging her daughter to join in games, teases her about being a scaredy-cat, intervenes if she sees her child make a mistake, and then scolds the child for not being perfect. In this way, the inhibited child learns not to take risks, draw attention to herself, or trust her own instincts.

Some overprotective parents feel that they are helping their shy child by allowing him to stick close to home and away from situations that trigger his shyness. After all, if the shy child is so uncomfortable around strangers, cries when he's in a new day care center or classroom, and has a hard time playing with new children, why make him so distressed?

Well, there's a very good reason why shy children shouldn't be overprotected. These children need to be in uncomfortable situations because they need to de-

"I was raised in an environment in which there was not much social interaction. My parents were basically homebodies and didn't have any friends themselves. Self-expression was not encouraged. There wasn't much communication or discussion between parents and children (children were to be seen and not heard). I was not raised in a warm, friendly, loving, touching family. There wasn't much self-esteem building done by parents. I was basically raised in a quiet, dull environment. We were not encouraged to be social."—twenty-five-year-old health care worker

"Growing up the only child is a major factor in my shyness. Since more of my time that I spent at home was with my parents I grew up entertaining myself and talking with my parents."—nineteen-year-old college student

"My parents' divorce led to instability, confusion, and feelings of neglect. I had feelings of inadequacy and I wasn't comfortable with my appearance."—twenty-one-year-old dental assistant[c]

velop a sense of frustration tolerance, or be able to cope with somewhat distressing or uncomfortable situations and feelings.[21]

All of us, not just shy people, need to be able to tolerate frustration in so many ways throughout our lives; it's how we reach our goals. When we're infants, we need to tolerate frustration when we're falling asleep by ourselves, when we're hungry, and when we want to be with our parents and they're too busy to hold us. When we're left alone during these distressing situations, we learn to cope with physical discomfort and find a way to soothe ourselves. It may be difficult to witness, but allowing a baby to fuss or cry is a good thing at times. Later in life, frustration tolerance is important when we're learning a new skill, working our way through a boring or grueling task, or simply not getting what we want as soon as we want it.

In many ways, shy people aren't able to tolerate frustration very well. During infancy, their mom swooped in to pick them up as soon as they started crying. When they went to a family party, they were allowed to hide behind the furniture or cling to their mom's leg. When they got a stomachache during their first morning at their new day care, they were allowed to stay home and avoid encountering new children.

When these kids were taken out of the stressful situation, these highly reactive children learned to cope with their discomfort by withdrawing into their narrow comfort zone and away from the distressing stimulation. In fact, they were rewarded for doing so, because they got to spend more time alone or in the safety of their parent's arms. It's a pattern that becomes harder to break as the years go on. And it shows how powerful environmental factors are on a person's physical responses to social situations.

The flip side, of course, is that some parents contribute to their child's shyness not by overprotecting them, but by providing inconsistent love and discipline. Research by Mark Eastburg and W. Brad Johnson at Fuller Theological Seminary Graduate School of Theology found that many shy adults say that their parents used inconsistent or improper discipline. As children, they didn't understand what their boundaries were, didn't know how to act in a way that wouldn't be criticized, couldn't predict other people's behavior, and lost confidence in themselves. They coped by withdrawing and avoiding people.[22]

Overly critical parents have an impact, too. In our review of a number of studies, Kaitlin King and I noted the relationship between verbally negative parenting styles and shyness-related feelings and behaviors.[23] To help explain this relationship, we have to remember that due to their excessive degree of self-consciousness noted in chapter 2, shy individuals have the tendency to internalize blame when failing to meet social expectations. So, in response to parental criticism for failing to meet their social expectations, instead of shrugging it off or learning from it, shy individuals are likely to take the criticism to heart and allow it to affect their self-esteem and self-confidence.

Siblings have an influence, too. Harvard University researchers Doreen Arcus and Cathleen McCartney found that children can develop shyness if their older sibling is naughty and requires a lot of attention.[24] This can start very early in life—as soon as the baby comes home from the hospital, in fact. If the older child throws tantrums to get attention, the parents will rush to that child. Then, the baby will learn that her needs aren't as important as her naughty sibling's. She'll learn to be quiet, withdraw from attention, and become a second fiddle to her older sibling.

## Your Friends Have an Impact on Your Shyness

Family members, of course, aren't the only people in a shy person's environment. No matter how small one's comfort zone is, it's populated with friends, teachers, neighbors, coaches and mentors, and acquaintances whom we may only see now and then.

Shy people say that some of the people in their lives caused their shyness. According to my study, about 16 percent of shy people said that interpersonal difficulties had an impact on their shyness. Examples include being teased, being called on in class, and trying to gain the approval of someone the shy person feels is important.[25]

Cristina, who believes she was born shy, also identified the influence of her peers on her shyness during adolescence. She claimed that being a shy child wasn't as bad as being a shy teen who was on the receiving end of her peers' cruelty.

Why would these factors cause shyness? When you look at these examples, they all involve a high degree of self-focus, self-consciousness, and negativity—all of the elements that are involved in a shy experience. For example, when a shy student is called on in class and feels unprepared to answer correctly, her dominant response kicks in. Physically, she feels uncomfortable because she's reacting so strongly to stress. She is focused on her pounding heart, sweaty palms, and shaking voice, and she feels that everyone else notices how stressed-out she is. And then, even if she answers correctly, she gives herself an F for her performance. And unlike other students who are less sensitive to criticism, she will dwell on this experience and avoid the spotlight in the future. Later in life, she'll believe that this adverse experience caused her shyness.

Friends, too, can be seen as a cause of shyness. Unlike introverts, shy people truly want to be with other people. They want to feel accepted, too, for who they truly are. This becomes a major issue during adolescence, when friendships become more important and complicated. So when a teen is teased, isn't allowed to hang out with the cool kids, feels rejected, fears being bullied, and cannot cope with the complexity of teen friendships, she withdraws, "becomes" shy, and learns that she only feels safe and comfortable when she's alone. In reality, the

"I think that one major factor that has contributed to my shyness has been past social rejection from my peers. In high school I had a great deal of difficulty fitting in and being accepted by the people in the so-called popular crowd. I was often teased and criticized by these people, both male and female, about almost anything, ranging from my body language to the way I talked, etc. I think that has been very damaging to my self-esteem, and although in college I was 'popular' and well liked, I'm not sure that I ever got over the negativity I was subjected to in high school. My father was also extremely critical of my appearance during adolescence. One particular remark I can still remember was, 'Those jeans show your saddlebags.'"

—twenty-four-year-old legal assistant[d]

teen doesn't have the social skills that will help her deal with the challenges of friendships in adolescence. Fortunately, social skills can be learned, and I'll highlight the most important ones for shy teens throughout this book.

## Transitions Are Powerful Shyness Triggers

Another cause of shyness that comes up again and again is the impact of major life transitions, such as moving to a new neighborhood, starting a new school, adjusting to parents' divorce or remarriage, beginning a new job or volunteer po-

Shy children and teens need more time to become comfortable in new situations. For example, they may not adapt as quickly as their outgoing peers to the beginning of a new school year. But, time and repeated exposure to their classmates will help shy teens feel comfortable and free to express themselves.

sition, or leaving home for college. All of these transitions bring out shy people's slow-to-warm-up dominant response. It takes them a little bit longer than their peers to adjust to their new surroundings, people, and activities. During this transition, they won't assert themselves, will be quiet and highly self-conscious, and feel uncomfortable, even if they don't show it. Some shy teens will feel so intimidated and so uncomfortable that they won't try to work their way through the transition.

But withdrawing from the challenge only serves to strengthen their shy dominant response. And that will make the transition more difficult and pull them further behind their more quickly adapting peers. Thanks to their slow adaptation to new life challenges—what's called being "off time"—shy teens will not benefit from having the support of their friends during their transitions. For example, if all of the shy teens' friends are starting to date but the shy one hasn't warmed up to this challenge yet, the shy teen won't be able to participate in conversations about dating, won't be able to go out on double dates or group dates, and won't feel as mature or knowledgeable as his friends. Being off time will make a shy teen even more self-conscious and isolated and serve to lower his self-esteem.

Being off time in adolescence can have consequences later in life. Slow-to-warm-up, off-time teens can become adults who date later, marry later, enter their careers later, and have a slower career path.[26] Of course, being slow to warm up doesn't mean that they will not ever find love or career success. It's just that being off time prevents them from having the social support and affirmation of their peers. They're always a little bit behind their peer group.

I felt off time when I was dating in high school. I was shy around attractive girls when I was a teenager, and I wasn't able to ask out the girls I really wanted to. At the same time, my guy friends were having no problem asking girls out and going on dates—at least, that's how it appeared to me. Eventually, I was able to ask out a girl I really liked, but at that point my guy friends were already experienced daters while I was trying to figure it all out. To make matters worse, I didn't want to betray my inexperience by asking my friends about how to act on a date or how to sort through my own emotions. That made me feel very self-conscious, isolated, and inhibited.

While it is true that I became successful at asking out girls and going on dates, I was slow to warm up to this new phase of life in which I saw girls not just as friends, but as potential romantic partners. I didn't avoid this challenge, but I was off time. If I had avoided asking girls out throughout adolescence and waited until I was a young adult, I would have been even more off time, inhibited, isolated, and frustrated. And that would have made it even more difficult for me to incorporate dating into my narrow comfort zone.

I suggest that all shy people tackle new transitions at their own pace and in ways that help them overcome their dominant response to withdraw and avoid

---

**Remember This**

Shy people can be just as successful as outgoing people, even though they may be a little off time. They just need to give themselves enough time to warm up to new social and life challenges so that they won't fall behind their peers.

---

new people, places, and activities. Although shy teens may be slow to warm up, they are able to succeed when faced with new social challenges.

## Shyness Around the World

Shy people—including shy teens—exist all over the world. In the United States, about 40 percent of us say we're shy. That's about the same percentage of shy people who live in Canada, Germany, India, and Mexico. The rates of shyness are higher in Asian countries. In Japan, about 57 percent say they're shy. In Taiwan, about 55 percent say they're shy. The lowest rate of shyness seems to be in Israel, where only 31 percent say they're shy.[27]

The way that shy people feel about their shyness varies by culture, too. It seems that some cultures value the individual over the group and self-assertion over silence. Other cultures value the group over the individual, where self-control and muted self-expression are encouraged. It seems that in the cultures that value the group over the individual—Asian cultures, notably—there is more shyness.[28] That said, a shy person in a culture that values assertive individuals probably feels that his or her shyness is more of a problem than the shy people in a group-oriented culture. That's why I believe that shy people in the United States feel that their shyness has a negative impact in their lives, while Japanese or Taiwanese shy people don't feel as burdened by their shyness. American culture simply doesn't value all of the wonderful qualities that shy people possess.

---

**Time for Reflection**

Now that you know all about the biological and environmental factors that can cause shyness, what do you think caused yours? Can you pinpoint one experience that made you feel shy, or do you think a mix of factors worked together to cause your shyness?

---

## Bringing It All Together

As you can see, there is no one cause of shyness. Some people were born with a temperament that can make them seem shy, but others with the same temperament show few signs of shyness as they get older. That's because life experiences have an impact on each person's shyness, especially when a shy person is making a major life transition, such as starting a new school or trying to make a new friendship. Those life experiences can make them feel more shy. For example, an embarrassing experience in the classroom can make someone avoid the spotlight in the future. But life experiences can also teach shy people that they can cope with stressful social situations and shine when they are the focus of everyone's attention.

This is one of the reasons why I think shyness—and shy people—is so fascinating. Shyness is a personality trait that shows the impact and interaction of nature and nurture and it continues to evolve during the course of one's life. Researchers may never be able to pinpoint the cause of shyness, but by listening to shy people we will gain a greater understanding of what shyness is and how shy people think about themselves and their lives.

# WHAT IT FEELS LIKE
# TO BE SHY

# SHYNESS OF
# THE BODY

hyness can feel overwhelming because a shy person's total being is involved in the experience. His body is reacting strongly to a threatening situation. His thoughts are racing. His emotions are heightened. And his self-esteem and identity are on the line. It's like trying to walk on a tightrope, on national TV, with a stereo blasting in the background.

No wonder why shy people feel so frustrated. A blast of shyness feels so powerful it's difficult to sort through, understand, and control.

Shy people do make good-faith attempts to try to solve their shyness, but I've found that they tend to do the wrong things to help themselves. Instead of approaching a social challenge with a plan to cope with their anxiety and assert themselves, they try to minimize their social participation by doing the bare minimum—showing up and hoping for the best.

For example, if they know that they will feel shy when speaking in the classroom, they won't raise their hand, won't rehearse an assigned presentation, and won't assert themselves in group projects. While they may think that they are "solving" their shyness by getting away with not talking, they're actually doing themselves a disservice—and making their shyness more intense—by not taking small yet logical steps that will make them more comfortable when speaking in class. Even worse, shy students will beat themselves up after flubbing a classroom presentation and will try harder to avoid public speaking in the future. Instead of putting effort into controlling their shyness, they focus all of their energy into avoiding situations that will trigger their shyness.

In this chapter and the following two chapters, we'll explore how a shy person's body, mind, and sense of self are affected during a shy episode. As you'll see, there are very logical reasons why a shy person reacts so strongly to difficult social situations, even if that reaction isn't always visible on the surface to others. Once you understand the logic and process of a shy experience, you can begin to break down the blast of shyness into manageable steps that can be conquered and controlled. Doing so will make you successfully shy—still shy at times but not a victim of your shyness.

## Emma's Story

Emma is a freshman in college who's studying to become a nutritionist. She seems to have a good handle on her shyness, since she said that few of her friends think of her as a shy person. But despite being able to control or mask her shyness with her friends, she feels that shyness has held her back and that the physical aspects of shyness get in the way of her ability to fully participate in all of the social and academic opportunities she's offered. Even though she knows that no one else is picking up on her physical discomfort, she still feels self-conscious about her social performance. That's a feeling that most—if not all—shy people can understand.

Emma's description of feeling shy is pretty typical—and revealing.

"As long as I can remember, I have always been shy," Emma wrote to me.

Because of my shyness, in school peers were sometimes cruel. My shyness is expressed by not talking, trying to get away from situations where I am uncomfortable, stumbling over words when I am nervous, not being able to talk well in front of groups.

I have physiological effects (shaking, sweating, feeling light-headed) that I feel but I have been told are unnoticeable. In a social setting, I am very uncomfortable with groups of people, especially when there are strangers in the crowd. I didn't date much through high school and was unhappy about that. Because I do not like to speak in groups, my class participation grades usually suffered. I wish I wasn't shy, but I am.[a]

This chapter will cover the physical component of shyness and how shy teens can alleviate their discomfort. Once you learn how to do so, you will be able to relax and allow your true self to shine in social encounters.

## Shyness Affects the Body, Mind, and Self

I think most shy people can relate to Emma's experience (above) when feeling shy. And her story shows why shyness has such a hold on people, whether they're children, teens, or adults.

Emma, like many shy people, believes that she has always been shy, probably because she remembers reacting so strongly—and negatively—to new, difficult social situations. Feeling shy made her a target for her peers, which undoubtedly was incredibly difficult and isolating.

Emma's description of how shyness "feels" is very vivid. She doesn't talk, avoids uncomfortable situations, has difficulty speaking, and feels that she looks far more distressed than she appears to others.

You can think of Emma's physical reactions as the "body" of shyness. This is how shyness feels under the skin, a shy person's highly reactive dominant response to a stressful social situation.

If shyness were merely a physical phenomenon, it would be easy to manage. Doctors could prescribe a pill to get rid of its symptoms or counselors could suggest stress-reducing breathing techniques. But any shy person will tell you that shyness isn't just a physical experience. Shyness also involves an individual's thoughts and emotions. Shy people's thoughts follow a specific pattern, and they're characterized by being self-focused and negative. This in turn affects their emotions, which are also negative, and can affect a shy person's identity and self-esteem. That's why people say that they "are shy," and not that they "have shyness." Shyness infuses their whole self so completely that it turns into their identity. And it's so powerful that many people feel that they were simply born shy.

Because the body, mind, and emotions are working together, a shy experience feels overwhelming. During a shy experience, it's hard to think clearly, act naturally, and feel good about oneself. Every part of a shy person is involved in shyness. And because it feels so awful, shy people try to avoid situations that make them feel this way. But that only intensifies their shyness in the future.

I've found that when shy people understand the specific physical, intellectual, and emotional elements of shyness, they can break it down into pieces that they can manage. In doing so, they become successfully shy, or still shy sometimes but not held back by their shyness because they are in control of it. Shyness is no longer in control of a successfully shy teen's life.

---

### Remember This

● Shyness feels overwhelming because it encompasses a shy person's body, thoughts, and emotions. But this overwhelming feeling can be dealt with when a shy person breaks down her experience into manageable problems that can be solved. That's what successfully shy people do, and I'll show you how to do it, too.

## The Shy Teen Experience

The shy experience feels the same, whether you're a child, a teenager, or an adult. It feels the same whether it's triggered by parties, speaking up in class, trying to speak to someone attractive, or dealing with an authority figure.

That said, shy teens have unique shyness-related experiences because adolescence is so unique. As I explained before, the purpose of adolescence is to build one's identity. This involves a lot of experimentation, whether it's with new identities, physical sensations, new school experiences, or new types of relationships, including romantic relationships.

This necessary experimentation during adolescence requires teens to act not shy—to be bold, outgoing, and fearless—and to constantly expand their comfort zone. But shy teens don't feel that way. In fact, all of these new demands can make them feel more shy, self-focused, and uncomfortable. When faced with all of these shyness triggers, their shyness is in full bloom. And instead of meeting their fears head-on, they withdraw from them, and their comfort zone becomes narrower just when it should become wider. While their outgoing peers are dating, speaking up in class, finding volunteer and work opportunities, and thinking about life after high school, a shy teen is slow to warm up to these challenges and becomes off time.

> "When I am in a situation where I am talking one-on-one with someone I do not know well, I start to feel like a shy little kid. My smiles feel frozen, I do not speak as articulately as I normally do, I get facial twitches, and my hands and voice sometimes shake.
>
> "However, I think I hide the shyness well. I don't think many people realize how uncomfortable I am. I think they just think I'm eccentric or unusual— not necessarily shy. I am often outgoing and friendly, but if I feel someone is watching me or judging me, whether they are in reality or not, I become exceedingly self-conscious. I can't eat if I feel someone is watching me. I feel as if I walk funny if people are watching me walk by, such as if I walk past a cafe and I know people are watching me.
>
> "I know this is incredibly stupid and narcissistic, but knowing that doesn't stop the behaviors."—twenty-three-year-old restaurant cook[b]

Being slow to warm up to a new challenge isn't the end of the world, but it can become problematic if it turns into being very off time or avoiding the new challenge altogether. While friends are talking about their dating experiences, for example, not only are they expressing themselves, but they're also benefiting from having the support of their peers. The shy teen, however, will be left out of these conversations and feel isolated. When they do start dating, they won't feel comfortable enough to share their secret fears and experiences with their friends, because the friends have already moved on to new or serious relationships and different life challenges. So while a shy person can be slow to warm up and successful, if he doesn't take on new challenges at roughly the same times his peers do, he will have to try even harder to find success.

The social complexity and near-constant experimentation of adolescence is why many people say that shyness wasn't a problem for them in childhood, but it became a major issue during their teen years. That's when they became shy, even though they may have been shy earlier.

## Shyness of the Body

Although most people think of shyness as an emotional or social phenomenon, every shy person—including Emma—will tell you that it's a very physical phenomenon that affects his or her emotions and social performance.

If you ask a shy person, she might tell you all about her physical symptoms during a shy episode. But one of my favorite descriptions of the shy body comes from a hundred-year-old article by British medical doctor Harry Campbell, which I dug up during some of my research. Here's how Campbell described the physical component of shyness:

> Blushing, a feeling of heat all over the body with a sense of suffocation, pallor even to the lips, a sensation of cold water down the back; cardiac disturbances, such as palpitation, fluttering or tumbling sensation at the heart; faintness, giddiness; perspiration, especially of the hands; dryness of the mouth, stuttering, headache, mental confusion; flurry, the employment of the wrong words, the making of ridiculous remarks, and the doing of ridiculous things; silence, garrulousness; wriggling, and choreic movements of the body; inability to hold the hands naturally and composed, resulting in restless movements of the fingers, twiddling of an object, such as a pencil or brooch, biting the nails, general tremor, bending of the legs, such as crossing and recrossing them—inability, as in the case of the hands, to dispose of them naturally; giggling, "nervous laugh," a "sheepish" expression, inability to look one straight in the face, the eyes glancing up, down, on one side, or askance.[1]

As you can see from Campbell's description, there's nothing new about the "shy body." Even in the twenty-first century, the dominant physical response of shy people during social situations is the same as Campbell's dominant response. We may not use some of these terms anymore. Today, we call them stress reactions, which is how the body fires up to respond to a short-term threat. Some common stress reactions include

- Blushing
- A rapidly beating heart
- Trembling hands, knees, and legs
- A dry mouth
- Inability to make eye contact
- A nervous laugh or stutter
- Racing thoughts
- A jittery feeling
- Feeling out of control and assuming that everyone can see how out of control you feel

Although these stress reactions may feel terrible while they're happening, they are mostly internal and invisible. It's almost impossible for anyone else to notice that you have a wildly beating heart, dry mouth, jittery legs, and dilated pupils, for example. The more you focus on these reactions, though, the more pronounced they will be.

All of these stress reactions may be in play when you're facing a social situation that you feel is threatening. What's important to remember is that this is your body's way of handling that threat. As you'll see throughout this chapter, you can use these stress reactions to your advantage and not let them get in the way of your social performance.

## Understanding Your Shy Stress Reactions

Although stress reactions can feel overwhelming, they serve a purpose. They are your body's response to a threat—whether it's a physical, emotional, or social threat—and they are very logical. They direct energy to what you should be paying attention to and divert energy from places in your body that don't need to be fired up.

Most shy people see their stress reactions as a sign that they shouldn't be involved in that stressful social situation. But I believe that a thorough understanding of stress reactions, whether they're triggered by public speaking or making

## Compare and Contrast

Even if you don't think of yourself as a shy person, you may feel stress reactions during a difficult social encounter. But some may start even when you're just thinking about a stressful social situation. For example, if you feel shy when dancing in front of other people, you may feel your heart thump, your palms sweat, and your mind race when you think about dancing in front of your friends and classmates at prom.

That's a perfectly normal reaction when you've got a new social challenge in front of you. But the way people solve this problem will vary depending on how they label their symptoms, their self-awareness, and their level of shyness.

- An outgoing person will think that all of this adrenaline pumping through her veins means that she's excited about dancing at the prom.
- A shy person will view those symptoms as a sign that he will have an awful time at the prom, won't fit in, will embarrass himself on the dance floor, and should cancel plans to go to the prom altogether.
- A successfully shy person will notice her stress reactions and realize that she's nervous about dancing in front of her friends. So before the prom, she might practice dancing at home, where no one can see her, or she might invite a friend or two over to dance, just to have fun. Then, when she's at the prom, the successfully shy person will feel kind of jittery but she'll be able to rely on the moves that she practiced at home and therefore feel more confident on the dance floor.

Notice that the outgoing and successfully shy dancers will have the same result: They'll enjoy themselves at the party. But the strategies they took to get there are different. The outgoing person interpreted her nervousness in a positive way. The successfully shy person, on the other hand, realized that her nervousness was a potential problem and took steps to solve it. It took her a little bit longer to get comfortable with dancing at the prom, a sign of being slow to warm up to this challenge, but the final result is that she succeeded in reaching her goal.

small talk with an attractive stranger, will help shy people take steps to alleviate them.

Here are four facts you need to know about your shy stress reactions.[2]

### Shy Reactions Are Comprehensive

Stress reactions involve your whole body, from the smallest parts of your brain to your major organs, such as your heart and lungs, to your muscles, eyes, and mouth. They even affect how your brain works, including the creation of your memories, perceptions, and emotions. You can't think clearly when you're consumed with your stress reactions, you look back on the experience with disappointment, and you feel anxious about feeling that way in the future.

For example, it's perfectly natural to feel stress reactions when you're trying to talk to someone you think is attractive. You blush, get tongue-tied, sweat, shake a little, and can't form a decent sentence—never mind getting up the courage to ask that person out. Instead of focusing on the conversation, you're focusing on how awful you feel and how you can reduce your symptoms. That whole-body experience may be so stressful and uncomfortable for you that you'll feel that you bombed during the conversation when you were trying to seem charming. Later, you will replay the conversation in your mind again and feel even worse about it, and you'll get nervous just thinking about trying to initiate a conversation with that attractive person in the future.

### Stress Reactions Are Economical

When your body is dealing with a threat, it arouses the parts of you that need to be engaged and it diverts energy from the parts of you that don't need to be involved. That's one of the reasons why stress reactions feel so horrible—your body isn't working as it normally does. But each symptom has a purpose, including those most directly involved in shy stress reactions:

- Dry mouth: Your body creates saliva to help you eat. But who eats during a crisis? Saliva also helps you to speak. That's why you get a dry mouth when you're feeling stressed. Your body isn't producing saliva because you aren't supposed to eat or speak. You're supposed to focus all of your attention on the threat, whether it's a predatory animal or a tough teacher.
- Sweaty palms: Your hands sweat when you're stressed because your body is heated up and the sweat helps you to cool down. Unfortunately, your sweaty palms can make you feel self-conscious, especially when you have to introduce yourself to a stranger and shake hands.

- Butterflies in your stomach: During stressful situations, your stomach releases a lot of acid so that it can digest food and provide a quick burst of energy to either confront the threat or run away from it. It also makes you less likely to stop and eat when you should be taking care of yourself. Unfortunately, these butterflies in your stomach can make you feel sick and less likely to feel comfortable during a stressful social situation.
- Pounding heart: Your beating heart means that it's working harder to send more blood to the parts of your body that need it.
- Lightheadedness: You may feel faint or kind of dizzy because blood is flowing away from your brain and toward the parts of your body that need it—your legs, for example.
- Trembling, stuttering, jittery knees: These are signs that you're very aroused and must take action.
- Tension headache: This is a sign that the muscles in your face and head are stretched and tight, just like all of your muscles are tight and ready for a fight. The muscles around your head eventually become strained and develop into a headache.
- Silence: During times of stress, the amygdala, a small but critical part of your brain, sends a signal to freeze your face muscles and jaw. That makes it difficult to speak—which could save your life if a predator is looking for you.
- Speaking in an unnatural voice: In addition to freezing your face muscles and jaw, the amygdala sends a signal to tighten the muscles in your throat, larynx, and vocal cords. This makes your voice sound dull, strained, and unexpressive.
- Sheepish grin, downcast eyes, crossed arms, head tilted away from threat: This is clear body language that you are trying to protect yourself by making yourself small, difficult to see, and submissive.

## Stress Reactions Involve Emotions

Not only do stress reactions involve your whole body, they also involve your emotions. So you don't feel well physically and you feel bad about feeling bad, too. That's one of the reasons why shy stress reactions feel so overwhelming at

 **Time for Reflection**

What are your physical symptoms when you feel shy? Can you explain how they are connected to your shyness? How do you try to deal with them?

times. It's not just a physical thing or an intellectual phenomenon. It's a physical-intellectual-emotional phenomenon.

Stress reactions create some specific emotions in shy people. When the physical component of shyness kicks in, shy people think, "I don't belong here," "I'm terrible at making small talk," "Nobody here wants to talk to me," "I'm safer alone," and "I'll never connect with anyone."

What do all of these statements have in common? They're all negative, and they're all untrue. The way that shy people think and feel about their stress reactions follows a specific pattern,[3] which will be discussed in depth in chapter 5. For now, just note that stress reactions are not only physical but emotional, too.

Shy stress reactions involve the body, mind, and emotions, making the shy person feel that she needs to be quiet or avoid the situation that triggers her shyness.

## Some Stress Reactions Are Automatic, Some Are Semiautomatic, and Some Are Strategic

There's nothing you can do to prevent some stress reactions from starting. You can't force your stomach to not produce acid, or reduce the amount of adrenaline flowing through your veins. These are automatic stress reactions. Think of them as reflexive physical responses to threats.

Other stress reactions are semiautomatic because they feel automatic but you have some control over them. Think of them as your dominant responses to stress. They seem natural but they are part nature and part nurture. For example, some people may start shouting when they're feeling defensive. They're acting on impulse (nature), but they've also learned that shouting or trying to intimidate someone will help them win the fight (nurture).

Shy people, in contrast, may feel nervous and leave a stressful situation because they're feeling threatened. They will tell you that their response is simply how they're wired or that they were simply born shy. But part of their dominant response is inborn, while some of it is learned behavior. They've learned over time that being silent and withdrawing is the easiest solution to their problems. They use this response over and over, so many times that it eventually feels natural, even though it is learned behavior.

Strategic stress reactions, on the other hand, are learned responses and utilize strategic thoughts and behaviors. These are responses that override the semiautomatic responses because they simply work better to achieve one's goals. When they're used successfully over and over, they become semiautomatic and can even feel natural.

For example, when shy people are at parties, they're nervous and have a fast-beating heart, sweaty palms, a dry mouth, and shaky knees—all of the classic automatic stress reactions that flare up before and during difficult social encounters. Their semiautomatic stress reactions—their dominant response—is to be quiet and hang out on the edges of the room so that nobody notices them, or to avoid going to the party altogether.

If shy people continue to avoid parties or other groups of people, it may seem natural to stay away. But what's really happening is that they are using one of the most powerful drivers of behavior—negative reinforcement, which is when any action you take that reduces or removes the source (trigger) of these unpleasant (negative) feelings becomes more likely to be repeated (reinforced) in the future. Don't like that nervous feeling you have before a party? Then you will more likely respond (reinforce) to that nervous feeling by continuing to avoid parties (the trigger). The problem, of course, is that pre-party shy stress reactions will become more intense and last longer the more often a shy person avoids going to parties.

> **? Time for Reflection**
>
> Now that you have a deeper understanding of your stress reactions, do you have a different view of the physical discomfort you feel when you are shy? Explain.

Instead of having moderate and manageable stress reactions, they'll become powerful, long-lasting, and painful to a shy person's body, mind, and self-esteem.

Fortunately, shy people don't have to avoid whatever makes them nervous. They can also use a strategic stress reaction that's developed by their intelligent mind. This may not feel natural at first, but their strategic reaction will help them out during this party. They could search for a friendly face and begin a conversation, offer to pass around a snack or pick out some music, compliment someone they're standing next to, or simply say hello to a stranger or someone they don't know all that well. For a shy person, all of these behaviors are learned, strategic responses to the threats they perceive at the party. If they use these strategies repeatedly, they will feel more natural or semiautomatic.

## Tips for Taming Stress Reactions

Stress reactions are no fun, but they are a signal from your body and brain that you're in a difficult and threatening situation. Here are some tips you can use to reduce them:

- Don't dwell on them. Not only do shy people notice their stress reactions, but they think about them to such an extent that they cannot think about anything else, such as listening to a teacher or introducing themselves to an acquaintance. But remember that stress reactions are short-term responses to fear. Getting stuck on them can turn your short-term fear into full-blown panic attacks or long-term anxiety.
- Refocus your attention. When stress reactions are in full bloom, shy people can only think about their nervousness and out-of-control feeling. Stop thinking about your blushing and clammy hands and focus on the people around you. Ask someone a question, offer to help someone, or give someone a compliment.
- Give yourself enough time to warm up. Your stress reactions are most pronounced when you're in a new social situation, such as the first days of school, meeting someone new, entering a group of people, or touring the

college you want to attend. But stress reactions will fade away. The longer you stay in the situation, the more comfortable you will become.

- Be realistic. Most stress reactions, like a rapidly beating heart and a dry mouth, are invisible and happen under the skin. Your stress reactions may feel terrible to you, but other people probably don't even notice them.
- Watch your words. How you think about and label nervousness before a difficult social situation such as the first day of school says a lot about how you will approach that situation. Stress reactions aren't a sign that you don't belong. They're a sign that you are nervous, excited, psyched up, and totally engaged in whatever you are doing. In other words, they're a totally normal reaction to whatever perceived threat you're facing.

## The Fight-or-Flight Instinct

Just about any shy person will tell you that his stress reactions are bothersome and get in the way of his self-expression. But these physical responses actually serve a purpose. In fact, the physical component of shyness is so old and so much a part of human behavior that it's rooted in some of our most ancient behavior. And, in addition, it probably kept us safe during very dangerous situations.

Shy people's dominant response of silence, wariness, and fearfulness can be traced back to our ancient fight-or-flight instinct. This is our primary defense mechanism. Although this instinctive response has been adapted to our modern times, it's still part of our physiological makeup.[4]

Back when we were living in more primitive times, we—and other animals—had to be alert to physical threats in our midst. Our lives depended on it, in fact. When we were out in nature, we had to notice motion that could indicate a predator, whether it was a snake, a lion or hyena, or even another human who wasn't part of our tribe.

When we noticed an immediate physical threat, we had two options: to approach and fight or to turn around and flee. Either way, our stress reactions kicked in. Adrenaline started pumping, our eyes dilated, our mouths became dry, our stomachs tightened up, and we became very alert and vigilant.

Fighting and fleeing can keep you safe, if done smartly. Fighting would be wise if you had a weapon or some friends to help you out, or could outsmart your predator. Fleeing can be wise, too, if you have a safe place to run to or if you can be still and silent enough that your enemy loses interest in you, or if you have a group of friends you can join and then develop a strategy to conquer this predator once and for all.

Nowadays, we don't have many physical threats like lions or warring tribes. But we do have more intellectual or social threats to our identity and social status.

"I feel that this is taking me away from myself, because even if I want to socialize, I feel that it is impossible for me, and it is making me more nervous. I feel that I am not living what I am supposed to live. This is making me more isolated."—nineteen-year-old college student

"Socially, I sometimes freeze up. I'm easily intimidated. However, sometimes I think people may mistake my nervousness for enthusiasm (because I try so hard for it to seem this way?). Furthermore, I'm pretty thin (my metabolism works like crazy!) and people say I'm hyper but I know I'm covering up major insecurities."—twenty-two-year-old waitress[c]

These threats include the fear of rejection, hits to our self-esteem, or simply not performing well during a social encounter. They are all triggered by evaluation apprehension, or the feeling that we're being judged by others.

So it's easy to see how shy people's response to challenging social situations—such as parties or speaking in public—is linked to our ancient response to physical threats. Like those who fled from predators, modern shy people are vigilant, have stress reactions, get a fluttering stomach, and clam up and become silent when their self-concept or identity is under attack. They often find a safe space and withdraw from the threat, hoping that it will pass without forcing them to conquer it.

It's also easy to see how fleeing from a threat, whether it's physical or social, can become a person's dominant response if that's the individual's default coping mechanism. But it may not be the best response in all cases. If a shy person constantly withdraws from threatening social situations, he will never build the social skills, network of friends, or community bonds that we all need in our lives. Rather than fleeing over and over, shy people need to strengthen their instinct to fight or approach social situations by putting themselves in somewhat threatening situations, armed with a strategy to conquer them.

## The Approach-Avoidance Conflict

If shy people only fled from social confrontations, and didn't feel bad about it, they wouldn't feel so bad about being shy. In fact, they would be introverts, who generally don't seek out the company of other people. Shy people, on the other hand, want very much to be with other people and to be accepted by them. They

"My shyness is not really expressed. I don't express because I am shy. I feel very inhibited around people I don't know in a large group. If I am talking one-on-one to a stranger I am okay, but if I don't know them very well then I feel really dumb."—sixteen-year-old high school student

"I try to act on impulse. I try not to think what anyone would think or say if I do what I want to do or say. Rather than thinking twice before I say or do something because of the fear of the reaction I may receive, I would like to attempt to change my shyness."—twenty-year-old receptionist and student[d]

want companionship, affection, and the feeling that they're understood. But at the same time that shy people want relationships, they doubt their ability to create them and they're certain that they're being judged negatively.

You can think of this ambivalence about other people as fighting and fleeing at the same time, because shy people are moving toward other people at the same time they hold themselves back. I call this the approach-avoidance conflict because shy people get stuck between these two warring impulses. In fact, it seems that the parts of the brain involved in this conflict also create the fight-or-flight instinct. But these reactions take different amounts of time. The fight-or-flight instinct is a short-term response to a short-term, specific threat, such as a bear prowling through the woods. Once the bear passes out of your area, you feel relief. The approach-avoidance conflict, however, isn't resolved as quickly. It begins when a person begins thinking about the threat and lingers for a long time.

Let's say that Dante, a shy teen, wants to try out for the school play. Even though he's quiet and well behaved at school, Dante loves to make faces in the mirror, and his close friends and family know that he can be very funny at times. Since he's very observant, he can even impersonate people he's just met very briefly because he's so good at picking up on their mannerisms and habits.

Dante gets excited about the announcement that his school's drama teacher will be holding auditions that week for the school play. He thinks about how he'd handle the audition, how much fun it would be to actually be on stage, and even what it would be like to land the starring role. You can think of his daydreams as his desire to approach this challenge. In fact, if the auditions were held that afternoon, he'd probably use this excitement to deliver a great performance. His excitement is the approach side of the approach-avoidance conflict. Dante is feeling all of the physical stress reactions that are fired up during this kind of challenge, but he thinks of them in a positive way.

Shy teens get caught in an approach-avoidance conflict when they want to try something new, such as auditioning for a school play, but feel anxious about doing so.

But as the days go on, Dante's excitement turns to dread. Sure, he still would like to star in the play. But the thought of reciting a monologue for the drama teacher at the audition, not to mention going up against some older students and more popular and good-looking students, scares him. Deep in his heart, he doubts that he can compete. For the next few days, he feels a pit in the bottom of his stomach, has headaches, and can't concentrate. He doesn't even memorize the monologue he'd like to perform. This is how he avoids the challenge of trying out for the play. His stress reactions become more intense, and he starts interpreting them negatively.

When Saturday rolls around, Dante's edgy. He didn't sleep well because he was so jittery, and overslept because he was so tired. He didn't have time to eat breakfast or look at the monologue one more time. He felt so bad that he had to talk himself into showing up, and was one of the last people to get to the audition. While he was waiting, he was comparing himself to the other budding actors, who

### Time for Reflection

● Dante didn't get a part in the play (see below) because he was so caught up in his approach-avoidance conflict. If you could give him advice, what would you say?

all seemed well prepared, upbeat, and very experienced. They all seemed to know each other and had no problem rehearsing lines with each other.

When he finally got in front of the drama coach to audition for the part, he stumbled over the dialogue, couldn't really hear the feedback and directions he was given, and didn't make eye contact with the drama teacher as he left the room. He wasn't surprised when he wasn't picked for the leading role—or any role in the play. He told himself that he just wasn't cut out to be an actor, no matter how much fun he had goofing around in private, and promised himself that he'd never put himself through that torture again.

That's unfortunate, because with a smart strategy and self-awareness, Dante could have let his natural talent shine through. But he was stuck in the approach-avoidance conflict, without a strategy to break through it and meet this challenge. Look at "Compare and Contrast" below for strategies for meeting this challenge.

### Compare and Contrast

Dante isn't the only actor who's nervous before auditioning for a play. Plenty of outgoing and successfully shy actors get nervous, jumpy, distracted, and full of anxiety in the days before the audition. But they handle it differently.

- An outgoing actress will label her nerves as a sign of excitement and use her nervous energy to rehearse her monologue over and over again, until she memorizes it and can do it six different ways to show the drama teacher how versatile she is. She aces it.
- A shy actor will get stuck in his anxiety and fear, and see his discomfort as a sign that he isn't cut out to be an actor. He'll procrastinate and play

video games instead of learning his lines. He'll show up to the audition unprepared, will mumble and rush through his lines, and will fail to show the drama teacher that he's got the charisma and talent needed for the role.

- A successfully shy actor will view his anxiety as a sign that he really wants this role and is worried about his performance and making a fool of himself in public. To get over his nerves, he rehearses his lines alone and then with a friend, so he can get some feedback and get used to speaking in public. He will also check out the audition room the day before so he can get a feel for it and imagine himself performing well. Although he feels a little strange doing it, he runs through the monologue in the room by himself so he knows how loud he needs to speak to be heard. He tries to sleep the night before but sets his alarm clock early so he has plenty of time to get ready before the audition. When he walks into the room he notices that the drama teacher is a little stern, but encouraging. The actor's voice shakes a little when he begins speaking, but he is confident that he knows his lines and can get caught up in the performance. He does so well that he gets the role that he really, really wanted.

As you can see, the successfully shy actor isn't held back by his fear of being judged in public because he wants to be in the school play. To get over his nerves, he rehearses and is well prepared for the audition. In that way, he can fall back on what he's memorized when he feels nervous.

Since many successful actors say that they are shy when they're not performing, it's obvious that shyness doesn't prevent them from expressing themselves on stage, on TV, or in film. Those who do conquer their fears are what I call successfully shy—still shy, but in control of their shyness.

## Risk-Taking and Rejection

Why is the approach-avoidance conflict so powerful? Because shy people need to take a risk to get from the avoidance side of the conflict to the approach side. And that risk requires them to expose themselves to other people and possibly be rejected.

Think about this on the primal, fight-or-flight level. Say there's a tiger roaming around the field you're walking through. You can hide in the bushes and wait for it to pass so you can run away, which is the flight response. Or you can lift your spear, stomp the ground, and shout at the tiger to scare it away—the fight response. That would mean exposing yourself and taking the risk that the tiger won't charge you.

Now, today's shy teens aren't physically threatened by other people, the way our ancestors were constantly looking out for animal predators. Today's shy teens are threatened by the judgment of others—or their belief that others are judging them—and are unsure of whether they can or should assert themselves. They fear approaching someone because they fear being rejected.

This is a powerful fear. In fact, according to research with the provocative title "Broken Hearts and Broken Bones,"[5] the same part of the brain that fires up when you're in physical pain is also fired up when you feel emotional pain, such as social rejection. That shows how painful it is to not have good friends, a strong social circle, and the ability to form new friendships with like-minded people. And that's how strong our bonding instinct is, too.

Many people—including outgoing people—do not fear rejection when they meet new people. If they do, they don't let that fear get in the way of meeting new people. But shy people get caught up in their fear, their evaluation apprehension, and get stuck in their approach-avoidance conflict. What they need to do is to take strategic, well-thought-out risks that will pay off. For example, instead of drinking a lot of alcohol to get through a party, they will bring an outgoing friend with them who's comfortable in crowds.

Smart risk taking seems to be a self-fulfilling prophecy. A small success on one front will lead that person to take another, slightly greater risk elsewhere. In that way, the person will build on his success a little bit at a time. In contrast, failing a challenge—or not even trying—can affect a person's self-image and self-esteem long after the so-called failure. As you'll see in the next two chapters, when we'll explore shyness of the mind and shyness of the self, the way that shy teens think of themselves is greatly impacted by how they feel about their social performance.

## Fear Versus Anxiety

Although few people would say that they like to be afraid, the fact is that fear is a good thing. Fear is a short-term response to a short-term, present, and specific threat. For example, if you see a coyote in the bushes, you feel fear and freeze. The stress reactions created when we're fearful alert us to the fact that something threatening is on the horizon. Fear is how we protect ourselves. In fact, we couldn't have survived all of these millennia without it.

Anxiety, on the other hand, is more general, long lasting, and vague. It's that low-level dread that's upsetting but doesn't necessarily stop you in your tracks the way that fear does.[6] Although many people think of anxiety as an emotional phenomenon, it's rooted in the body. Signs can be stress headaches and stomachaches, racing thoughts, and general jitteriness and worry. Over time, the physical stress of anxiety can really cause wear and tear on your body because you aren't supposed to be in this constant state of agitation.[7]

Shy people fear social situations, but I believe that the anxiety related to shyness causes them more problems. Yes, some shy people fear some specific social situations, such as speaking in public. When called on in class, a shy student may clam up, stutter, or have a very shaky voice. But once the stressful situation passes, he recovers fairly quickly.

But other shy people feel anxiety about a wider range of social situations, and they let that anxiety affect them before, during, and after stressful social situations. People who feel anxious sometimes cannot put their finger on the cause, although shy people can often say that a certain social event on the horizon is worrying them.

I think this anxiety is caused by the approach-avoidance conflict, which is more long lasting than the fight-or-flight instinct, which surges up and is resolved fairly quickly. Shy people become anxious at the thought of asserting themselves with someone else but aren't happy with the thought of running away, either. They get stuck—and anxious. And without a resolution, they will stay anxious about being sociable.

## When Anxiety Is a Good Thing

Anxiety can feel terrible at times, but at other times it's a very good thing. In fact, according to the Yerkes-Dodson Law, anxiety is necessary for motivation.[8] It just

> **Remember This**
>
> Some antianxiety medications are prescribed to allow shy people to cope with their anxiety. Some shy people, most specifically those whose lives are disturbed by social anxiety, benefit from them. But I suggest that shy teens try other strategies before taking medication. These strategies include changing the way they think about their shyness and stressful social encounters, finding ways to physically calm themselves that don't involve drugs or alcohol, learning social skills, and finding smart ways to expand their comfort zone. Taking a pill may give a shy person some physical relief, but it will not make her a better conversationalist.

depends on how much anxiety is being generated. If you feel too little anxiety, that means you're bored, drowsy, and unmotivated to take on a challenge. If you feel too much anxiety, you'll be consumed by it and freeze up, feel confused and unable to think straight, and be in a state of frenzy.

But there is an optimal level of arousal between those two extremes—just enough for you to feel charged up and focused, but not so much that you are scattered and hyper. You are alert and engaged but not consumed by your energy. In fact, at times people want to generate some anxiety because it readies them for a big task. For example, actors and athletes try to psych themselves up before a big game or performance, and pep rallies and loud music and cheering are designed to fire up a crowd so that fans will provide some motivation for their team.

Many people are held back by performance anxiety, which is the anxiety that results when you are competing, taking a test, or being judged. Too much performance anxiety can make someone's mind go blank when he's taking a big exam or make her miss a free throw in the final minutes of a big game, in front of a big crowd. Too little performance anxiety will mean that the test taker or basketball player doesn't really care about the results.

Shy people can feel performance anxiety when they are called on in class, have to introduce themselves to a stranger, go on a job interview, or talk to someone they feel is attractive. During these challenges, shy people can freeze up, stumble over their words, or rush through the encounter because their minds and bodies are supercharged and full of adrenaline. These shy people need to learn how to manage and focus their anxiety so that they can approach someone else with energy and not shrink away because they feel so stressed out.

## Try This

While the "shy body" describes what happens under the skin when someone is in a difficult social situation, it also describes what happens when an individual is threatened in any way, whether it's driving through heavy traffic in the rain, feeling anxious about an upcoming test, or coping with procrastination before a big project. When you produce stress reactions that make your body seem like it's out of control, don't let your anxiety spiral out of control. Stop, think about the purpose of your stress reactions, and begin minimizing them by shifting your focus to something productive.

## Using the Mind to Cope with the Shy Body

Now that you have a greater understanding of how shyness is expressed physically in the body, in the next chapter I'll explain how to use your thoughts to cope with these shy stress reactions and anxiety. As you'll see, shy teens need to learn how to use their intellect to become successfully shy. It requires some self-awareness, practice, and focus, but it definitely can be done.

# SHYNESS OF THE MIND

Now that you have a deeper understanding of the physical component of shyness—what I call shyness of the body—you can take steps to reduce those shy symptoms so that you can turn your focus from your shy stress reactions to your social interactions.

Since shyness is holistic, meaning that it affects your body, mind, and self, shy people cannot simply shut down their stress reactions and expect to be free of shyness. Instead, they need to use their minds to reduce their shy physical reactions, thoughts, and emotions. Every part of your being is involved in shyness, so every part will be involved in controlling and limiting it.

Antianxiety medication can help make someone with extreme stress reactions feel calmer, and that can help her feel relaxed and focused when she's outside of her comfort zone so that she can utilize her social skills and make conversation. That said, medication won't cure shyness. The pills won't help that same person become an interesting conversationalist. It's true that she will be able to go to a party under the influence of medication, but the pills won't teach her how to introduce herself, make small talk, or crack jokes. Another potential effect of medication is that when she does feel calmer in situations that typically make her stress out, such as a party, she will chalk up her success to the pill, and not to her own efforts. She won't give herself credit for using all of the strategies that a successfully shy person uses, such as staying at the party long enough to warm up to her environment, finding a friend to accompany her, actively approaching new people instead of avoiding them, and not listening to the critical voices in her head that are telling her that because she feels uncomfortable, she doesn't really belong there. The medication can rob her of a well-earned feeling of success and satisfaction.

In this chapter, I'll show how shy teens can use their minds to cope with their shy physical reactions. I've found that shy people's thoughts follow a pattern that enhances or amplifies their stress reactions, which then leads to more shy experiences and more frustration. Changing those thought patterns may require some

---

**Fernanda's Story**

Fernanda is in her sophomore year at a small college and, like most shy young adults, found that her shyness became a problem during her teen years. I think most shy teens can relate to her constant second-guessing of herself, which prevents her from feeling natural during conversations with strangers. Here's what she had to say.

"I had friends in elementary school but I was very quiet," Fernanda wrote to me.

That's what I was known for. I sat in the back of the classroom. I just tried to be invisible.

I think being a shy teenager was worse than being just a regular teenager. I think I did the same things I did when I was a kid and tried to be invisible. But in some ways high school was a bit easier than being in elementary school. It's bigger, so it's easy to get lost because there are more students. I wasn't forced to be social and do things that I hated.

Social events bring it out now. I don't know how to deal with people, or how to talk to them. I'm nervous before, during, and after I go out. I think about it after it's over. I think, "How am I going to talk to them? How can I approach them? What am I going to say?" I try to figure out how I'm going to break out of it. But then I go and I do the same thing as always. I sit in the corner and hope nobody notices me. I think about things I should have done or said. I think about that forever. It never ends. It just goes on and on.[a]

---

practice, but it certainly can be done. In that way, shy teens can become successfully shy teens.

## The Shy Mind

The previous chapter explored what happens under the skin of a shy person—all of the physical sensations that are triggered by stressful social situations and make interacting with other people so difficult. Chapter 4 also showed how these physical stress reactions are rooted in our ancient fight-or-flight instinct, when we had to either charge into danger to slay an attacker or run away to safety.

The modern shy person's fight-or-flight instinct kicks in during stressful social situations, not when they're in physical danger. And, what's more, they get caught in an approach-avoidance conflict that produces anxiety, dread, and excessive self-consciousness even when they're not interacting with other people. Or, as Fernanda explained (see page 80), she feels nervous before, during, and after she goes out and she thinks about it after it's over.

This is where the shy mind comes in. Shy people's thoughts are linked to their shy stress reactions. Although each shy person is unique, his or her thoughts follow a pattern that is very powerful and serves to isolate that person, makes him or her feel helpless and hopeless, and leads to even more shy behavior in the future. Think about Fernanda's statement: "I try to figure out how I'm going to break out of it. But then I go and I do the same thing as always." That's a sign of hopelessness, even though Fernanda has the ability to become successfully shy.

What triggers the workings of the shy mind? Excessive self-consciousness, which is an individual's tendency to pay attention to his or her self.[1] Self-conscious people—including shy people—are focused on themselves to a high degree. In general, they can be publicly self-conscious and focused on their appearance or behavior, or privately self-conscious and focused on their internal feelings and thoughts.[2]

Shy teens feel excessively self-conscious during social situations in which they feel they are being judged.

Shy people tend to be both publicly self-conscious and privately self-conscious. They are publicly self-conscious because they are focused on how they are being perceived by others. ("Everyone is watching me walk down the hallway.") They're also privately self-conscious because they are paying attention to their internal thoughts and bodily reactions and physical arousal. ("I'm so nervous I'm starting to stammer.") With all of these competing thoughts trying to grab their attention, shy people find it very hard to focus on the discussion at hand, respond to a question, or keep track of all that is going on in a conversation. Even remembering someone's name immediately after being introduced can be difficult because shy people are thinking about everything but what that new person is saying—including her name. Instead, they're thinking about their own stress reactions and how the other person is viewing them.

Although any stressful situation can create self-consciousness, social situations trigger them to a much greater degree in shy people. When excessive self-consciousness kicks in, it's like turning up the volume in your brain. It's hard to think clearly when you are being distracted by this very loud background noise. Imagine trying to study when you have a loud stereo speaker blaring in your ear—and then have an audience watching your every move. That's how shy people feel when they are in a stressful social situation. Instead of thinking about the people they're encountering, they're thinking about themselves, their thoughts, feelings, emotions, physical sensations, and identity—and the judgments that other people are making about them.

These self-conscious thoughts get in the way of social interactions. Instead of thinking about what their conversation partner is saying, a shy teen like Fernanda will think, "My heart is pounding so hard I'm sure everyone can hear it. My palms are so sweaty—I hope that nobody shakes my hand. Do I have bad breath? Is something stuck in my teeth? Did I just laugh at the wrong thing? Why am I interrupting her? Why didn't I just tell her that joke that I heard the other day? I wish I could remember that joke. I can never remember jokes when I need to. Did she just roll her eyes at me? This is the worst conversation I've ever had. Why did I come here? I'll never do this again."

As you can see, Fernanda is having a parallel conversation with herself. The conversation she is having with herself is getting in the way of her conversations with others. It's like trying to carry on a conversation with two people at the same time but with each person saying something different into each of your ears. As complex as the brain is, it can only do one thing at a time. When you multitask, your brain is actually flipping back and forth between tasks. With easy, well-learned tasks, such as scanning through TV channels on the remote control while eating, it isn't difficult for the brain to flip back and forth. The brain has a much harder time when it is processing a new or complex task, such as trying to follow a conversation while thinking about what you are going to say next to someone you just met at a party.

See how the shy mind gets in the way?

In many ways, you could say that shyness is a form of narcissism, because shy people are only focused on themselves, not other people. However, there are some important differences. Narcissists in general want everybody's attention and they get angry when they don't get it. Shy narcissists, on the other hand, think that everybody is focused on them but they do not want the attention they imagine they are receiving. For example, a narcissist will walk down the hallway and assume that everybody notices them and how wonderful they are. Those who aren't paying attention to them will be the target of the narcissist's anger. A shy narcissist, though, will walk down that same hallway and assume that everybody notices them. But instead of relishing their time in the imagined spotlight, they will try to deflect that attention by slouching, not making eye contact, keeping quiet, and feeling anxious.

As a result of the variety of changes associated with this period of development that can create erosion in many important aspects of the self-concept,[3] self-consciousness can become even more intense during adolescence. One of the natural changes that occurs in the teen years is the increased importance of friendships with other teens. These friendships help teens get through all of the difficulties of adolescence. Instead of looking to parents and childhood friends for support, teens look to their peer group to see if they are acting properly. This is what's called social comparison. Teens are constantly using social comparison to evaluate whether they are doing the right thing. A fundamental principle of social comparison is that we turn to others for information about what to do when we don't know what we should be doing. Since adolescence is a time of much uncertainty, teens turn to other people who are in a similar situation for guidance.

For example, a younger kid will have no problem wearing hand-me-downs from her older sister. They may not be the most stylish things, but she doesn't really care too much. In fact, she loves her older sister so much that she's happy to wear anything that her sister once picked out and wore. When she gets older, though, her attitude may change. Instead of liking her sister's castoff sweater, she'll begin to compare that sweater to the ones other girls in her class are wearing. "Selena's sweater is brand-new," she'll say to herself. "I saw that exact one in a magazine last month. Mine looks really out-of-date compared to hers. And Bryn's, too. She's wearing the same one as Selena, but in a differ-

> "I think other people think of me as a 'stuttering idiot.'"
> —twenty-year-old psychology student[b]

> ### Remember This
>
> ● All teens use social comparison to try to fit in. But shy teens use it more often because they are so unsure of their ability to socialize. And, in addition, they compare themselves to the most outgoing person in the room. Shy teens would have a more realistic view of their social abilities if they compared themselves to the quieter people who surround them. After all, shy teens cannot see all of the stress reactions that others are experiencing.

ent color. I bet they went shopping together. My old sweater is something a loser would wear. I hope nobody notices it. If I skip lunch today and hang out in the computer lab nobody will see me. Maybe I can wear my jacket over it for the rest of the day. Everyone's going to think I have bad taste in clothes and not want to hang out with someone as ugly as me."

Two major reasons why peer influence is so important during adolescence is that peers can serve as a source of social, emotional, and practical support during difficult times and provide a standard by which teens can measure their behavior.[4] It seems that every social encounter is a stressful one. They are constantly comparing themselves to their friends and peers. They are always looking at other teens' behavior, level of comfort and ease, sense of humor, popularity, intelligence, attractiveness—you name it—because they are never quite sure if they fit in and are accepted. But instead of copying the behavior of their socially successful peers or realizing that they do fit in, shy teens get caught up in their own stress reactions and try to clam up to prevent them from spiraling out of control. That's the approach-avoidance conflict at work.

Another problem is that shy teens tend to feel that they are the only ones who are shy, so they don't realize that there are similarly shy teens wherever they go and they don't compare themselves to these teens. Instead, they look at the wrong people, those who are very unlike them. They look at the most outgoing person in the room, or even actors, supermodels, and other celebrities. Obviously, these are unfair comparisons. Shy teens don't have scripts to follow, press agents to coach them, or the desire to be the loudest person in the room.

## Turning Up the Volume

Although all teens may feel self-conscious when they are not feeling confident about their ability to fit in, some situations seem to make their self-consciousness more intense. Researchers have found that some outside objects—like a camera, mirror, or video recorder—create what's called objective self-awareness. Quite literally, the object makes people more self-aware or self-conscious and focused on their internal feelings or beliefs.[5] The object turns up the volume on your feelings and takes you out of yourself. Under these circumstances, you become more aware of what you do or say, and the imaginary mirror or camera will exaggerate your feelings.

For example, we've all been in a situation where somebody pulls out his cell phone to take a picture—a very common trigger for objective self-awareness. But have you ever noticed how people respond to that cell phone camera? The outgoing individuals will smile broadly, pose provocatively, or make faces. Those who aren't particularly outgoing or shy will smile naturally. But the shy people will duck behind someone else or slouch or paste a frozen smile on their face. And while doing so, they'll think to themselves, "Hurry up! I hate having my picture taken! I always look terrible in photos." That's classic objective self-awareness.

Think about what happens when you look at yourself in the mirror. If you are feeling good about yourself, you'll smile, touch up your hair, and think, "Hey, I look pretty good." The image you see in the mirror will make you more confident. But if you don't think highly of yourself, you'll see yourself in the mirror and think, "I've got a new pimple. Everyone can see it. I'm having a bad hair day.

Some outside objects—like a camera, mirror, or video recorder—create what's called objective self-awareness. The object makes people more self-aware or self-conscious and focused on their internal feelings or beliefs. Shy people will become more inhibited, while extroverts will act even more outgoing.

**Time for Reflection**

Are you more likely to focus on your perceived flaws or the flaws of others? Do you think your friends or classmates spend time picking apart your flaws? Or do you think you are your own worst critic?

Why is my nose so big? This T-shirt makes me look like a wimp. And these braces are so gross. I wish I could hide for the next two years."

The analogy that illustrates this point is that it is as if shy people tend to walk around with an invisible mirror or camera focused on them when they're in social situations. The imaginary mirror or camera turns up the volume on their social discomfort. Every conversation is an evaluation. This makes them consumed with their negative feelings about themselves, their stress reactions, their social skills, their likeability, or their appearance. They feel judged in social situations, but, in reality, they are the ones holding up the mirror or camera and judging themselves so harshly. And they are the ones creating a standard that is impossible to attain. Shy teens are their own worst critic and the volume of these negative thoughts is so high that they are unable to hear anything else.

When all of us are feeling stressed and under scrutiny, we rely on our dominant response and exaggerate it. So when outgoing people feel that they are being evaluated, they will act even more bubbly and chatty, laugh louder, and try to win over whoever they are speaking to. Shy people, on the other hand, will be quiet

**Try This**

Although objective self-awareness can make shy people more inhibited when they're in public, objective self-awareness can actually help people act in ways that they desire. For example, sitting in front of a mirror can help you do something you normally dread—like studying—because seeing yourself doing the desired action will make you feel more comfortable. But having to watch yourself fidget, check your phone, daydream, and drum your fingers on the desk will be so uncomfortable that you will change your behavior and get to work. Try this as a study aid the next time you are procrastinating.

so that they don't misspeak, offend anyone, or draw attention to themselves. Like Fernanda, they will try to be invisible so that nobody will notice them.

## Evaluating Your Social Performance

We all think about and judge our own social behavior, whether we're outgoing, shy, intelligent, popular, kind and sympathetic, or mean and intimidating. But we don't always make accurate judgments about our own behavior because we often do not evaluate ourselves objectively. Our emotions are involved in our evaluations. We don't always have all of the information we need. We may be focused on either positive or negative aspects of ourselves. Or we simply fall into a thought pattern that is hard to break.

Research indicates that the shy mind follows a specific pattern when evaluating social interactions.[6] Not surprisingly, this pattern is overwhelmingly negative and very powerful. It's also unfair and inaccurate, too.

One of the thought patterns that shy people rely on is a pessimistic attributional style that makes them shrug off any control over their social successes but forces them to take the blame for social failures. In other words, they attribute success to luck or someone else. They think, "I just happened to remember that joke when I was talking to Luis," or "Kara is so easy to talk to." But when they

"My shyness is expressed by not expressing my opinions, not saying how I really feel sometimes because I'm afraid of the rejection I might receive. Another way is when I avoid calling or writing people back because I'm not sure what to say and if I do say things, that I won't have a lot to say and that I feel that I'll somehow feel rejected if I ever ask to get together with them.

"I become jealous a lot in my mind because I wonder why I can't be like another person. I feel as if I'm worthless in my social aspects because I can't always talk about 'fun' stuff.

"I am becoming more and more frustrated, like I don't know how to just calm down and take one day at a time. Every time I try to overcome it, I rush it so much and then always have a more depressing day once in a while and go downhill from there."—nineteen-year-old manicurist[c]

have a bad social experience, they blame themselves. They think, "That conversation stalled because I couldn't think of anything to say," or "Matthew thinks I'm boring."

A more positive attributional style would allow shy people to claim credit for succeeding socially. After a good conversation, they'll think, "I told Sasha things she was interested in discussing," or "That joke always works." On the other hand, when they have a conversation that doesn't flow so well, they won't blame themselves. They'll think, "Tim was really distracted and wasn't really listening to me," or "Mrs. Mayer isn't the warmest person."

The following story about Hashim and Jenna will show how this works.

### Evaluating Hashim and Jenna

Hashim is a shy sophomore in a large high school. The good thing about the size of his school is that he can blend in and hide in the crowd. The bad thing is that it's hard to meet new friends, because most students stick to the friends they've had since junior high. Hashim does that, too, but he wishes that he could find some new friends to help him enjoy being at school a little bit more.

Hashim is a really good student. He's so successful at math that he takes calculus with juniors. The good thing about that is that it challenges him intellectually. The bad thing, of course, is that he feels really awkward in class. And he had to reschedule his lunch period, which means that he can't hang out with his buddies.

On the first day of his new schedule, he felt totally lost in the cafeteria. He picked out his food, then scanned the loud room for a place to sit. He isn't a jock, doesn't think of himself as a nerd, and didn't want to hang out with the rowdy kids. He also didn't want to sit at a table full of girls, since that would be really uncomfortable. The thought of it made him sweat and get all nervous.

He was just about to sit down at a table by himself so that he could wolf down his lunch quickly, hoping that nobody would notice him, when he saw Jenna, who was sitting by herself with a few empty seats around her. He doesn't know Jenna all that well, but she lives down the street from him and always said hi to him when they crossed paths.

He took a deep breath to try to calm himself and decided to go for it.

"OK if I sit here?" Hashim said as casually as he could.

"Sure," Jenna said. She gave him a little smile, then stuck a fork in her lasagna.

Hashim still felt nervous, but he thought that he could fight it and calm down enough to get through the lunch.

"My schedule changed so I'm taking lunch this period," he said, trying to explain himself. "I'm taking calculus."

"Calc's tough," Jenna said. She took another forkful of food, then pulled out her phone and started paging through her texts. She became so engrossed in her messages that she didn't look up again for the rest of the lunch. Hashim sat there in silence, wondering what he did to tick her off and hoping that nobody would notice that Jenna was totally blowing him off. He left as soon as he could and hung out in the resource center until his next class started.

The next day, Hashim sat by himself at lunch. He didn't see Jenna in the crowd, but he didn't want to sit with her anyway.

## Making Attributions

Hashim's experience is shared by a lot of shy teens. They try to reach out to other teens but they have a hard time making that connection and developing friendships. I've found that the way that shy people think about their social experiences—the shy mind—prevents them from breaking out of their shyness because they get stuck in a cycle of negative thinking. They have a pessimistic attributional style, which means that they don't feel like they caused their successes but they definitely caused their failures in social situations.

We all make attributions about events in our lives, whether it's tripping over a crack in the sidewalk ("I'm clumsy" or "This sidewalk is in terrible shape") or getting a top score on an exam ("I studied really hard" or "It was really easy"). Attributions help us understand our world because we are able to assign causes for events that would otherwise seem confusing or random.

In general, attributions can be

- Internal or external: Internal attributions are those that are caused by you ("She stopped talking to me because I'm boring"). External attributions are due to something outside of you ("She stopped talking to me because she was reading important texts").
- Stable or unstable: Stable attributions are those that are caused by something that doesn't change ("I'm not attractive to girls"). Unstable attributions are those that are caused by something that can change at any time ("Jenna had to deal with those texts, because they were about her babysitting job that night").
- Specific or global: Specific attributions are those that are caused by something unique to that situation ("I caught Jenna at a bad time"). Global attributions are those that apply to all situations ("I turn girls off").

Shy people, however, seem to use the same attributions over and over. In fact, they rely on these attributions so often that they become a predictable pattern

Shy teens tend to use a pessimistic attributional style, which creates a cycle of negative thinking that separates them from others.

called a pessimistic attributional style. When shy people succeed, they don't attribute their success to themselves. They use external ("Sarah is doing all of the talking in this conversation"), unstable ("I got lucky"), and specific ("I feel comfortable around Sarah because she's known me forever") attributions. When shy people fail, they use internal ("This conversation is full of uncomfortable pauses because I can't think of anything to say"), stable ("I've never been good at making small talk"), and global ("I'm a terrible conversationalist") attributions.

Here's how Hashim, a shy high school student, made attributions about his uncomfortable lunch with Jenna:

- Internal: "Jenna's usually pretty outgoing. She must be standoffish with me because I'm boring."

- Stable: "I can never get past 'hi' with Jenna."
- Global: "I can't make conversation with girls."

It's no wonder that Hashim doesn't seek out Jenna at lunchtime anymore. His negative attributions make him believe that he will never be able to talk to her. Even worse? Hashim, like other shy people, generalizes this belief so that it applies to other people and situations. He believes that not only can he not talk to Jenna at lunch but he cannot talk to all girls. And, unbelievably, it gets even worse than that. Hashim's attributions affect his behavior now ("I have a hard time talking to Jenna") and well into the future ("I can never talk to girls").

With such a pessimistic attributional style comes a sense of helplessness and hopelessness. The shy person just stops trying. They think, "Why should I even try? It's not going to get any better. I repel other people." By making general statements about specific situations, shy people feel that it's impossible to change who they are. They feel that they have to become an entirely different person to have different results. It's like saying that they need to throw out their computer just because it has glitches now and then.

Isn't that unfortunate? Instead of shrugging off his bad lunch with Jenna, Hashim's pessimistic attributional style affects his desire to reach out to other people in the future. Why bother, if he's only going to be rejected? Well, Hashim should try to reach out to other people in the future and become successfully shy.

## Successfully Shy Attributions

Hashim, like all shy people, isn't forced to use a pessimistic attributional style. While this shy thought pattern may seem inborn, like a reflex, it is not. It is a choice. That means that Hashim can choose to think like a successfully shy person by changing the attributions he makes about negative social experiences. Hashim

> **❘ Remember This**
>
> ● We're rarely aware of the internal dialogue that we engage in constantly. Thoughts come and go and we don't usually remember them. But this self-talk can be very powerful if it begins to affect one's sense of self. For example, a lot of damage can be done by thinking, "I'm dumb," "I can never get this right," "I suck," or "Nobody will ever really love me." If or when these thoughts arise, remember that they are unfair. You are your own worst critic, and you shouldn't turn a single negative incident into a powerful, permanent belief about yourself.

can seek out more information and reevaluate his encounter with Jenna. He could ask her if she had important texts to read, and she could have told him that she needed to confirm her babysitting job that night. That information would allow Hashim to make successfully shy attributions:

- External: "Jenna is busy right now with the texts about her babysitting job tonight."
- Unstable: "Jenna needs to deal with her texts right now."
- Specific: "Jenna is nice to me when she isn't preoccupied with her texts."

As you can see, a successfully shy person won't always blame himself when things go wrong. Unlike people who are held back by their pessimistic attributional style, successfully shy people will find reasons for failure other than themselves. They won't always assume that they are at fault when a conversation turns cold. Nor will they believe that one bad conversation automatically means that all conversations will be awful. Successfully shy people are much less critical about their social performance, which gives them more confidence in the future. They can shrug off problems because they know that they can learn from them and not repeat them in the future.

### Hashim and Jenna, Again

Here's another scenario involving Hashim and Jenna, one that is more positive.

The following week, Hashim was biking down his street to go over to his friend Mike's house and saw Jenna trying to pull a heavy box out of the trunk

**Try This**

Now that you've seen how shy Hashim and successfully shy people make attributions about negative social experiences, think about the last time you had a difficult social encounter. Then pretend you're Hashim and write down the internal, stable, and global attributions you can make about it. Then write down the attributions that a successfully shy person can make about the same encounter. Lastly, circle the answers that you think would help you feel more confident and positive about yourself.

of her mom's car. Hashim slowed down a bit, torn about what to do. On the one hand, Jenna is usually nice to him and she really looked like she was struggling. On the other hand, she wasn't that nice to him when he tried to talk to her in the cafeteria.

As he was dragging his foot on the ground to slow down, Jenna looked up and saw him. He couldn't duck her now. He took a deep breath and turned into her driveway. She needed help.

"Hey," he said, then took the box out of Jenna's arms.

"Thanks!" Jenna said. "I was wondering how I was going to get this thing in the house. I saved up my babysitting money for a new TV for my room and I can't wait to set it up."

She led him into the house and told him he could put it on the kitchen table. His arms were sore but he didn't think she could notice.

"I can't thank you enough. There's no way I could have done this alone."

"It's nothing," Hashim said.

"It was really nice of you. Are you hungry? My mom made brownies if you want some."

She handed him two brownies on a napkin, and Hashim didn't feel he could refuse. He relaxed a little bit as Jenna started chatting about her new TV, her babysitting job, and her day at school. He found himself really engaged in the conversation and even made her laugh a few times. When he finished eating his third brownie, he was truly sorry that he had to leave to go to Mike's. He really enjoyed hanging out with Jenna. She was so easy to talk to. Then again, she was doing most of the talking and Hashim was doing most of the listening.

## Taking Credit for Success

Most shy people, like Hashim, find it difficult to take credit for social successes. They discount all of the smooth and easy conversations they have and only focus on the difficult social situations that trigger objective self-awareness and excessive self-consciousness. And when they do think about their social successes, they use attributions that give all of the credit to someone else, and not themselves. This is the other half of the pessimistic attributional style. They use external, unstable, and specific attributions for positive situations:

- External: The positive experience is due to someone else ("Jenna is chatty and easy to talk to").
- Unstable: The social success is a fluke and can't be repeated ("Jenna's in a good mood").
- Specific: The easy conversation can't be repeated ("Jenna's only being nice to me because I helped her carry in her new TV").

It's easy to see how this pessimistic attributional style impacts shy teens like Hashim even when they have positive social interactions. Not only do they internalize all of their negative experiences, but they give themselves no credit for positive ones. That style of thinking robs them of any feeling of success because they let others take credit for it. And it makes them feel like they'll never be able to repeat that success in the future.

However, if Hashim made different attributions, he'd have a more optimistic attitude about his conversation with Jenna. He could make successfully shy attributions about this positive encounter, which are internal, stable, and global:

- Internal: Hashim is responsible for the successful conversation ("I helped Jenna and had interesting things to say").
- Stable: Hashim can talk to people he's familiar with ("I'm usually relaxed and talkative with people once I get to know them").
- Global: Hashim is an interesting person who can hold his own in a conversation ("I'm not shy with everyone").

Hashim's successfully shy–style attributions are far more positive than his shy attributions. They allow him to realize that he has control over his behavior and can succeed. Not surprisingly, this attitude increases his self-esteem and allows him to build an identity that isn't based on shyness. Yes, Hashim is still shy. But if he continues to use realistic attributions that allow him to take credit for success and not always shoulder the blame when things turn south, he will be able to develop friendships and a sense of self that's isn't connected to shyness.

## You Are More Powerful Than the Shy Mind

The shy mind is a powerful thing. Its patterns and belief system serve to isolate shy individuals and send them the message that they are alone, are not good at making conversation, and will always be this way. That, of course, is untrue. But shy people tend to believe these myths because they feel true. After all, isn't that what their intense stress reactions are all about? Shy people believe that because they feel uncomfortable and stressed out during social encounters, they're simply unable to break out of their shyness.

Although the shy mind is powerful, it isn't more powerful than an individual who is armed with information and has the desire to break out of her shyness. The first step is to understand how the shy body, mind, and self interact to create the dynamic phenomenon that is shyness. In this chapter, we explored how the shy mind makes shy people feel like they're being watched and judged, holds them responsible for failure and doesn't allow them to take credit for success, and makes them feel helpless and hopeless. Fortunately, this thought pattern can be changed once a shy person notices her self-talk that turns one difficult encounter into a permanent aversion to being with other people. That's how people become successfully shy.

# SHYNESS OF THE SELF

Shyness is so powerful because it encompasses an individual's thoughts, behavior, and emotions. It's a tangle of uncomfortable physical reactions, a specific thought pattern, and negative feelings. Ultimately, shyness can have an impact on one's identity and self-esteem and can lead a person to label herself as a shy person instead of thinking that she feels shy during specific situations.

In this chapter, we'll explore how shyness affects one's identity and self-concept, its impact on one's self-esteem, and how shy people can better understand the role of shyness in their own personality.

## Gigi's Story

Gigi is a recent high school graduate who, like many shy people, believes that her shyness is worse than other people's shyness. She isn't shy in every situation, but she's very inhibited and anxious in social situations that mean a lot to her—meeting people at parties. She said she's tried to change her shyness, but hasn't had any luck. Here's her story:

"I don't express myself because I am shy," Gigi wrote in her letter to me.

I feel very inhibited around people I don't know in a large group. If I am talking one on one to a stranger I am okay, but if I don't know them very well then I feel really dumb saying anything to an adult or someone my age.

Being shy has really put a damper on my enjoyment of parties. Recently I went to a party where I only knew two people. It was really awkward for me because I did not feel comfortable going up to anyone and introducing myself because I did not know what to say after "Hi, I'm Gigi. What's your name?" Even when my friend introduced me to people I did not know what to say.

Part of my shyness may stem from the fact that I have had a stuttering problem for most of my life. I am not shy with people I know and who know me. It's just a group of strangers that I have trouble with.

Overcoming shyness has been something I wish I did not have to deal with, but I do. I have tried to tell myself I am harder on me than anyone else will ever be, and that I should just forget it. I have even purposefully put myself in situations where I would be forced to talk to strangers. But nothing has worked. I went to camp out of state this past summer for six weeks. I was a little bit more outgoing there, but when I got home I slipped back into my old inward self.

What has happened before is that I would meet someone, talk to them for a while, hit it off really well, then say goodbye for the evening. Then, the next day, I'd see them again, but I'd feel shy/dumb and say hi, then give a weak wave and keep on walking.

I hate it! Maybe my problem isn't shyness. Maybe it's self-confidence and/or self-concept. But I hate myself and I hate what my shyness has made me. I think the way I see my shyness is a little bit warped because I know my friends are a bit overconfident. So I see myself as a little bit more abnormal than I am. Also, if I don't know how a person will react to something—like my going up to them—I won't try it.

Shyness is something I probably will have to deal with for the rest of my life. It is also something that will only hold me back as much as I allow it to. Which I'm afraid will be a lot.[a]

## Understanding Your Self

First, let's clarify some basic concepts. We may all think that we know what the "self" is. It's you, your identity, your personality, right? Well, those definitions may be adequate for casual conversation, but psychologists have defined the term *self* to set it apart from other distinct terms, such as *identity* or *personality*.

The self is the core part of an individual's personality that unites all aspects of it.[1] It seeks unity, harmony, and balance. It ties together the masculine and feminine aspects, the conscious and unconscious aspects, and the private and public aspects of one's personality. It holds together all of the opposing and harmonizing parts of us. When all of these aspects are in balance, the self is healthy. When the self isn't able to stay in balance, such imbalance can lead to a sense of frustration and feelings of depression, stress, anxiety, or anger.

The self-concept is what an individual believes about himself.[2] A portion of the self-concept is about one's physical attributes. Do you believe you are average looking? Better than average? Another part of the self-concept concerns one's personality attributes. Are you sensitive, empathetic, friendly, sociable, active, dominant, passive? These can all be part of one's self-concept. Other elements of the self-concept include beliefs a person has about herself, for example, religious or philosophical beliefs ("I believe in an afterlife"), beliefs about one's intelligence ("I'm just as smart as anyone else"), interests ("I like to bake"), or approach to life ("I don't sweat the small stuff").

Interestingly, we aren't born with a self-concept; we develop it as we age. It appears when we're about six months old, the age at which we are able to recognize ourselves in the mirror—a theory created by Charles Darwin, the noted biologist. That's when babies will reach out to a mirror to touch the image. They think that they are reaching out to another child.[3]

## Try This

Take an inventory of your self today. Include your beliefs about your physical attributes, interests, social or psychological attributes, abilities, and beliefs. Physical attributes can include your height, weight, face shape, nose shape, hair color, skin color, and general body type. Your interests can include what you like to do to when you're alone or when you're with friends, which subjects you like in school, what you'd like to pursue as a career, and more. Your social or psychological attributes can include your sense of humor, your sociability, your level of assertion, your independence, or your sensitivity. Your abilities should be your strengths and talents. Your beliefs can touch on your spiritual or religious beliefs, your political ideas, and your general thoughts about other people and the world.

Keep this inventory handy, because we'll refer to it throughout this chapter.

The self-concept becomes more concrete in the next few years and becomes stable by the ages of eight to ten. Very young children will be able to identify themselves and others by age and gender. By the time children enter school, their self-concept includes group membership—for example, their family or their grade—as well as psychological traits ("I'm a silly boy") and interests and abilities ("I'm good at puzzles").[4]

Between the ages of six and twelve, our self-concept becomes more refined as we compare ourselves to our peers. Younger kids will consider whether they can do an activity, such as being able to do long division, being a Boy Scout or Girl Scout, or being able to bake brownies from a premade mix, and they compare those abilities to their peers'. Older kids will have a more sophisticated way of making those evaluations of their abilities—for example, getting a high grade on a trig exam, being an Eagle Scout, or cooking an elaborate dish from scratch—and make comparisons to other kids.[5]

## The Shy Self

Shyness is part of many people's self-concept. There isn't a tipping point between being a "shy person" and "feeling shy" in specific situations. Identifying as a shy person happens when that individual cannot think of himself apart from his shyness. Either it infuses so many of the person's social interactions that he cannot think of a life free of shyness or it influences him during specific interactions that mean so much to him that it takes over his self-concept.

This is a subjective definition, of course, and it would be wrong to say that shy people don't understand themselves. But in many ways, becoming successfully shy requires individuals to begin untangling their sense of self from their shyness. Once they adjust their self-concept to include more than just their shyness, they can take note of all of the aspects of their life that have nothing to do with it.

Gigi, for example (see page 97), feels shy in certain encounters—when she's in a group of strangers and when she encounters acquaintances she doesn't know

> "When people tell me I'm a quiet person, I am surprised because I guess my mind always seems loud to me. Wait a minute. Come to think of it, I don't consider myself to be 'shy.' Other people might. Mainly, people who don't know me just think I'm quiet, unless it is someone I hit it off with. People who do know me would not consider me shy at all."
>
> —eighteen-year-old community college student[b]

> **Remember This**
>
> ● Your self-concept is made up of a wide range of elements. Shyness may be one of those elements. But it isn't the only attribute in your self-concept, nor is it the most important one that determines your fate. Don't let your shyness define you; it's only one aspect of your self-concept.

well. She doesn't report feeling shy when she's with friends or family, when she's at school, or when she's doing activities she loves. It's likely that these social situations make up the vast majority of her day. Yet her experiences in large groups—which likely happen less often—have become such a problem for her that she allows them to affect her whole identity. She doesn't say that she's among the 90 percent of people who say they feel shy in specific situations. Gigi says that she's among the 40 percent of us who identify as being shy. Whether that's a fair or accurate assessment is up to her, but learning more about her own self-concept and self-esteem can help Gigi develop a more well-balanced sense of self.

## Self-Esteem Isn't What You Think It Is

Like the self and self-concept, self-esteem is often misunderstood. Many people think of it as simple statements such as "I like myself" or "I'm a good person" or simply just self-confidence or "my happy place."

Self-esteem is a person's overall sense of self-worth. Where the self is made up of all of the elements of yourself, self-esteem is how you feel about those elements. It's how you evaluate yourself.[6]

The self-concept is value neutral. For example, you may say that you are a good skateboarder. You would have to have the skills to prove that. In contrast, self-esteem is how you feel about being a good skateboarder. You may think, "Being a good skateboarder makes me feel special; I like the feeling I get when I master a new trick." Or you may think, "Anyone can become a good skateboarder. It's really no big deal. I'm not as good as people I've watched on the Internet."

There are various ways of thinking about self-esteem. One is general self-esteem or specific self-esteem. General self-esteem is how you think of yourself as a whole. "I'm a good person," "I'm a piece of garbage," and "I'm a quality person" are all statements of general self-esteem. Specific self-esteem is how you think about individual elements of your self. "I'm a great joke teller," "I'm a math whiz," "I'm terrible at small talk," and "I'm not a good driver" are all examples of specific self-esteem.[7]

"I have suffered severe depression, loneliness, and isolation as a result of my shyness. Once I was very attracted to a girl at work. In the morning, rather than risk talking to her, I would use a path to go around the entire room, a distance of 300 feet. Awful! In therapy, my psychiatrist concluded that I am mainly shy with females, as opposed to being a basically shy person. That conclusion did wonders for my self-esteem."
—twenty-four-year-old computer technician[c]

Think back to Gigi's story. From what we know of her, she seems like a good person. She's intelligent, thoughtful, and considerate, so her general self-esteem should be fairly high. Her letter indicates some insight into her specific self-esteem elements. Gigi likes going to parties, so we can assume that "I'm a friendly person" is part of her specific self-esteem. That's a positive note. But, more negatively, Gigi would likely include "I'm not a good small-talker at parties" in her specific self-esteem inventory as well. If she analyzes her self-esteem in this way, Gigi can learn to develop a healthy perspective about her shyness and her self-esteem. Instead of allowing her lack of party skills to affect her self-esteem,

### Try This

Let's take a look at your general self-esteem. Consider how you would rate yourself overall on a scale from 1 to 10. Give yourself a 10 if you think you are an awesome person. Give yourself a lower score if you don't feel good about yourself. This is your general self-esteem.

Go back to your self-concept inventory. Look at each element of your self-concept and assign a value to it. Working with a scale from 1 to 10, give the items that you don't feel good about a low score. Give higher scores to the items that you feel good about. Now, look at your scores overall. Are they high? Low? Somewhere in the middle? The way you rate parts of your self-concept indicates your self-esteem on these specific items. Does it match your general self-esteem and sense of self-worth?

she can keep her doubts about her self-esteem in check and develop a sense of self-worth that takes into account all elements of her self-concept.

Another way to think about self-esteem is to consider stable self-esteem versus temporary self-esteem. Stable self-esteem is how you generally feel about yourself over a long period of time. In contrast, temporary self-esteem depends on context and is more variable. For example, you may be having a good day and you have generally healthy self-esteem. But if you trip in front of a group of people and become embarrassed, your self-esteem may dip a bit if you care about how you appear to other people.[8]

Going back to Gigi, her stable self-esteem should be pretty high, based on what we know of her. But she's likely to experience a drop in her temporary self-esteem after going to a party where she doesn't feel she's as outgoing and sociable as she'd like to be. If Gigi learns to separate her stable and temporary self-esteem factors, she'll be better able to not let a brief, negative experience affect her greater sense of self-worth.

## Your Real Self and Your Ideal Self

Another view of self-esteem comes from clinical psychologist Carl Rogers, who looked at why people may have high or low self-esteem. For Rogers, an individual's level of self-esteem comes from comparing one's real self to one's ideal self. Rogers's real self is a fairly accurate snapshot of one's self-concept. The ideal self is the person you want to be. The key seems to be whether someone reaches her

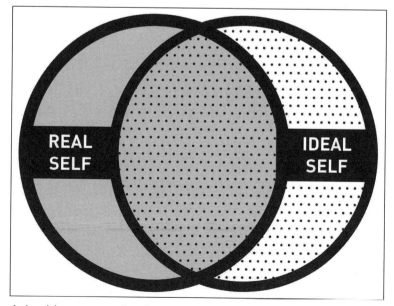

A healthy personality has a large degree of overlap between one's real self and ideal self. *Image courtesy of David Zylstra*

**Try This**

Write down elements of your ideal self. Now, compare them to the elements that make up your self-concept. How much overlap is there? Where are there differences? How can you close the gap between your ideal self and your real self?

goals or succeeds in what she set out to do. If the real and ideal self are similar, then one has relatively high self-esteem. A fairly wide discrepancy between the real and ideal self results in relatively low self-esteem.[9]

Once again, let's look at Gigi's experiences. Among the factors of her real self is her difficulty making small talk with strangers at a party. Her ideal self would be a good small-talker who's comfortable at parties. If she wants to raise her self-esteem in this area, she has a few options. Gigi would need to bring her real self more in line with her ideal self. She could learn to make small talk, a topic that will be covered in depth in chapter 9. That would bring her real self closer to her ideal self because she would meet her goal. Or she could adjust her perception of her ideal self and not worry about making small talk. If she doesn't aspire to be able to make conversation with strangers at parties, then she won't evaluate her performance and let it affect her self-esteem.

## What's Important?

Another view of self-esteem incorporates value judgments made by each person.[10] According to this viewpoint, self-esteem is affected by the importance an individual places on each element of his self-concept. In other words, the individual's physical, emotional, social, and psychological attributes that are important to him are the ones with the most impact on self-esteem. The attributes that aren't important have less influence on one's self-esteem. For example, if being a good guitar player is important to you, then your musical ability will affect your self-esteem. It will raise your self-esteem if you believe you are a good player while it can put a dent in it if you struggle with simple chords and can't even play an easy song after practicing it over and over. However, if guitar playing isn't important to you, then your ability to play the guitar—whether you're good at it or not—will have no impact on your self-esteem.

> "While I don't like shyness in myself, I think it's an attractive quality in others. I like shy people, perhaps because they're easier for me to approach and relate to."—twenty-four-year-old teacher
>
> "My shyness has made me feel very bad and alone in the past. There's nothing that I would like more than to have the self-confidence and self-esteem to be able to talk to anyone at any time in any place. I think it would enable me to live not only a happier life, but a better, more fulfilling life."
> —nineteen-year-old cashier[d]

Once again, let's turn to Gigi. Being sociable at parties seems to be very important to her. Since she has a difficult time talking to strangers at parties, her perceived deficiency will have a negative impact on her self-esteem. If she didn't care about it, then her social struggles wouldn't matter to her self-esteem.

One note about what's important to each person. As discussed in chapter 1, psychologists have found that people focus their attention on the qualities that are important to them and what they feel they are missing. This phenomenon is called perceptual saliency. It happens when you're hungry and fixate on the fast-food commercials on TV, or when you're nursing a broken heart and all of the songs on the radio seem to be about romance, or when you're feeling lonely and find yourself surrounded by happy couples, laughing friends, and rowdy groups of people.

It's only natural that when evaluating one's self-esteem, people, shy or not, will focus on what they lack, whether it's a physical attribute ("I'm so short!") or a social ability ("I can't speak up in class without getting nervous") or an emotional aspect ("I can't share my true feelings with my girlfriend").

But while focusing on what one lacks is natural, it shouldn't be the focus of every evaluation. In fact, people tend to ignore what they do well and take that natural talent for granted. These natural talents can be everything from being a good friend and listener to being good at math, being generous or being physically strong. The problem with ignoring or discounting things that we do well means that we don't incorporate these talents into our self-esteem—we only focus on our struggles or what we lack. This misperception skews our self-esteem in a negative direction. Gigi, again, is a good example of this. She isn't good at small talk with strangers, so she focuses on it. But she likely doesn't focus on all of the things she does well, including being able to have a one-on-one conversation with someone once she gets to know him or her.

**Try This**

Go back to your self-concept inventory. Circle the attributes that are important to you. Draw an *X* through the factors that don't mean much to you. Do you place greater importance on factors that you feel are your weak spots? Do you discount what you do well? Do you think you strike a fairly even balance between what you do well and what you'd like to improve?

## Internal and Social Sources of Self-Esteem

Self-esteem is a subjective way to evaluate one's self-concept. But where, exactly, do these values come from? How do we figure out which of our traits are important, or highly regarded, or detrimental? How do we develop the yardstick by which we measure ourselves?

One source of self-esteem comes from ourselves. We consider our personal attributes and abilities and rate them according to our individual, internal yardstick. Each person's evaluation will be different. For example, Tony may think he's a great cook because he can warm up a frozen snack in the microwave, but Aiden may think he's a terrible cook because one of his dinner guests needed to add just a pinch of salt to his elaborate meal.

Tony and Aiden are measuring themselves on different yardsticks. Even though Aiden is a better cook than Tony, he'll likely have lower self-esteem regarding his culinary skills than Tony. Being a good cook will likely mean different things for each young man so their perceptual saliency of cooking will differ. Tony may not care too much about cooking, while Aiden may want to apply for culinary school and become a chef one day. Or their ideal selves may be different. Tony's ideal self may not encompass cooking, while Aiden's ideal self includes being a world-class chef. The gap between Tony's real self and ideal self will be narrow. For Tony, being able to heat up a frozen meal will equal being a great cook. Aiden's yardstick is much different. Being a good cook means being able to create a five-course meal from scratch. The difference between Aiden's real self and ideal self will be wider because his aspirations are higher.

Another source of self-esteem comes from our peers. When we're in doubt, we turn to others to see how we rate—the phenomenon of social comparison, which was discussed in chapter 5. Think about walking into a roomful of strangers. As soon as we enter that room, we take a look around to see who's there, what they're wearing, who is talking to whom, what the energy is like in that room, and whether we will fit in. We'll wonder if we're dressed appropriately and if the room is full of people who are similar to us in age and social status. We'll notice if the crowd seems rowdy or relaxed, tense or somber.

When making these mental notes, we'll use social comparison to evaluate ourselves and those in the room. We'll think, "I'm dressed too casually for this gathering," or "All of these people are too important to notice me," or "I'm not as outgoing as these people," or "I'm the oldest one here," or "These people are all geeks."

We use social comparison to size up ourselves and others so that we can figure out where we fit in and how to act appropriately. In fact, using social comparison is a vital social skill. Just think about what would happen if you never used social comparison when in a new situation. You'd act inappropriately, not care about group dynamics, and constantly stick out, for better or worse.

We use social comparison when we're uncertain about our behavior, typically during life transitions—such as moving to a new city or starting a new school—or during specific social encounters that are new or unusual to us. Social comparison helps us size up situations and allows us to fit into larger groups. As discussed earlier, teens use social comparison often because adolescence is full of transitions—from a smaller junior high school to a large high school, for example—and uncertain situations, such as asking someone out on a date.

While social comparison can help us fit in, it can also affect our self-esteem.[11] After all, if your response to walking into a room of strangers is all positive or all negative, it's going to affect how you feel about yourself. For example, an internal dialogue that's full of "I'm hotter than these people," "I'm more experienced than these beginners," "My clothes are the trendiest," "I'm more interesting than these people," or "I could take any of these guys in a fight" will provide a boost to one's self-esteem. On the other hand, thoughts such as "I'm the least attractive person in the room," "My clothes are out-of-date," "I'm not as smart as everyone else," "I'm not as popular as this crowd," and "These people intimidate me" can have a negative impact on one's self-esteem.

> "As a young child and into my early adolescence, I was overweight. Therefore, I was wide open for ridicule. I admit this time in my life was difficult and not feeling one with the crowd I withdrew. I built my own little world with only a few friends who accepted me as I was, fat and yet a good human being."—twenty-three-year-old social media producer[e]

Comparing yourself to others can be a useful way to discover how to fit into a new social situation. The most helpful comparisons are made with people who are similar to you.

What's critical here is which yardstick is being used. To be useful, the comparisons one makes should be fair. The people to whom you are comparing yourself should be similar to you. This will help you make realistic comparisons. Comparing yourself to exceptional people—such as the most extroverted person in the room or a celebrity—will provide biased, unfair, and useless information for you. Remember, every group is full of people like you. Only a handful of people—or perhaps just one person—is the exception. Comparing yourself to people who are exceptional will only lead to negative and unfair comparisons and diminish your self-esteem.

**Try This**

Go back to your self-esteem inventory and look at the elements you circled. What are the sources of your evaluations? Are they internal, based on your own evaluations and goals? Are they based on your use of social comparison to others? How fair are your comparisons? Do you see a pattern?

# Shy Teens and Self-Esteem

While common wisdom indicates that most teens struggle with low self-esteem, in general, self-esteem tends to be pretty stable over time.[12] In fact, if there is some change in an adolescent's self-esteem, it's likely to change in a positive direction.[13]

Studies indicate that if you think pretty positively about yourself as a child, there's a good chance that you will carry that with you as you move through adolescence into adulthood. The converse is true, too. If you think that you're no good, stupid, worthless, or ugly as a child, this negative self-assessment will likely stick with you as you grow up.[14] These feelings about yourself could have been influenced by your family, especially your parents, or by your peers.[15] If you think about the messages that your family or friends give you, you can see how they can have a long-lasting impact on your sense of self-worth if they are overwhelmingly positive or negative.

Self-esteem can change, however. Obviously, temporary self-esteem changes according to what's happening in an individual's life. It can rise when you've succeeded on a certain task—for example, if you got a good grade on an exam—or it can lower if you received negative feedback or failed at something, perhaps by getting a bad grade or learning that you didn't earn a spot on the soccer team. These are temporary bumps and dips that occur all the time. And if you have a healthy and stable self-esteem, then these fleeting changes won't have a major impact on how you generally see yourself in the long run.

That said, self-esteem can change for longer periods of time during adolescence. According to a variety of studies, a teen's self-esteem can drop if he or she experiences a number of life changes all at once, such as changing schools, struggling with a changing body, going through a family breakup or other problems, or having a hard time dating. This happens to a small minority of teenagers.[16] Not surprisingly, these can impact an individual's self-esteem negatively until that teen begins finding solutions to these problems. And it's easy to see why teens coping with these negative experiences can feel down about themselves, lonely, and isolated.

Shy teens may fall into this category of teens who experience lower self-esteem during adolescence. As discussed in chapter 1, adolescence is the time in life in which young people experience a number of transitions, physically, emotionally, socially, and intellectually. Since shy people tend to struggle with transitions and become "off time," the many changes endured during adolescence can cause shy teens to feel more insecure about themselves.

Shy teens also use social comparison more often, and more unfairly, than other teens, which will have an impact on their self-esteem.

As discussed in chapter 5, shy teens rely on social comparison more often than other teens because they are more likely to feel uncertain in social situations than

> "I was not shy in elementary school. In fact I was really popular.
> But then you get older and kids become aware of society's standards and
> what's attractive and I certainly wasn't that type. Like I remember one
> teacher gave a pool party for our class and I wouldn't go because I wouldn't
> put on a swimsuit. I mostly avoided things that would make me stand out."
> —nineteen-year-old college student[f]

other teens. While outgoing teens can size up a situation quickly and feel comfortable, shy teens are slow to warm up to new situations, and while they're warming up, they're sizing up the people around them. Not only are they comparing themselves to others, but they also feel that others are judging them. They feel that an imaginary audience surrounds them, which makes them feel even more self-conscious. This heightened use of social comparison affects shy teens' self-esteem. Every social situation becomes an opportunity for judgment.

Not only do shy teens use social comparison more often, but they do so unfairly. As discussed in chapter 5, the "shy mind" creates a loop of negative self-talk. When shy teens compare themselves to others, they tend to compare themselves to the exception in the room—the most outgoing partygoer, the most beautiful person, the wittiest conversationalist, the most popular student, the class president. Or they compare themselves to an expert. So, for example, when they evaluate their joke-telling skills, they compare themselves to a professional comedian, not their own friends. In this way, shy teens don't compare themselves to their peers who are more like them. They don't notice the kids on the edge of the crowd, the ones who are quieter, those who don't spend excessive amounts of money on clothing, the ones who aren't drawing attention to themselves through their outrageous antics.

In addition to making the wrong comparisons, shy teens compare themselves negatively to these exceptional people. Instead of thinking, "Wow, I'm glad that I'm not an attention hog who has to create drama in every situation," they think, "I wish I could be as important as that person." These biased, negative comparisons will chip away at a shy person's self-esteem.

Think about Gigi, who wrote, "I think the way I see my shyness is a little bit warped because I know my friends are a bit overconfident. So I see myself as a little bit more abnormal than I am." Gigi notices her friends' overconfidence. She doesn't see that they may be overcompensating and acting out because they don't feel confident. In fact, they may feel just as shy and insecure as she does, but she is only looking at their superficial behavior, not their real selves. And, in addition,

> ! **Remember This**
>
> ● Social comparisons only provide useful information when they are fair. When you find yourself comparing yourself to another person, think about how similar that person is to you and notice the attributes that both of you share. In addition, find a positive comparison each time you compare yourself negatively to that person. For example, if your classmate has a newer cell phone than you, which makes you feel uncool, notice also that you got a better grade than she did on the last exam. In this way, you are providing more balance to your biased social comparisons.

she's glossing over and ignoring all of the times she feels confident, sociable, and able to express her true self with another person.

These negative evaluations can affect one's specific and global self-esteem. But they can also impact a shy teen's desire to act in the future. In a sense, their unfair social comparisons make them want to give up. They think, "Why bother attending parties and being part of the crowd if I'll never measure up to the class clown or most popular clique?" Eventually, shy people will avoid situations in which they feel they don't belong, which will deprive them of opportunities in which they can practice their social skills, expand their comfort zone, and become successfully shy.

## Successfully Shy Teens and Self-Esteem

Now that you have a deeper view of the complexity of self-esteem and how it relates to shyness, you can begin to change your perception of yourself and your shyness. Remember—shyness is just one facet of an individual's self-concept. It doesn't determine one's identity. Nor does it doom that individual to a life of low self-esteem.

Successfully shy people have a healthy view of their shyness and their self-esteem. They realize that shyness is part of them—but not their entire identity. In addition to being shy at times, they take stock of all of the other attributes and abilities they possess, whether it's being a loyal friend, meeting specific academic goals, or being able to speak out when another person is being cruel or unfair. And instead of allowing their shyness to lower their self-esteem, they realize that almost everybody feels shy at some point, so shyness must be part of the human condition and therefore shouldn't make them feel "less than" someone else.

The following scenario, told to me by a teen who attended one of my workshops, will help you understand how successfully shy people think about their self-concept and their self-esteem.

## Isabelle's Story

Isabelle is a successfully shy sixteen-year-old who just landed her first job working behind the counter at a busy fast-food burger place in the food court at the mall. She felt kind of awkward when she was filling out job applications and going on interviews to get a job, but her desire to earn a paycheck outweighed her nervousness. She's saving up for a new computer, which she really wants because she's trying to write personal essays to use when applying to colleges over the summer.

Isabelle felt intensely nervous on her first day at work. Even though everyone was wearing the same uniform, she thought it was dorky and didn't fit her well. She felt really self-conscious, as if everyone could notice that the shirt was too baggy and the pants were too tight. Nevertheless, she showed up at work a little early for her training, which consisted of shadowing the assistant manager, Cole, as he flipped burgers and waited on customers. As she watched Cole behind the counter, she felt more relaxed and at ease, probably because he was kind to her and told her that she'd make mistakes at first but would get better as she got the hang of things. He was right. The first time she assembled a double-decker burger she squirted too much mustard on it and forgot to add tomato. But Cole was cool about it. He laughed and told her to do it again, reminding her to double-check her ingredients before wrapping up the burger. She made another burger, more slowly this time, then checked it and smiled when she knew she did it properly.

Waiting on customers was a little bit more nerve-racking. It was super noisy behind the counter and her coworkers were running around behind her, so it was easy to get distracted when she was trying to take orders. She smiled and had to ask a few customers to repeat themselves. And she punched in the wrong order once. Cole told her to slow down and study her training manual when she got home that night, because the cash register was kind of confusing at first.

Isabelle left after her four-hour shift tired but proud of herself. She'd made a ton of mistakes, but she earned some money and learned a lot, too. She couldn't wait to go back on Saturday afternoon. Until then, she'd read the training manual a few times to make sure she wouldn't be a total flop.

On Saturday, Isabelle made fewer mistakes when putting together orders, so she felt good about that. But when some jocks from her school stood in front of the counter, waiting for her to take their orders, she felt anxious and nervous. One of the jocks made her so jumpy that she double-charged him for a chocolate shake. When she gave him his order, with two shakes, he got a little mad and wanted her to give him a refund. When she told him she needed a manager to do it and looked around for Cole, the jock just laughed and said she shouldn't bother—he'd drink both of them anyway. Isabelle blushed and wanted to hide, but when the jocks left and she had to take more orders she focused on her new tasks, not her recent goof.

## Reality Checks

Isabelle is a pretty typical successfully shy teen. While she gets nervous at times, she is able to change the focus of her attention from herself to the task at hand,

A shy teen's self-concept and self-esteem can be affected by testing her skills at a job that seems difficult, such as working at a fast-food restaurant.

whether it's applying for jobs, flipping burgers, or waiting on customers. When she's immersed in these tasks, she isn't able to dwell on her nervousness or awkwardness.

Isabelle's self-concept includes being shy. But it also includes a wide range of attributes ranging from being goal oriented and a quick learner to being independent and self-motivated.

Isabelle's global self-esteem isn't negatively impacted by her shyness. If you asked her what she thought about herself, she'd probably rate herself as "above average." She knows that she can improve herself in various ways, but she also knows that she is a person of value who has much to contribute to others, no matter how imperfect she may be. Plus, she has a pretty good track record of setting and achieving her goals, so she isn't daunted by setting more difficult goals, like going away to college. As Isabelle takes on more challenges, her real self becomes closer to her ideal self.

Contrast Isabelle's self-assessment with a typical shy teen's view of himself. While Isabelle has a healthy view of herself, a shy teen will allow his negative view of his shyness to cloud his entire view of himself. And since shy teens often opt out of challenges, they'll tell themselves that they shouldn't attempt to take on new ones in the future. This pessimistic attitude will likely lead to lower self-esteem and a wider gap between their real self and ideal self.

Now let's look at how Isabelle's new job has affected her self-esteem. Since she was in an uncertain situation, she compared herself to others. She thought she looked ugly in her uniform and wasn't as skilled as Cole in making burgers and waiting on customers. But then she realized that she looked just like everyone else in their uniforms—no worse, no better—and decided to learn from Cole, the assistant manager, instead of comparing herself to him. That's in contrast to how a shy person would evaluate herself in the same situation. She'd think that she looked terrible in her uniform and let her mistakes drain her confidence and sense of self-worth.

Look, too, at how Isabelle handled her encounter with the jocks. She got flustered and made a mistake when taking an order. Although the flub affected her temporary self-esteem, she didn't allow that embarrassment to impact her stable self-esteem. She realized that the jock wasn't that upset and probably forgot about the incident as soon as he finished his second chocolate shake. The mistake didn't affect her self-esteem. A shy person, on the other hand, would tell herself that the jock was just as focused on the mistake as she was—and would carry that negative impression around in the future.

As you can see, Isabelle's self-esteem is affected by her choices. Her shyness during some encounters doesn't have a negative impact on how she views herself. As a successfully shy person, she realizes that shyness is a part of her personality, but it doesn't form her entire entity.

# Enhancing Your Self-Esteem

Since self-esteem is made up of a wide range of components and decisions, it can be raised or lowered by one's choices. Here are some tips to think about evaluating your self-esteem:[17]

- Remember that you are in control. Your self-esteem is based on your beliefs about yourself, your abilities, attributes, and talents. It shouldn't be determined by what others think of you. Nor should it be controlled by your shyness. Shyness doesn't equal low self-esteem.
- Remember that you set the standards. You determine the factors that make up your self-esteem. These are factors that you feel are important to being a good, well-rounded person. And, in addition, you—not society, not another person or social group—create the yardstick by which you measure those attributes.
- Make realistic comparisons. If you are constantly going to compare yourself to an unattainable ideal, you will feel like a constant failure. Remember that surfaces can be deceiving. Images of beautiful people on TV or scripted scenarios in which everyone has a witty comeback are unrealistic. You will gain more valuable information about yourself if you compare yourself to someone who shares your interests, abilities, and weaknesses. And, in turn, you will likely raise your self-esteem when you realize that you are more similar to other people than you first realize.
- Notice the positive. It's natural to overlook and take for granted the things that we do well. But that's unfortunate, because those positive components won't impact your self-esteem. When you begin dwelling on the negative, remember to notice the many things you do well.
- Stop the negative self-talk. It's easy to dwell on small mistakes and allow them to become major errors through negative self-talk. That's how thoughts like "I'm the only shy person in this room" turn into "I don't belong here." When you start thinking this way, stop this negative spiral in its tracks. Realize that one small mistake is just that. It can only impact your self-esteem if you let it.

# The Shy Body, Mind, and Self

Now that you know more about the interaction of the shy body, mind, and self, you have a greater awareness of why it can be difficult to be rid of shyness. If shyness only affected the body, you could take a pill to alleviate your physical symptoms. If it only affected your mind, you could learn to divert your thoughts to something else. If it only affected your self, you could just think "happy thoughts" about your self-concept and become an extrovert.

But shyness is more complex than that and breaking out of shyness requires a little more thought. Fortunately, shy people can use their intelligence and desire to become successfully shy to change their body, mind, and self so that they don't feel like they are missing out on life because of their shyness. A good step to take is learning more about one's comfort zone—each person's familiar people, places, and activities—and how to expand it so that more unfamiliar elements are incorporated into it. That's what we'll cover in chapter 7.

# BECOMING A SUCCESSFULLY SHY TEEN

# GETTING READY TO GET OUT THERE

In the previous sections of this book, we discussed the internal, private experience of shyness. This private world of shyness includes how shy people think about themselves, the roots of their shyness, and how shyness affects their body, mind, and self-concept.

In this section and the following one, we'll turn to the external expression of shyness, or how shy people behave when they're in unfamiliar social situations and outside of their comfort zone. As we'll explore in depth in this chapter, the comfort zone is made up of familiar people, activities, and environments. Going outside of the comfort zone, whether you're shy or not, requires a bit of risk taking. But with some smart problem-solving skills and the ability to break down the comfort zone into manageable components, shy teens can begin to take safe but effective risks that will expand their comfort zone and put them at ease in new social encounters. With each step forward, their comfort zone will expand to include more people, places, and environments.

## Iggy's Story

Iggy loves the outdoors and is in his first year of college, where he's majoring in environmental studies. He says he feels shy a few times a week, usually in groups or with strangers and authority figures, such as professors. Like most shy people, he doesn't feel inhibited around his close friends. Although he only feels shy occasionally, he does feel that he's more shy than others. He isn't sure if he can take control of his shyness, but he's willing to try. Here's what he wrote to me.

As long as I remember, I have always been shy. Because of my shyness, in school peers were sometimes cruel.

My shyness is expressed by not talking and trying to get away from situations where I'm uncomfortable. I stumble over my words when I am nervous. I'm not able to talk well in front of groups. When I feel shy, I shake, sweat, and get light-headed. I've been told that these effects are unnoticeable.

In a social setting, I am very uncomfortable with groups of people, especially when there are strangers in the crowd. I didn't date much through high school and I was unhappy about that. Because I do not like to speak in groups, my class participation grades usually suffered. The required speech course was the worst class I had to take.

I have tried to make myself speak in social and occasional class settings. This has worked somewhat but I am still uncomfortable in these situations. One thing I didn't try consciously, but has helped me in overcoming my shyness, is using social media to express myself, especially if it's about environmental causes. Being able to express myself online rather than face-to-face has given me more confidence in myself in face-to-face situations and in meeting people I had previously only known through a computer.

I have found that as I get older and have more experiences, my shyness decreases. With a group of friends, especially those I've met online first or in one of the environmental groups I've joined, I am quite outgoing and comfortable. Still, when I meet new people or when I am required to give a presentation or speak to someone I don't know well who is an authority, I am extremely shy.[a]

## Everyone Has a Comfort Zone

When we are at ease and able to express ourselves without fear, self-consciousness, or anxiety, we are in our comfort zone. Take Iggy, for example (see page 119). Like most shy people, he feels at ease and free of shyness when he's in his comfort zone with his friends and doing what he loves. Although he feels shy and tense with strangers in person, he has no problem chatting with strangers when he's online.

The comfort zone is made up of familiar people, activities, and environments. Everyone has a comfort zone, although it changes throughout the course of one's life. When we're very young, it's very small. Young children are usually only at ease with a few people, perhaps their caregivers, other children in their play group or day care, and siblings or other relatives they see often. When they encounter someone outside of their comfort zone, they may hesitate a bit at first to see if that person is friendly. The activities of young children will be limited, too. They will have favorite toys, games they like to play, videos they like to watch, and a general routine that governs their day. And, lastly, young children will be familiar with a few places—their home, their care center, their relatives' houses, or the grocery store or neighborhood playground.

As you can see, it's only natural that our comfort zone will expand as we age and have more encounters with the world at large. We'll meet new people, who will eventually become so familiar that they will become a part of our comfort zone. An example is a student's classmates. On the first day of school, they'll be virtual strangers. But eventually, after a series of encounters, one's classmates will move from strangers to acquaintances to friends and become part of each student's comfort zone. Activities work this way, too. In fact, almost everything you know how to do was once outside of your comfort zone. But as you learned

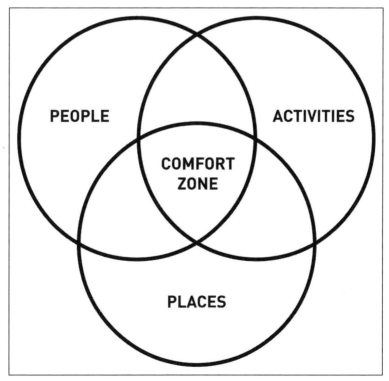

Everyone has a comfort zone made up of familiar people, places, and activities. *Image courtesy of David Zylstra*

new behaviors, you incorporated them into your comfort zone. For example, you weren't born knowing how to speak, walk, feed yourself, tie your shoes and dress yourself, brush your teeth, write and type, use a cell phone and computer, read—you name it; just about everything you can do now was once outside of your comfort zone. Likewise, the number of places in which you feel comfortable has expanded with age, too. Instead of just feeling comfortable in a few places, you've acclimated to new environments at school, in your neighborhood, at your friends' houses, and beyond, if you've been fortunate enough to travel outside of your hometown.

Although everyone has a comfort zone, it is as unique as that individual. Your comfort zone will not look like your sibling's, your parents', or even your best friend's comfort zone. These unique comfort zones will likely overlap, however. You will be included in your relatives' and close friends' comfort zones, and they'll be in yours. If you like doing the same activities—playing volleyball, perhaps, or listening to the same kind of music—they'll overlap here as well. And if you feel comfortable in specific places—in your classrooms, at home, or your regular hang-out spots—you'll have this in common as well.

## Try This

Take an inventory of your comfort zone. Begin with familiar people, the ones with whom you are totally at ease. These people will likely include your parents or caregivers and your friends. These familiar people will also include the people you encounter regularly and have a relationship with, such as your teachers, classmates, coaches, parents of friends, boss, and neighbors. They may even include people you encounter occasionally but feel a connection to, such as relatives who live in another state, your doctor, or a former teacher or babysitter. Now, list the activities that you do often or that you love to do. These activities can be social, such as hanging out with your best friend, or solitary, such as playing the keyboard or making videos you share with your friends. Finally, make note of the places that are comfortable to you. These will likely include your home and school, specific hang-out spots, and your neighborhood.

Keep your personal comfort zone inventory at hand, because you'll need to refer back to it throughout this chapter.

# A Shy Teen's Comfort Zone

Shy teens are just like everyone else—they have a comfort zone made up of familiar people, activities or behaviors, and environments. But shy teens' comfort zones have unique aspects that are dissimilar to other teens' comfort zones. Shy teens have small and rigid comfort zones that they want to expand beyond their current boundaries.

## A Shy Teen's Comfort Zone Is Smaller Than Other Teens' Comfort Zones

A shy teen's comfort zone will include a handful of people (close friends and family members), a few activities (playing online games, talking to close friends, or listening to music, for example), and a small number of safe spaces (at home, in the back row of the classroom, or online, perhaps).

Iggy, for example, likely has a small comfort zone. He's at ease with his close friends and his online acquaintances. His classmates are probably in his comfort zone as well—but not when he's making a presentation. His relatives are probably in his comfort zone as well. Definitely not in his comfort zone are strangers and authority figures. Of course, few people would include strangers in their comfort zone, perhaps only extremely outgoing people. From what we can tell, Iggy's comfort zone includes fewer people than his outgoing peers' or a successfully shy person's comfort zone.

Iggy didn't say much about the activities he enjoys, but we do know that he likes to chat online, is an expert on the environment, and is likely a good student. Meeting his online friends is something he feels comfortable doing as well. Speaking to strangers and to groups of people is not in his comfort zone.

Lastly, we know little about the environments in which he's comfortable, but Iggy is probably comfortable at school and at home, at his regular hangouts, and online. He's not comfortable at the podium, speaking to a crowd.

Taken together, Iggy's comfort zone seems pretty small. In this he is a typical shy teen, because he relies on his close-knit circle of friends for his social life. He may have known them forever, or he may have gotten acquainted with them online first before deciding to meet in person, but Iggy's familiar friends are probably fewer than those who comprise an outgoing teens' social circle.

## Shy Teens' Comfort Zones Are Rigid

While outgoing teens have fairly fluid comfort zones, which incorporate new elements with ease, shy teens' comfort zones have thick barriers that provide a wall between their familiar people, places, and activities and unfamiliar factors.

"Over the years, I would avoid going places and doing things so that I would not make a fool of myself in the eyes of those around me. Today, I recognize that the problem exists and that recognition makes it easier for me to deal with it. Overcoming the behaviors behind my shyness has not been easy, nor do I expect they will get any easier. But as long as I am aware of what is going on inside my head, it isn't as difficult as it could be."

—twenty-four-year-old video game programmer[b]

Shy people are at their best and most at ease when they're inside their comfort zone. They are not shy when they're with their friends, doing what they love, in a setting that's familiar to them. Iggy, for example, isn't shy with his longtime friends or even acquaintances he's meeting in person for the first time, if he has encountered them first online and has discussed environmental issues with them.

But stepping outside of the comfort zone triggers the shy experience for many people. The attempt to test uncharted waters outside of the comfort zone creates anxiety. For shy people, the social aspect of the experience is what triggers the shy experience. They feel self-conscious, assume there's an imaginary audience judging them, and become overwhelmed by their anxiety. For those who are not shy, they may feel frustrated when attempting a new activity (such as learning to play a musical instrument) or not feel comfortable in a new environment (such as traveling to another country). Shy people may feel all of those fears and frustration as well, but the social component is what is most critical to them.

Because shy teens feel blasted by the anxiety of stepping outside of their comfort zone, they retreat back into their familiar routine. They rely on their small circle of friends, do their habitual activities, and stick to familiar territory. This may reduce their anxiety in the short term, which makes them feel good in the moment. But their retreat into their comfort zone reinforces their dominant response to avoid or flee new situations. As this response is repeated over and over again, their limited comfort zone becomes more restricted and frustrating. Iggy, for example, is comfortable talking about environmental issues, such as the local recycling program, with his friends. But talking about the environment in front of a group seems to be very difficult for him. If he continues to avoid opportunities to speak to groups, it will become more difficult to do so as time goes on and the boundary of his comfort zone will become a solid brick wall that's difficult to break through.

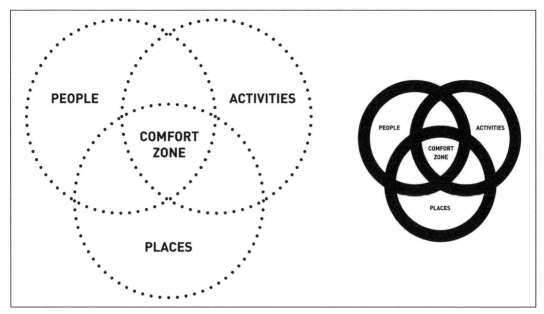

A shy teen's comfort zone is smaller and more rigid than a more outgoing peer's comfort zone. *Image courtesy of David Zylstra*

## Shy Teens Want to Enlarge Their Comfort Zone

Although many non-shy people think that shy people are happy when left to themselves, that's not the case at all. Remember—shy people want to be connected to other people. They want to act differently in social settings. They want to feel at ease so they can express themselves in a variety of situations that currently fill them with dread and anxiety. As a result, their small, rigid comfort zone makes them unhappy.

Think about Iggy. Iggy wants to enlarge his comfort zone. He wants to expand his social network (by turning strangers into friends), learn a new activity (how to speak in public), and become a part of the wider world (attend college).

Iggy's desire to expand his comfort zone is a common goal of a shy person. The problem that Iggy is having is that while he wants to expand his comfort zone, he isn't able to do so to his satisfaction. He puts himself in situations that will force him to meet strangers or speak in public. That's a good thing. But he feels that he fails when he does so. Instead of patting himself on the back for speaking up in class or approaching strangers in group settings, his shy mind kicks in and he tells himself that he can't do it or that he was visibly nervous and drawing negative attention to himself when he was speaking publicly.

Shy people also need to consider that their tendency to warm up slowly to new situations will be apparent when they try to expand their comfort zone. Shy teens want to be with others so badly that they assume they should be able to strike up

## Time for Reflection

Shy teens feel that their comfort zone is too small and too rigid to break through. Shy teens also want to expand their comfort zone beyond its current boundaries. Do you share these feelings? If so, when? Write down the areas in which you'd like to expand your comfort zone. Would you like to meet more people? Would you like to take a solo activity public? Would you like to feel free to be yourself in a new place? If so, you share the same desires as all other shy people.

Remember, shy people may feel alone and isolated, but they are surrounded by other people who feel the same feelings they do.

a connection in an instant. So when they feel anxious and nervous while they're warming up, they assume those uncomfortable feelings are a sign that they should clam up and run away or that they are terrible at making new friends. They tell themselves that they are shy and are destined to live a life of social frustration.

Shy teens' discontent with their small comfort zone is a positive sign. It shows that they are interested in meeting new people and fully expressing themselves with others. They aren't happy doing the same things over and over again with the same small group of people. Shy teens need to harness this desire to go beyond their current limitations and channel it into taking smart but calculated risks to expand their comfort zone. The rest of the chapter will show how this is done.

## The Factorial Approach to Expanding the Comfort Zone

In this section, we'll show how a shy teen can use a factorial approach to expanding his unique comfort zone. This will require some forethought and strategy, but it will diminish risks and increase the likelihood of success. This factorial approach will turn a shy and scared teen into a more confident, successfully shy teen.

Taking a factorial approach means breaking down the comfort zone into its three components—people, activities, and places—and working with each factor individually. The people in one's comfort zone will increase gradually; one's established activities will be built on and added to; and the places in which one feels comfortable will expand as well. Shy teens who use the factorial approach will focus on each component individually so that only one new factor—people, activities, or places—has to be dealt with at any time.

The factorial approach is unlike what shy people usually do to overcome their shyness. Oftentimes, shy people say that they tried to be outgoing and it was difficult so they don't want to continue trying.

A typical example is receiving an invitation to a party from someone you don't know all that well. A shy teen—

**Remember This**

● Changing one factor at a time is easier and more likely to be successful than changing everything at once.

we'll call her Jasmine—wants to go to the party, but it's filling her with anxiety. On the night of the event, Jasmine turns up alone, without any friends to help her through it. When she walks into the crowd in the backyard, Jasmine is riddled with anxiety and isn't able to approach the other kids with confidence. Although she recognizes some of them from school, Jasmine hangs out at the margins of the crowd, uncomfortable, and leaves as soon as she can. Actually, this is an improvement over the last time Jasmine received an invitation for a birthday party. That time, she felt so anxious and full of dread in the days leading up to the party that she interpreted that anxiety as a sign that she shouldn't go. She canceled at the last moment and beat herself up for allowing her shyness to control her life.

Like many shy people, Jasmine took an all-or-nothing approach to expanding her comfort zone. She was trying to incorporate new people (the partygoers), activities (making small talk with strangers), and place (the host's backyard) all at once, which is a very difficult task. She felt blindsided by anxiety and didn't give herself enough time to warm up to her new environment. Although Jasmine didn't drink alcohol, sometimes shy people will try to take a shortcut to becoming comfortable at the party by having a drink, but this isn't the best approach to dealing with a party.

At least Jasmine went to the party. The other alternative that shy people like Jasmine often take is to decline the invitation and not go to the party. This is their way of admitting that they can't break through the rigid barriers of their comfort zone. And, making the situation even worse, their refusal to go to the party will make the barriers surrounding their comfort zone even thicker and forbidding. The next time the teen receives an invitation, she'll have to work even harder to break through and expand her comfort zone.

Both of these approaches will likely end in frustration and failure. But the problem isn't that Jasmine cannot go to parties and have a good time. The problem is that shy teens like Jasmine who try to jump in without a strategy—or avoid the challenge altogether—are confronting too many new things at once. Remember, shyness is triggered by new social situations, people, and environments. If all of these factors are new, shy teens will be blasted with shy symptoms and be overwhelmed by their discomfort. But if shy teens learn how to minimize the new factors they encounter, they will be able to warm up and be themselves more quickly and with less stress and anxiety. This is the approach that successfully shy people take when they are faced with a new situation that can bring out their shyness.

## How to Change One Factor at a Time

The factorial approach to expanding one's comfort zone begins with isolating one component and changing it while keeping the other two components the same. In other words, keep two factors and add a new factor to gradually expand your comfort zone with little risk.

- People: If you want to incorporate more people in your comfort zone, keep the activities and places the same. If you and your best friend like to hang out at your local taco joint, you can bring an acquaintance (new person) to eat tacos (old activity) at your favorite hangout (old place). Or you can turn a solitary activity into a social one. For example, if you jog around your neighborhood every Saturday morning, you can ask a friend (new person) to jog (old activity) in your neighborhood (old place) with you.

Shy teens can expand their small comfort zones by changing one factor at a time. For example, instead of doing homework alone in the library, a shy teen can ask some classmates to join him.

- Activity: If you want to learn a new activity, keep the people and place the same. Let's say that you want to learn how to make a friendship bracelet. You can grab your friends (old people) and hang out in your family room (old place) and get to work on your bracelet (new activity).
- Place: If you want to feel comfortable in a new environment, keep the people and activity the same. Perhaps you play basketball with your pals in your driveway but it's getting kind of boring. Suggest that your pals (old people) play basketball (old activity) at the basketball court in your neighborhood park (new place).

As you can see, it's easier to cope with one new factor rather than three, and it's easier to go to a new place or try a new activity if you've got some old friends to support you. Shy teens, of course, will likely have more trouble expanding the people portion of their comfort zone than expanding the other factors of their comfort zone. After all, shy people have lots of talents (activities) and feel comfortable in some places (their homes, their friends' homes, school) but have a harder time incorporating new people in their comfort zones. And, in addition, shy teens have tried all sorts of things to avoid being with new people, so the barrier around the people component of their comfort zone will be pretty thick and seem insurmountable. But even though shy teens' dominant response is to avoid new social situations or clam up when they're with new people, that is a choice—not an automatic response or reflex. It's a choice that only feels automatic. Shy teens will need to learn new responses that will feel more automatic and easier until they become habitual or seemingly automatic. If shy teens are willing to put in some effort, they will become successfully shy.

## Help Iggy Expand His Comfort Zone

Let's go back to Iggy, whose story opened up this chapter. Iggy has some close friends; can express himself online, especially if it's about environmental issues; and can take some of his online friendships offline, to some extent. Iggy shows interest in other people, but he feels that he can't speak to strangers in a group setting.

Iggy can use the factorial approach to help him expand his comfort zone. Here's what he can do:

- Change the people in his comfort zone: Iggy can keep the activities the same (discussing environmental causes), and the place (school, perhaps, or one of the environmental groups in which he's a member), but incorporate new people into his comfort zone. For example, he can invite one of his online friends to one of his environmental group meetings. Or he can

**Try This**

When you decide to take a risk, don't just jump off a cliff with your eyes closed and hope for the best. Develop a strategy so you will take a moderate risk. Not only will you be more likely to reach your goal, but you will raise your self-esteem at the same time. Studies show that people who have high self-esteem take moderate risks. It seems that their realistic goals and risk taking enhances the odds they will be successful. Then, they can take credit for their successes and their self-esteem will rise. In contrast, taking a big risk, in which you have a low likelihood of success, will more often than not result in failure. In addition, taking a very low risk, in which success is easy, produces no sense of achievement and competency.[c]

When you decide to take a risk and go outside of your comfort zone, make sure you are taking a moderate risk. Using the factorial approach and other problem-solving skills will help you develop a smart strategy to lessen your risk. Instead of walking into a party full of strangers and becoming blasted with anxiety, for example, you might try taking a friend with you, arriving early so you can introduce yourself to others individually, and giving yourself enough time to warm up to the event. This will allow you to expand your comfort zone in a smart way and take credit for the challenges you have overcome.

check out a different environmental group so that he can meet new people with the same interests. As he continues attending these meetings, and warms up to his new friends, he will feel more free to speak up without fear of criticism.

- Change the activities in his comfort zone: Iggy can attend one of his environmental groups (old people) at the meeting place (old place) and create a demonstration or presentation for the group (new activity). Since there is safety in numbers, Iggy will have the support of his friends while trying something new. For example, Iggy can introduce a documentary the group can watch. He can prepare a brief report about an issue that's close to his heart. Or he can volunteer to help out during the group, such as handing out supplies or helping a guest speaker set up before the group begins. At the very least, Iggy can arrive early and greet members individually so that he can introduce himself and launch some new friendships. This foundation will help him build relationships and increase his self-confidence. From there, Iggy can try new activities with his friends—perhaps by participating in a neighborhood cleanup or raising funds for a good cause.

- Change the places in his comfort zone: Iggy can invite his environmental group friends (old people) to discuss environmental issues (same activity) at a different location (new place). For example, Iggy can go out for coffee after the group, carpool, or agree to meet outside of the group to learn more about the environment. In this way, Iggy will become more comfortable in a wider variety of environments and incorporate them into his comfort zone.

As you can see, Iggy can become successfully shy and expand his comfort zone without overhauling his personality and taking on a new identity. He can work with his current friends, interests, and environment to explore the world beyond his comfort zone. These small but steady steps forward will lead to great progress and increased self-confidence as he builds on his success.

## Help Jasmine Expand Her Comfort Zone

In Iggy's case, he was in the driver's seat. He was the one choosing how and when to expand his comfort zone. But what if a shy teen is faced with a situation in which everything seems to be outside of one's comfort zone? Go back to the scenario in which Jasmine was invited to a party. There are three new factors—a new friend (the host), a new activity (making small talk at the party), and the new place (the host's house). Even though this may feel like a lot of novelty, with a

**Try This**

Like Iggy, you can use the factorial approach to expand your comfort zone. Go back to your comfort zone inventory and select one person and one activity. Now add a new place. Next, select one activity and place, and add a new person. Finally, select one person and place, and add a new activity. Do you think you can put this into action in your own life?

little investigation Jasmine can identify elements that are in her comfort zone that can make her feel more secure and at ease.

- People: Jasmine may feel that the partygoers are a bunch of kids she doesn't know, but in reality she may know some if not all of them. She knows the host, of course, even if Jasmine doesn't know her well. They must have some connection they share, even if it's just being in the same geometry class this year. In addition, Jasmine can ask questions before the party to find out who else is invited. If she feels comfortable doing so, she can reach out to one of them to find out if they can go to the party together. Or Jasmine can wait until she gets to the party to locate someone she knows and hang out with him until she feels more comfortable.
- Activity: Jasmine may not feel like she can have fun at the party, but that's because she is worried about her social performance when she's outside of her comfort zone. In reality, attending parties, or at least doing the things that people commonly do at parties, is likely in her comfort zone. Jasmine can think about all of the parties she's attended in the past that she enjoyed and identify what she liked about them. Perhaps she liked watching her friends' faces as they opened up her gifts or had fun playing certain games, dancing, helping the host pass around food, or eating birthday cake. All of these activities are within her comfort zone.
- Place: Jasmine hasn't spent any time at the host's house, so it's outside of her comfort zone. But she's definitely been to parties at other people's houses, and perhaps she's been to that neighborhood before. If she hasn't, she might want to take a trial run and drive past the host's house, just so she knows where it is, or she can research it online and make sure that she knows where it's located.

## ? Time for Reflection

Think about a time when you, like Jasmine, had to deal with a very unfamiliar situation outside of your comfort zone. Like Jasmine, it could be attending a party, or it could be facing the first day of school, going away to camp, joining a new after-school club, or applying for a job or college. Write down the people, places, and activities that were inside your comfort zone when you faced this challenge. Now, write down the people, activities, and places that were outside of your comfort zone. Could you have taken a factorial approach to stretching your comfort zone by expanding one element at a time? Would that have helped you warm up to the challenge a little bit easier?

As you can see, even the most unfamiliar situations have elements that are already in your comfort zone. Successfully shy people rely on these familiar components and build on previous successes when they're stretching their comfort zone beyond its current boundaries. Like Iggy, Jasmine can take a factorial approach to expanding her comfort zone when she's faced with a challenging social situation. In doing so, she will increase her chances of coping with them successfully.

## A Word about Change

Change isn't always easy, but it is worth attempting. Change doesn't happen at a steady pace and in a straight line. In fact, changing a behavior has choppy progress. Think about the last time you vowed to work out more often, or set up a study schedule, or learned a musical instrument—all endeavors that required changed behavior. You probably got off to a fast start because you were motivated to adopt a new behavior. Soon, though, change became more difficult. This is because you were altering your dominant response and rewiring your body, mind, and self. But your struggle wasn't a sign that you can't change. It's a sign that you're making progress.

Remember: Change gets worse before it gets better. Changing your shyness by stretching your comfort zone and your responses to what's outside of it may be difficult at times because you are taking risks and changing the people, activities, and places that are familiar to you. When you first begin venturing out of your comfort zone, you may feel anxious, tongue-tied, or that you are rushing through your introductions to other people and bumbling through a conversation. That may be true for a little while, but as you build on your successes these difficulties will lessen. Don't quit when it gets difficult. That's when success is just around the corner.[1]

## The Four I's of Problem Solving

The factorial approach to expanding one's comfort zone is an example of a problem-solving skill for coping with shyness. But it's not the only problem-solving skill that

> "I have no fear when I am doing what I love. I am not preoccupied with my shyness. I don't feel I suffer all that much. When I feel ill at ease, I look for a comfort zone. When I feel really nervous and blush, I smile and say I am a bit shy. Once I say it, I don't feel so alone."—twenty-one-year-old cupcake decorator[d]

shy teens can utilize to navigate difficult social situations—or any other situation that requires a creative solution.

Some very basic problem-solving skills are known as the Four I's: identification, information, incorporation, and implementation.[2] The Four I's are so helpful in such a wide range of situations—including expanding one's comfort zone—that they can be used again and again to minimize risk and enhance success.

## Identification

When you go to a doctor or a mechanic, you need to know precisely which problem to fix. This is the first step of problem solving—identification. After all, if you have the flu, you don't want to be treated for a sprained wrist, nor do you want to fix a car with a dead battery by changing the oil.

Likewise, shy teens will want to identify when they feel anxious about a social situation, and why. For example, Iggy identified the main problem of his shyness as being uncomfortable when speaking to strangers in a group setting. He seems to have no problem turning online friends into offline friends, hanging out with his friends, attending group meetings, or speaking to girls. This precise identification of his main shyness-related problem will help Iggy develop a smart solution to that specific issue.

## Information

Once you've identified the problem you must fix, you need to gather information. If you've got the flu, you'll want to find some remedies that will make you feel better, perhaps by speaking to a doctor or nurse, researching on the Internet, or talking to friends and classmates who have the same symptoms.

In that same vein, shy teens will want to get more information about their shyness. Reading this book is a good start for an overview of shyness in adolescence. But for the problem you've identified and targeted, you'll want to gather more specific information. Iggy, for example, noted that he doesn't like to speak in front of groups. He can gather information by researching public speaking tips, learning more about the people in his group so he isn't so intimidated by them, or becoming an expert on a topic he wants to talk about in front of his group. In this way, he'll show up to the next meeting with more information and confidence in his ability to speak publicly.

## Incorporation

The whole point of solving a problem is incorporating potential solutions into your life. This means becoming more self-aware, committing to solving the problem, and making room in your life for change. In the flu example, incorporation could include setting aside enough downtime to heal and perhaps staying away from other people if you are contagious.

Iggy, like other shy teens, can incorporate solutions into his life that will expand his comfort zone. He will need to stick with his plan even when it gets difficult, give himself time to warm up in new situations, continue to act on his social interest by reaching out to other people, evaluate his behavior fairly and not become overly self-critical, and pat himself on the back when he's been successful.

## *Implementation*

Armed with identifying the specific problem that needs to be solved, information about solutions, and ways to incorporate those solutions into your life, a problem solver must implement his strategy in real life. A teen sick with the flu will need to set aside time to recover, take the right remedies, and allow herself to heal, for example.

A shy teen will need to act on everything he knows about the cause of his shyness and smart strategies before implementing a solution. Iggy, for example, will need to act on opportunities to expand his comfort zone by speaking up in his group gatherings—and also create opportunities by trying the

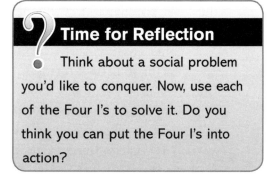

**Time for Reflection**

Think about a social problem you'd like to conquer. Now, use each of the Four I's to solve it. Do you think you can put the Four I's into action?

factorial approach and incorporating one unfamiliar element while keeping two familiar elements in his comfort zone. As discussed earlier, he could prepare a short presentation for his familiar group or help the group leader run a gathering.

As you can see, the Four I's can be used in a variety of sticky situations, whether shyness related or not. But, of course, any successfully shy teen will use problem-solving skills to help her cope with difficult social situations.

## More Problem-Solving Skills

In addition to the Four I's, try incorporating these additional problem-solving skills into your social life:

- Plan ahead. Researching the people, activities, and places you will encounter will help to lessen your anxiety and make you feel more comfortable when you confront a new situation. For example, if you are going to a new restaurant, check out its menu online; if you are going to try out for the tennis team, watch some practices and emulate the best players; if you want to ask someone out on a date, consider your date's favorite activities so you can share them.

- Go to your strengths. Shy people say that they are not shy when they are doing something they love. When they are immersed in their favorite activity, they feel a sense of control and mastery and are not concerned with being judged negatively by others. This is especially helpful if you are used to solitary activities that don't involve others. If you are shy but you're great at cooking, swimming, word puzzles, or writing, find a way to make these activities social. You can join a swim club, volunteer your time cooking, mentor a younger student by doing puzzles, or start a writers' group or write for your school newspaper. When you are doing one of your favorite activities, you will not feel shy as you share your talents with others.

- Manage your expectations. Not everyone can be the life of the party or the most popular kid in school. If you are trying to expand your comfort zone, take small but steady steps toward your goal. You shouldn't expect to become an extrovert overnight—nor should you want to. Judge your progress on your own terms.

- Brainstorm. A great way to get out of a rut is by brainstorming, just letting your mind roam free so that you can think creatively. The problem, of course, is when you let your internal critic begin shooting down ideas as soon as you can think them up. Instead, write down your ideas, no matter how outrageous they are, without censoring them. Then, take a break and come back to your list. This is when you can weed out the good ideas from the bad ones. So when you are developing ways to expand each factor in your comfort zone, don't eliminate ideas before you've given them a second chance.

- Practice. The best way to become successful is to practice the activity you want to master over and over again so that it becomes routine. That's what top athletes, musicians, and actors do so that they don't get caught up in their anxiety when they are performing in front of an audience. Shy people can practice making a presentation alone in their room or introduce

"I believe that my shyness can be changed if it becomes important enough for me to change. That isn't to say that I don't want to change it. Shyness is not a character defect. It just is."—twenty-one-year-old college student[e]

themselves to and make small talk with people they don't care about impressing, such as a clerk at a store.

As you can see, becoming successfully shy doesn't happen by magic. It is the result of taking small but significant steps toward expanding one's comfort zone. Utilizing the factorial approach and other problem-solving skills, such as the Four I's, can help to minimize risk and enhance your chances of success.

In the next chapters, we'll continue discussing the public aspects of shyness—making small talk and conversation and establishing friendships. Just like expanding the comfort zone, these activities aren't the result of magic and can be broken down into logical and manageable steps that any shy teen can take.

# 8

# MAKING CONVERSATION

........................................................................

When you think about it, every relationship begins with small talk. Very few friendships begin with deep conversations about intimate details that you only share with very close friends. Rather, relationships start with light conversations—small talk—that are more or less just chats about inoffensive topics that merely show that you are interested in talking further.

Unfortunately, a critical problem for shy people is making small talk. In fact, shy individuals tend to make a series of standard mistakes when attempting to make conversation with individuals they are meeting for the first time.[1] This is unfortunate because the leading course of action shy teens attempt to deal with their shyness is to try to make conversation with people they would like to know.[2]

These light conversations with people who aren't in their comfort zone bring out a shy individual's insecurities and heighten their self-consciousness. During these chats, they feel that they are being judged, and, in turn, they judge their performance harshly. This begins the shy process of self-consciousness and self-criticism as they struggle to feel at ease in this stressful social situation.

## Kenya's Story

Kenya is a college freshman who's interested in medical research. She feels that she is more shy than other people and is shy around most people she doesn't know well, whether they are attractive men she'd like to date or authority figures. But she feels that she can cover up her shyness by going out socially, even if she isn't talkative when she's in public.

"My shyness is difficult to see," Kenya wrote to me.

I am one of those people who ache on the inside while managing to look extroverted on the outside. You could pick up on it, if you looked, because I often run out of things to say in a conversation. I never speak up in a group or meeting of more than four people and I will almost never say more than hello to someone I do not know unless they start a conversation with me. I know some people see me as snobbish (until they really talk to me).

I try—but my mind goes blank—and nothing seems important or interesting enough to say. I know that I often look down and smile because I have nothing on my mind.

I have had many problems because of shyness. I don't speak up or ask questions. That was the same thing in school. I never asked the teacher a question in class. Maybe after class if I was really desperate.

Socially, it has been hard. I never dated much because I couldn't imagine someone actually liking me enough. I was involved with someone for four years. I was social because he was very outgoing and social. He knew everyone. We also had a regular group of friends so I knew them and did not have to go out of my way, consciously or unconsciously. I learned a lot from him but not enough to really make a difference. I still feel invisible and forgettable when I make the effort to talk to someone new.

Lately, the hardest part has been meeting people. I have never really been approached by anyone when I am out. The only times I might go on a date is if I meet someone a few times and they get to know me.

I am not ugly or fat or stupid. I am active, fit, and intelligent with a good sense of humor. But I always feel so unattractive because nobody ever seems interested in me. I can't help but feel that my shyness clouds the reality of the world.[a]

Fortunately, making small talk isn't a skill that we're born with. It's a skill that can be learned by anyone—including shy teens. In fact, successful small talk follows a specific formula, one that will be discussed in depth in this chapter.

## The Importance of Making Small Talk

Many people dismiss small talk as shallow, uninteresting, uncomfortable, and superficial conversation that is beneath them. They believe that small talk isn't

> **Remember This**
>
> ● Don't underestimate the power and importance of small talk. Small talk is the temporary bridge that we build to another person, a bridge that can become permanent if we wish to build a friendship.

important, while deeper, more intimate conversation is what really matters in relationships.

This belief is erroneous. Small talk is very important. Small talk is the temporary bridge that we build to another person, a bridge that can become permanent if we wish to build a friendship. In fact, almost every relationship begins with small talk. Small talk is how we show that we're interested in making a connection with another person. It indicates that we're friendly and polite, willing to share ourselves and able to make our partner comfortable and feel included. It's a vital skill in each person's social repertoire.

Another reason why people dismiss small talk is because they believe that small talk is shallow and pointless. This is true in some sense. We don't spend our lives only engaged in polite exchanges about the weather. But small talk is only superficial at the beginning. It leads to deeper conversations if both people want it. Small talk is the vehicle that carries the conversation to a more intimate destination.

## Why Making Conversation Is Difficult for Shy Teens

Making small talk is the cornerstone of every relationship. But not everyone can make small talk easily or without anxiety. Shy people, in general, are among those who struggle with small talk apprehension, or a concern for how others are evaluating them while they are making small talk.[3] They feel that they are being judged by their partner and judged harshly. But it goes even further. Not only do shy people feel that they are being judged on what they're talking about, they also feel that their whole self is on the line as well. This pessimistic attitude makes them think, "I'm totally boring him with my story about how I adopted my puppy from the local shelter. He must think I'm a boring and dull person." Shy people rarely think, "He's really interested in this story. I must be a charming, intelligent, engaging person."

Shy people feel this small talk apprehension because meeting new people is so important to them that each conversation is loaded with meaning. They want to make a good impression and be accepted and liked. They don't just want to say interesting things—they want to be interesting people.

Making conversation with new people is difficult for shy teens because they feel small talk apprehension, a concern for how others are evaluating them while they are making small talk. Shy teens may seem cold or disinterested in speaking to others despite their desire to make contact with new people.

In fact, one of the biggest myths about shy people like Kenya is that they want to be alone and aren't interested in others. But the fact is the opposite is true. Shy people want to be with others, a desire that's also shared by extroverts. The problem is that shy people get caught in an approach-avoidance conflict or, more specifically in this case, small talk apprehension. They want to reach out to others and meet them, but they get caught up in the anxiety of doing so. All of the physical signs of shyness come out—shy people get nervous, blush, stammer, have a dry mouth and sweaty palms, and are jittery. This makes them feel self-conscious, as if they are in the spotlight with a laser pointer focused on their flaws. Shy people interpret their discomfort as a sign that they aren't good at meeting other people and shouldn't try again in the future.

This theme is echoed in what shy teens say that they do to overcome their shyness. Since they're interested in meeting others, they place themselves in social situations.[4] They show up. They go to parties. They attend class, join groups, linger in the classroom and hallways, and eat in the cafeteria. The problem is that they don't know what to do after they show up. They don't know how to approach someone outside of their comfort zone, introduce themselves and strike up a conversation. They say that their mind goes blank and all of the shy stress reactions kick in. Or, as Kenya puts it, she simply runs out of things to say. (For a refresher on shy stress reactions, go to chapter 4.)

What makes their minds go blank? A few variables work together to create small talk apprehension:

*Small talk takes shy people out of their comfort zone.* When making small talk, at least two factors within their comfort zone are new. They are chatting (new activity) with a new acquaintance or stranger (new person), and they may even be doing it in an unfamiliar place. This wide, quick expansion of a shy person's comfort zone loads them up with anxiety and gets in the way of a successful conversation.

*Shy people believe small talk is all about them.* When trying to make small talk, shy people focus on themselves. They are excessively self-conscious as they try to expand their comfort zone. They dwell on their shy stress reactions (blushing, racing heart, sweating), their thoughts turn inward ("I'm so nervous I can't think of anything to say") and their emotions (feelings of failure and lack of self-confidence, as well as believing that their partner isn't interested in what they have to say). In reality, small talk is all about the other person. Small talk is how you express your social interest and make someone else feel comfortable during a new social encounter.

*Shy people have excessively high expectations.* Shy people think that when they make small talk they must be brilliant, witty, sophisticated, attractive—you name it. They feel that they need to knock out the other person with their wit and charm. That kind of pressure makes them anxious and nervous. In reality, they merely need to be polite and show an interest in their partner.

*Shy people make unfair comparisons.* Shy people believe they need to be as witty and sociable as the most extroverted person in the room, and don't even notice all of the slightly outgoing and quieter people who surround them. So, when they try to introduce themselves to a stranger and make small talk, they feel they need to overperform and be the most outgoing person in the room. This gets in the way of their ability to act naturally and think clearly.

*The imaginary audience is listening.* Small talk triggers the imaginary audience phenomenon, which makes individuals feel that the entire room is focused on them and judging them. (Go back to chapter 1 to review the imaginary audience phenomenon, if necessary.) It's as if they are in the spotlight and have cameras focused on them as well. Shy people feel that they need to perform for this audience, not just speak to another person in a one-on-one conversation. This heightens their self-consciousness and makes them act unnaturally and, obviously, impedes their ability to talk freely with their partner.

*Shy people's pessimistic attributional style kicks in.* As explained in chapter 5, "The Shy Mind," shy people tend to use a pessimistic attributional style that's internal ("I'm boring her"), stable ("I always bore new people"), and global ("I'm a boring person, period"). So when they make small talk and it is a little strained or

"As I see people around me surrounded by their groups of friends, I feel almost abnormal as I do not have a 'group' of close friends. This leads to an almost constant feeling that I am 'missing out on life' as I am not able to share these experiences. This is especially apparent as I see groups of people at public places (for example, at a bar) enjoying each other's company while laughing and having a good time. I am constantly very self-conscious and worried about others passing judgment on me. I project a negative self-image and as a result I am viewed by others as stuck up, unfriendly and unapproachable."—twenty-one-year-old college student[b]

uncomfortable at times, they analyze the situation with their pessimistic attributional style and take all of the responsibility for that conversation's failures—and they blow up that specific failure into a larger, more serious character flaw.

*Shy people believe that you're just born with the ability to make small talk—or not.* Shy people believe that small talk is an inborn talent. You either have it or you don't, they assume. But, in fact, making small talk is a social skill that can be learned and practiced until it becomes so familiar that it feels natural. Successful small talk follows a specific pattern, which will be covered in detail in this chapter, and is not any more difficult to do than typing, reading, or using a computer—skills that were once outside of a teen's comfort zone and are now firmly inside of it.

*Shy people make the same common mistakes but don't know how to fix them.* As will be discussed in this chapter, successful small talk follows a specific formula. But shy people are unaware of this formula and also make common errors when trying to make small talk. These mistakes will be covered in depth in this chapter, but for now it's important to note that once again, shy people are not alone in their shyness and social discomfort. It just feels that way sometimes.

As you can see, making small talk triggers the shy process. Fortunately, shy teens can learn how to make small talk—and practice this skill—and reduce their

## Time for Reflection

Think about the times you had difficulty making small talk. How did you feel before, during, and after this episode? Do you feel that your experience is unique? Or do you think that many shy and not-shy people feel the same way?

anxiety and expand their comfort zone. It will take some time and effort, but acquiring this skill is definitely worth it.

## The Small Talk Formula

A common misconception about small talk is that it is just mindless chatter that only superficial people engage in. In fact, the opposite is true. Small talk is an important kind of conversation that serves a purpose: It indicates to another person that we are willing to talk. Without it, we'd either be completely isolated when standing in a crowd or rush into an intimate conversation with a total stranger. Both options make us—and those we encounter—very, very uncomfortable.

A fascinating study by Philip Manning and George Ray at Cleveland State University analyzed successful small talk and found that each example follows a specific pattern that moves a conversation from initial meeting, to showing interest, to finding areas of common ground and follow-up.[5] A key element is knowing what to say and when to say it.

I've expanded on that pattern and developed a small talk formula that works like this:[6]

### *Step 1: Setting Talk*

Setting talk is the initial comments you make to a stranger or acquaintance, commonly known as icebreakers. These can be benign comments about the environment—"Is it hot in here?" or "I can't believe how crowded it is" or "This is my favorite song"—or a nonprobing question, such as "Have you been here before?" or "Have you seen Logan?"

These icebreakers can seem uncomfortable at times. But without this first step of setting talk no conversation will transpire at all. What matters is that you say something to indicate that you notice your partner and you're establishing that you want to converse. You don't need to be wildly witty or say something unique that will blow their socks off. You just need to be polite and show that you are interested in your partner.

> **! Remember This**
>
> ● You don't need to be incredibly witty or brilliant when breaking the ice or making quick talk. You just need to be polite and show you are willing to talk.

If the conversation ends here and doesn't move into anything more personal, then it's called quick talk. You can think of quick talk as the brief encounters you have with people every day, such as the polite comments you make with the barista who makes your favorite coffee drink, the bus driver who greets you, or a fellow student you see in the hallway. These brief encounters show that you are friendly and interested in making contact with others, but that you don't want to engage in a more lengthy conversation. Quick talk is how you fill your day with friendly people.

## Step 2: Personal Introduction

After establishing setting talk, the next step is to introduce yourself. If you fail to introduce yourself now, it will become more awkward as the conversation unfolds. And it's a nice transition from setting talk into something more personal. In fact, it's a good idea to include some personal information about yourself when you make your introduction. For example, you can say, "My name is Martina. I'm looking for Logan because he needs my thumb drive." Or "My name is Martina. I go to East Side High School."

Oftentimes, people will say that they are so nervous about introducing themselves that they immediately forget their partner's name. This is created by small talk apprehension. Their shy body and mind are producing so much anxiety that they cannot focus on their anxiety and listening at the same time. A good solution is to introduce yourself first. This will allow you to focus on your partner's introduction without having to think about how you will introduce yourself, or when. Another tip is to repeat your partner's name, which will help you remember it.

## Step 3: Pretopical Exploration

Once you and your partner have established that you want to talk, you can take the conversation further. You can do this by trying pretopical exploration, which is trying to find a topic that both of you can discuss in depth. What's key is that you need to find a topic that both of you want to discuss. You can do this by expanding on your partner's introduction—"My cousin Natalie is a junior at East. Do you know her?"—or by building on something else you may have in common,

**Try This**

The next time you find an opportunity to introduce yourself to a stranger, do so. Don't wait for an introduction or fail to do so at all.

> "I have tried to overcome my shyness by being around people as much as possible and getting involved in the conversation. However, after a few seconds I become very quiet. I have a problem keeping conversation flowing."—eighteen-year-old mover

such as the purpose of the gathering ("Have you been here before?" "How long have you been involved in this group?") or something you can offer ("I'm going to get some water. Would you like some?").

The important thing to remember about pretopical exploration is that it may take a while to settle on a topic. Your partner may rebuff your efforts to move the conversation further, or you may find that you have to make a few attempts to find common ground. For example, your partner may not know your cousin, or may not be willing to offer personal information about why she's at the event. If so, you can keep trying or take your partner's disinterest as a sign that she doesn't want to talk. Of course, your partner may be shy and caught up in his approach-avoidance anxiety and will be slow to warm up to your overtures.

Another key point is the rule of reciprocity: Pretopical exploration shouldn't be too superficial, nor should it be too personal. You want to match and reciprocate your partner's level of intimacy and self-disclosure. For example, you don't want to go back to setting talk and continue talking about the weather. That's boring and superficial. Nor do you want to rush into a deep conversation with a stranger—that's the dreaded Too Much Information phenomenon that turns people off. You don't want to talk about the details of your recent breakup and why you don't want to see your ex, for example. This will make your partner feel uncomfortable. You want to match your level of intimacy with your partner's. If your partner is discussing her thoughts on East High, you can discuss your opinions of East High or your own high school. But take care to mirror your partner's level of comfort and interest.

Lastly, questions or open-ended statements can help you find a topic to discuss. It's how you can test topics of interest and learn more about your partner.

## ! Remember This

When you want to move a conversation forward, remember to match your partner's level of intimacy. Don't go back to impersonal setting talk or rush into an intimate discussion with a stranger.

But don't allow some friendly questioning to turn into an interrogation. When you ask a question and receive an answer, follow up with a comment—"East Side High does seem really big"—or provide an example from your own life, such as "I don't know many upperclassmen, either." In this way, you will share something of yourself, just as your partner is sharing herself with you.

## Step 4: Posttopical Exploration

As you and your partner banter about potential topics to discuss, it's only a matter of time before you will find a subject that both of you want to talk about. This is where conversation really begins to flow. Think of it like a tennis match and respond to each comment that your partner makes. You can do so by offering personal information ("I can't wait for the school year to end"), asking more questions ("Are you taking Driver's Ed?"), offering an opinion ("These events are always boring"), or responding to what your partner says ("I spend my summers at camp, too"). Remember to keep matching your partner's level of intimacy so that both of you are comfortable. And when you feel that you've exhausted your current topic, you can introduce a new topic when it seems appropriate.

Small talk apprehension can be overcome by using the small talk formula. The five steps in the formula will help you move from the awkward, initial phases of small talk to a more substantial, free-flowing conversation in which you feel at ease.

> **! Remember This**
>
> ● Talking about your favorite topic is a good thing if you are engaging in a balanced conversation with your partner. But don't turn a dialogue into a monologue by shutting your partner out of the conversation and talking at them, not with them. Listen as much as you speak.

Although the most awkward parts of small talk are most likely behind you, there are a few things you need to know to keep conversation flowing. Remember to check your partner's verbal and nonverbal cues. Your partner may not want to chat with you, which he may signal through terse answers or silence. If so, don't take it personally. Simply take the hint, thank your partner for talking, say that you hope to meet again, and leave. Your partner may be preoccupied, shy, or simply in a bad mood. It's not totally your fault if he doesn't want to talk.

Another potential pitfall is relying on your favorite topic, or the subject you know a lot about and love to discuss. Many shy people are not shy when they're talking about their favorite topic, because it's within their comfort zone and they feel confident when discussing it. However, this is a double-edged sword. Although they don't feel shy and are happy that they're talking, at the same time they run the risk of dominating the conversation and not allowing their partner to chime in. When that happens, they are violating the rule of reciprocity because they are not allowing their partner to match their level of self-disclosure and intimacy in this one-sided conversation. To prevent this from happening, remember to take breaks to ask questions, give your partner a chance to talk, and read her nonverbal clues, such as looking around the room, seeming disengaged, or totally clamming up and looking bored.

## *Step 5: Ending the Conversation*

Terminating a conversation politely is just about as important as starting it well. You don't want to leave your partner with the impression that you are rude or that she is boring. A good way to end a conversation is by expressing your appreciation for your partner, excusing yourself, and offering opportunities to talk again. For example, you can say, "I had a great time talking to you and it was nice to learn more about East High. But I see Logan over there and I need to give him this thumb drive. I'll talk to you later."

A good tip to remember is reminding your partner of something you discussed. For example, you can say, "I didn't know East offered Driver's Ed classes.

**Try This**

The next time you end a conversation, express your appreciation for your partner. You can say, "Thanks for letting me know about that home-work assignment" or, simply, "I'm really glad that I met you." In this way, you are signaling that you are open to developing a relationship beyond this initial conversation.

Thanks for letting me know. I'll see if I can sign up." In this way, you are letting your partner know that you were listening and what he told you was valuable. You will leave him with a good impression and make him feel good, too.

In addition, you can make plans to connect in the future. You can tell your partner that you are on Facebook or another kind of social media, offer to give out your e-mail address or phone number if you are comfortable doing so, or make plans to talk together again later. In this way, you are building the bridge to a deeper friendship.

## Help Milo and Nina Make Small Talk

Now that you understand the formula for making small talk, you can put it into action. Let's help Milo and Nina, two shy teens who don't know each other, strike up a conversation while they're first encountering each other at a neighborhood block party. Neither one of them wants to be there. Milo's family just moved into the neighborhood, and his parents thought it would be a good idea if they attended and met their neighbors. Milo, a shy junior in high school, would rather stay at home and play games on his smartphone with his old friends than have to go to this block party and hang out with his parents. In contrast, Nina's family is one of the organizers, but Nina, who's shy in crowds, doesn't feel like she fits in. As a sophomore, she's too old to hang out with the young kids and her peers and the older teens are too cool to attend. A few neighbor kids who go to different schools are there, but she doesn't really know them. She's spending most of her time helping her mom set out snacks and sitting on the front porch, texting her friends about getting together later that evening.

Milo and Nina noticed each other from a distance, as groups of neighbors and little kids circulated throughout the afternoon, but both teens stayed close to their own homes and showed more interest in their phones. After talking to Nina's mom, Milo's mom kept nudging him and nagging him to approach Nina and introduce himself, but he resisted each time. He didn't know what to say to her, and he thought that she'd think he was stupid.

Let's help Milo talk to Nina. The place to start is step 1, setting talk—a brief icebreaker that shows that Milo is interested in speaking to Nina. Many shy people like Milo get stuck on this first step, because they believe that they need to say something incredibly witty and brilliant that really impresses their partner. But that isn't necessary. Those who want to break the ice simply need to show that they are nice, polite, and interested in their partner.

People who engage in small talk can have a few icebreakers that they rely on, such as "Is it hot in here?" "Hi, how are you?" or some sort of canned line. But if you don't have a standard greeting, a good way to do setting talk is to look at what you and your partner have in common in the environment. (That's why many people talk about the weather—it's a shared component of the environment.) But there are many other environmental factors you can talk about. For example, Milo can talk about the block party, Nina's house, her phone, the neighborhood in general, or the fact that their two moms were just talking to each other. Another good strategy is to ask a question that isn't too invasive and personal. And offering to help someone or complimenting them is always welcome.

Milo can say, for example,

- "Are you Nina? My mom said you go to Lincoln High."
- "So, what do you think of this party?"
- "They just broke a piñata. Do you want some candy?"
- "That's a cool phone. What kind is it?"

Notice that all of these icebreakers are not incredibly brilliant or witty. But all of them serve their purpose—to show Nina that Milo is interested in talking to her. That's all that you need to do to strike up a conversation through setting talk.

## Try This

Write down two icebreakers that Milo can say to Nina. Now, reverse their roles and put Nina in the driver's seat. Write down two icebreakers that Nina can say to Milo so that Nina is starting the conversation through setting talk.

> ! **Remember This**
>
> • Small talk is all about your partner, not you. It is the bridge that you are building to another person. Offer information that will put your partner at ease and show that you are not a threat. Introducing yourself early in the conversation is a good way to reduce your partner's anxiety about you—and, in turn, reduce your own anxiety about being rejected or judged harshly by your partner.

Now that Milo has signaled to Nina that he wants to chat, he can move on to step 2, the personal introduction. This is the best time to introduce yourself and move the conversation forward by offering some information about you. A personal introduction puts both you and your partner at ease, since you are identifying yourself and perhaps why you are there. By offering contextual information about yourself, you are reducing your partner's potential fear of speaking with you. She doesn't have to wonder why you are there or who you really are.

If you don't introduce yourself now, you may end up having a long, involved chat with someone but not have the opportunity to introduce yourself naturally. Some very socially adept people can introduce themselves later in the conversation without much awkwardness, but it can be difficult for shy people, who are already coping with the stress of making small talk.

Here's how Milo can introduce himself:

- "Hi, I'm Milo. We just moved in down the street in July."
- "Hi, I'm Milo. I'm going to attend Lincoln this fall. I'm going to be a junior."

Once again, nothing Milo is saying is incredibly brilliant. But he is showing that he's polite and ready to share himself with Nina. And, in addition, nothing is inappropriate. He isn't invading Nina's space ("Hi, I'm Milo. What are you doing on your phone?") or saying anything too personal ("I had a dream about you last night") or rude ("This block party is lame"). Milo is keeping things nice and light and showing that he can be trusted, exactly what he needs to do when introducing himself.

After the introductions, it's time to move the conversation forward with pretopical exploration. This is when you begin throwing out topics until you find one that both of you want to discuss. A good way to do this is to build on information gained from your introductions ("I go to Lincoln, too, but I'm a sophomore"), ask a question ("Which teachers do you have this fall?"), build on common ground

**Try This**

Write down two more ways that Milo can introduce himself to Nina. Now, write down two ways that Nina can introduce herself to Milo. Remember: Both Milo and Nina should offer some inoffensive personal information about themselves along with their names. For example, they could talk about the school they attend, the grade they're in, how long they've lived in the neighborhood, or whether they are having a good time at the event they're attending.

("Did you get a burger before they ran out?"), or offer a compliment ("I like your phone; I wish I had that one"). The key is to respect the rule of reciprocity and not get too personal with your partner ("I know your ex-boyfriend") or get too impersonal by going back to setting talk ("Nice weather we're having"). And remember that it may take some trial and effort before you can find a topic on which both of you can build a conversation.

Here's how Milo can move the conversation forward:

- "I'm new to Lincoln. What's it like?"
- "Does the neighborhood hold a block party every year?"
- "Is that a band on your T-shirt? I've never heard of it."

Milo and Nina may need to try a few threads of conversation before they can really settle in. But they shouldn't interpret any silences or awkwardness as signs that the conversation is going nowhere. They've already established that they want to talk to each other and get to know one another better. They should act on their interest in each other to make a connection. It will get easier as they warm up and become more familiar.

As Milo and Nina find a topic they both want to explore, they will settle into the phase of posttopical elaboration. This may seem easier than initiating a conversation, because you've both established that you want to get to know each other, but it can still be difficult at times. One thing to remember is to go to your strengths but not get stuck on your favorite topic. This is a common mistake that shy people make, because they tend to think that if they are talking, then everything is okay. But the problem is that shy people become so consumed with their favorite topic that they don't allow anyone else to speak. They dominate the conversation, which turns into a monologue. Remember to look at your partner and ask her questions at times to ensure that she is participating in the conversation, too.

Posttopical elaboration also requires transitioning from topic to topic when one thread of conversation runs its course. It may be signaled by silence or some awkwardness. To transition to a new topic, you can pick up on information you learned earlier in the conversation ("How long have you been studying French?"), from your environment ("Those little kids are really loud"), or bringing another person into the conversation ("My friend speaks French fluently").

Here's how Milo can take the conversation deeper:

- "Does Lincoln require sophomores to take a foreign language?"
- "Do you know those guys over there?"
- "My sister plays in a band. Do you want to meet her?"

Remember that it may take some effort to build a new topic of conversation. But it'll get easier to talk when you know more about your partner and have more information to turn into a topic of discussion.

At some point, Milo and Nina will have to end the conversation. A good way to do so is to say that you need to leave and express your thanks for your partner ("I have to go, but I really enjoyed speaking with you") and then extend the opportunity to speak in the future ("I'll let you know the next time I go to the beach to see if you're available"). If you feel comfortable, you can give your new friend your e-mail address or phone number, or ask if you can contact him in the future on the phone or via social media. Remember: You are in control of your shyness and social life. If you want to build new friendships, you will need to take the initiative and create opportunities to develop your relationships.

Here's how Milo can end his conversation with Nina and initiate a friendship with her:

- "I have to go, but thanks for telling me about that band. I'd like to check them out in the future."
- "I see my dad needs to talk to me, but I had a great time talking to you. Can I friend you on Facebook?"
- "I need to go, but thanks for the tips about Lincoln. Would it be all right if I called you if I have more questions?"

Notice that Milo is being polite and thanking Nina for sharing herself with him. In this way, he's creating a positive, lasting impression and ensuring that Nina doesn't feel rejected because he is ending the conversation. Notice, too, that he is creating ways to include her in his comfort zone—and expanding his comfort zone by including her and her interests in it.

## Golden Rules about Making Small Talk for Shy Teens

In addition to knowing and practicing the small talk formula, it's good to know some other golden rules about striking up a conversation with a stranger or acquaintance:

**Try This**

Write down two ways that both Milo and Nina could end the conversation. Then, look back at all of your responses in this section. Do you think that you could use this conversation as a model for your small talk opportunities in the future?

- Focus on your partner. Shy teens often dread making small talk or putting themselves in social situations in which they'll have to mingle with a lot of strangers. That creates small talk apprehension, which gets in the way of their ability to connect with other people. They can overcome their small talk apprehension by focusing on their partner, not their own internal discomfort. This will help shy teens be able to act naturally, listen carefully, and approach others with confidence.

- Give yourself time to warm up. Small talk apprehension will create some anxiety. A good way to take control of your anxiety is to give yourself time to warm up and get used to the new people, places, and activities outside of your comfort zone. For example, if you're at a party, take some time to settle in before you approach someone else to make small talk.

- Respond to the small talk efforts of others. Recognize the efforts of other people to make small talk with you and get to know you better. Don't brush off others' attempts to talk to you. Respond with a smile, some setting talk, and an introduction.

- Create opportunities for small talk. Shy teens tend to avoid strangers when they can, and some may go to great lengths to stay away from situations in which they'll encounter new people. But that strategy will only hardwire their aversion to small talk. Instead, take advantage of all of the opportunities for small talk or quick talk that exist every day. These include talking to a store clerk or cashier, school acquaintances, teachers, coaches, mentors, or neighbors. Think of this as practice for more difficult small talk opportunities, such as parties or group gatherings.

- Silence doesn't mean rejection. Shy teens often interpret silence or awkwardness as a sign that they are failing. But conversation naturally has ebbs and flows of chatter and silence. Silence during small talk isn't necessarily a sign that your partner doesn't want to talk to you. If your partner doesn't seem responsive to you, don't take it to heart. He may be anxious or nervous and unable to really focus on the conversation, preoccupied by something else, or trying to formulate a response or a new topic of conversation. You can terminate the conversation ("It was nice speaking with you") or continue trying to move the conversation forward by finding a new topic to discuss.

- Make eye contact. Shy teens tend to not make eye contact with their partners as a way to reduce their overwhelming anxiety. But not looking at your partner can lead to the mistaken assumption that you are not interested, are bored, or rude.[7] The next time you are speaking with someone else, whether it's a stranger or a good friend, make sure that you make eye contact with her. It will get easier the more often you do it.

- Don't rush to become best friends. Many shy teens go too deep during conversations and reveal too much personal information too quickly. They do this because they want to be accepted by their partner, and revealing personal information is one way to do that, and because they are unsure about how to develop a conversation naturally. But this rush to intimacy doesn't work. It turns off their partners, who are wondering why they are learning inappropriate information about strangers. It makes people uncomfortable. Remember the rule of reciprocity and match the level of intimacy of your partner.

- Go to your strengths but don't get stuck there. Shy teens like to talk about their favorite topics, because they know a lot about those topics and feel confident discussing them. That's great. But watch out and don't get stuck on your favorite topics and bore your listeners. Remember to take breaks and ask questions and allow your partner to speak as well. And look for unspoken clues that your partner is getting bored, perhaps by looking around the room, going totally silent, or looking uninterested in your monologue.

Overall, shy people can overcome their small talk apprehension by acting on their sincere interest in other people. What's critical is that they focus their thoughts on others, not themselves. As long as shy people take and create opportunities to make small talk, they will find it easier to talk to people who are outside of their comfort zone, and to become successfully shy.

## Breaking into a Conversation

Although creating small talk in a one-on-one situation can be difficult, it's also awkward at times to break into a conversation that's already underway. For example, you may be at a party and a few people are talking about a basketball tournament. You want to join in. But how?[8]

The best way to get involved is to show that you want to be involved. Stand near the people who are talking and listen intently—and show that you're listening intently by smiling, nodding, laughing at jokes, or otherwise showing that you're a silent participant in the discussion. This is called the wait-and-hover

> "The most obvious sign of my shyness is silence. I am much happier listening to the conversation than actively taking part in it. However, if I do speak, I make jokes to compensate for my nervousness. I laugh a lot, wring my hands, sweat, and fidget."—twenty-one-year-old digital illustrator[d]

approach—which will be covered in depth in the next chapter—and it serves a few objectives. It allows the shy person to get used to the others and pick up the thread of the conversation, which will help to alleviate small talk apprehension. And it allows the others to get used to the shy person as well and realize that he is not a threat to their discussion.

Then, it's time to wait for a lull in the conversation, which provides an opportunity to join in. But how? Here are some options for joining a conversation about the basketball tournament:

- Compliment the speaker: "I had no idea that the Falcons were in the tournament. How did you know that?"
- Ask a question: "Do you know if the Wildcats are in the tourney?"
- Build on the previous comment: "The Falcons had a great season. They're my pick for making it to the finals."
- Offer something new: "I'm going to get another soda. Does anyone want one?"
- Join in: "I couldn't help but overhear you discuss the Falcons. Mind if I join in?"

As you can see, joining an existing conversation doesn't happen by magic, nor must you rely on luck to get involved. Just like making small talk in general, breaking into a conversation is something anyone can do as long as you are polite and show a genuine interest in other people.

## Building the Bridge to a Friendship

Many people dismiss small talk as being shallow and superficial, but it's actually the launchpad of every relationship. Unfortunately, making small talk is a major obstacle for many shy people, who get caught up in their small talk apprehension because they have difficulty thinking clearly and speaking with confidence while they're entangled in their anxiety. Fortunately, shy people can reduce their small talk anxiety by learning and practicing the small talk formula. As explained throughout this chapter, shy teens don't need to be incredibly brilliant or witty when doing so. They merely need to be polite and genuinely interested in their partner. Remember: Small talk is about your partner. It's how you build the bridge to another person.

In the next chapter, we'll explore how small talk can be used to create lasting friendships and an expanded comfort zone.

# MAKING FRIENDS

In the previous chapter, we explored the importance and purpose of small talk. It's the bridge that we build to another person and no relationship begins without it. In this chapter, we'll discuss how to use small talk and other social skills to establish a friendship. Like all teens, shy teens want to be friends with their peers. But they aren't sure how to make that happen, which creates approach-avoidance anxiety that gets in the way of making a connection with another person and forming a bond.

Like all social skills, the art of making friends isn't something that someone is born with. It's a skill that can be learned and practiced until it feels like a reflex that happens automatically.

In this chapter, we'll explore the role of friendships during adolescence, how childhood patterns of social interaction are carried into adolescence, and how shy teens can implement new strategies for creating a friendship and becoming successfully shy.

## Why Friendships during Adolescence Are So Important

Olivia's story (see page 160) strikes at the heart of friendships during adolescence, especially the friendships that shy teens develop—or aspire to develop. Like all teens, shy teens want companionship. They want to be understood, especially by those who are going through the same experiences they are. And they want to be admired and feel attractive, too, even if they don't fit accepted physical standards of our society.

There's a very good reason why adolescents value friendships so much. According to noted developmental psychologist Erik Erikson, adolescence, as explained in chapter 1, is a time of turbulence and incredible change during which we learn new tasks and develop a more mature identity that we carry into adulthood.[1] Teens undergo a huge growth spurt—not just physically, but emotionally, intellectually, and socially as well as they experiment with new roles, new behaviors, new types of relationships. This wave of change upon change makes teens feel uncomfortable, vulnerable, and highly self-conscious. Teens feel that they

## Olivia's Story

Olivia is a seventeen-year-old high school senior who also has a part-time job as a cashier in a big-box store. She says that she's always been shy and that she feels she's much more shy than others. Olivia is trying to overcome her shyness, but she doubts that she can do it. Still, she has some good friends she hangs out with, and she's really into music—not only does she listen to it, but she tries to compose her own songs on her guitar. She hasn't worked up the courage to perform in public yet, but she'd love to be able to do so. That may surprise many people, because Olivia is a "shy rebel" whose outward appearance is outrageous, a mask for her shyness and vulnerability. On the outside, she may seem fierce, but inside Olivia is a very sensitive young woman who doesn't know how to express her true self with others.

"I think that one of the factors that has made me a shy person is the way that I look," she wrote to me.

I am much shorter than other kids my age. For example, at my first concert, other people laughed at me like I was out of place.

When I first meet someone I'm very quiet until they talk about something I'm interested in. And then I think I tend to over-do my part of the conversation. I try hard to impress other people.

Since I am very shy, I don't get close to very many people, even when I want to.

When I was fourteen, I thought that if I acted like I didn't care what other people thought of me, that would help me overcome my shyness. I shaved my head, pierced my nose and eyebrows, my lip, and my tongue. My ears were pierced six times on each ear. As I got older, my rebellion brought me more negative attention than positive.

I want to get over my shyness. I want to be able to walk into a room with other people and not feel like an outcast.[a]

Friendships provide teens with much more than companionship. Friends help each other navigate the many changes encountered during adolescence.

are the only ones who are going through these changes and that their personal journey is so unique that no one will ever understand them, a phenomenon called the "personal fable."[2] They don't feel like they belong, but they desperately want to belong to some group, not only for companionship, but to affirm their identity and their place in the world.[3]

During this time of incredible uncertainty, all adolescents look for cues from their peers, the phenomenon called "social comparison."[4] They look for social signals about how to behave, how to dress, how to try out new behaviors, and how to date and form a romantic relationship. This is a significant shift from childhood, when younger kids are more likely to turn to parents or authority figures for guidance on how to behave. That's why teens are so caught up in their friendships—their friends are their comrades and their guides through the rocky years of adolescence.

Friendships help teens navigate all of these changes in very important ways.

Friendships help teens develop an identity. When teens belong to a social group or clique, the group gives them a sense of identity, perhaps as a jock, brain, burnout, loser, rocker, or popular kid. Even Olivia, who changed her

> ! **Remember This**
>
> ● Adolescence is a time of incredible change. To reduce uncertainty during this phase of life, teens turn to fellow teens for cues on how to behave, present themselves, develop romantic relationships, and create an identity. But as teens become more confident in their identity, they will act on their own unique beliefs instead of following the crowd.

physical appearance to keep people away from her, did so to build what's called a negative identity, an identity that's the opposite of what is expected.

Friendships also provide security. During times of threat or anxiety, numbers create security. If you can join a group or strike up a partnership or alliance with another person, you will be able to fend off challenges or threats from outsiders.

In addition, friendships help set the stage for intimacy. While childhood friendships tend to be simple, adolescent friendships become more complex. That's because teenagers' lives and emotions are more complex, so the bonds they share will be, too. This complexity shouldn't be dismissed or minimized. It's setting the stage for more intimate relationships that teens will build when they reach adulthood.

And, finally, friendships help expand a teen's comfort zone. When you think about it, adolescence in general is about expanding one's comfort zone, a time when we incorporate new people, activities, and places into our lives at a rapid rate. Having companions along the way helps us make the unfamiliar less threatening.

As you can see, friendships play a critical role in an adolescent's life, and having a wide social circle will help a teen get through the uncertainty of adolescence a bit more easily. After all, if you are able to reach out and connect with a number of peers who are going through the same thing as you, you will feel less isolated, more "normal" than someone who isn't as connected and protected.

## Gender Differences Become More Pronounced

Besides being more complicated, adolescent friendships are also marked by gender differences. During childhood, boys and girls tend to play differently and separately. But as boys and girls age and become preteens and teens, the impact of gender on one's friendships becomes more pronounced.[5]

In general, boys' friendships and social groups are based on shared activities and physical strength.[6] Boys do things—play sports, video games, take risks, and make their mark on the world. Boys vie to be at the top of the heap, to be the best

**Time for Reflection**

● Do you feel your relationships changed when you became a preteen or teenager? How? Do you notice the gender differences in teen friendships? Do you feel that the gender differences feel right, or would you like to break out of their limitations?

athlete, the most adept gamer, the most courageous risk taker, and the highest achiever. When that happens, their status among their peers rises. In fact, it even rises among girls, since girls tend to be attracted to boys with the highest status within their group.

Shy teen boys tend to feel that they lose out on this battle for dominance. They're less willing to take risks—unless they resort to alcohol, which is never advised—and are more likely to become the lower-status members of the group. Boys who develop shyness in adolescence will point to their off-time development as the cause. They may be late to physically mature, which hampers their athleticism and makes them targets for bigger boys. And since they are low status, shy teen boys will probably feel that they are less attractive to girls and will be less likely to approach them for a date.

Girls' relationships are also infused with battles for power, but status isn't achieved by what they do. It's achieved by their interpersonal connections and appearance. In comparison to boys, the network of friends for adolescent girls tends to be small and exclusive.[7] Girls tend to share information and support; their friendships are all about connections. Due to their exclusiveness, the pressure to connect with others can turn into the pressure to conform. That's why you see adolescent girls dress the same as their friends, own the same possessions, and ostracize other girls who are different. This isn't because girls are inherently shallow and superficial. It's a general means by which to cement connections and identify who's in the group and who's out.

Shy teen girls are probably less likely to play this connection game because it takes them longer to warm up to new people than their more outgoing peers. They are also likely to have fewer relationships than most extroverted girls, or they will be the passive ones in a relationship and lose their true identity.

## Shy Teens' Friendship Barriers

Contrary to conventional wisdom, shy teens—even shy rebels like Olivia—want to be friends with other teens. But they face barriers that keep them separate from others. They want to make connections with their peers, but they doubt their ability to do so and be accepted by another person. Also contrary to conventional wisdom, shy teens do have friends. They just have fewer friends than they'd like to have.

One barrier shy teens have when trying to create a friendship is that they feel an approach-avoidance conflict when faced with new people. Shy teens want to connect with a new person, but they become filled with anxiety and acute self-consciousness because they fear being judged and rejected by the new person. This approach-avoidance conflict makes shy teens feel uncomfortable and less inclined to take a moderate risk by introducing themselves to someone new.

In addition, shy teens are slow to warm up to other people. We all have a warm-up period when acclimating to a new person. But it takes a shy teen a bit longer to get used to someone new. So it will likely take him a longer time to become friends with someone, typically after a period of repeated encounters, as happens when we routinely see another person in school, at work, or during a regular social activity.

Shy teens may not feel at ease with new people because they're off time. Since shy teens have a longer warming-up period than their more outgoing peers, it takes them longer to adapt to new activities and social challenges. So when they are ready to take a small risk, like asking someone out on a date, their friends have moved on to another challenge, leaving them behind. This tendency to be off time creates a disconnection in one's relationships because the shy teen isn't going through the same thing as his or her peers and loses critical social support. In addition, some teens may feel shy because they are early or late bloomers who are off time physically, which makes them feel self-conscious. If a teen boy physically matures later than his peers, he'll be less likely to dominate his group. If a teen girl matures earlier than her peers, she may not be ready for the attention she generates from others and may withdraw from social encounters. Or, like Olivia, she may be a late bloomer and seem younger than her age, which makes her feel self-conscious and uncomfortable.

Another friendship barrier is a shy teen's rigid comfort zone. Since shy teens feel more resistance when expanding their comfort zone, it will be harder for them to reach out to an unfamiliar person and find areas of common ground.

"I prefer to get lost in a crowd. I'm reluctant to dance and make small talk, or arrange immediate social activities with new acquaintances. I prefer to have others approach me and I have difficulty expressing my emotions to others. I'm easily bored."—twenty-one-year-old welder[b]

And as they repeatedly withdraw from new encounters, their dominant response to them will be withdrawal and avoidance. The thought of approaching a new person seems too risky and threatening for them.

Shy teens' mind-set can become a barrier to forming friendships because they make unfair comparisons. During times of uncertainty, we use social comparison to figure out how to fit in. The best, most instructive comparisons we can make are to the people who are most like us. But shy teens tend to compare themselves to people who are exceptional—for example, distant celebrities or the most popular or extroverted person in the room—and overlook the quieter, more average people who surround them. Unfortunately, these unrealistic comparisons may make shy people feel negatively about themselves and their social behavior and status, making it much more difficult for them to create a friendship with someone new.

Lastly, shy teens' social skills deficit makes it difficult to connect with new people. For example, shy teens find that making small talk is difficult for them so they avoid it or, like Olivia, wait for someone to break the ice with them and talk about a subject close to their heart. Fortunately, social skills are something that can be learned, and shy teens who are willing to practice them and incorporate them into their lives will find that they can become successfully shy with relative ease.

As you can see, shy teens have some barriers to forming friendships. Fortunately, these barriers are not permanent obstacles that will stand in the way of making a connection with someone else. What's more, once these barriers are overcome and they incorporate new people into their comfort zone, shy people find that they are free of their shyness. That's why so many shy people say that their good friends have no idea that they are shy. Their shyness falls away once the novelty of the relationship wears off and the relationship is incorporated into the teen's comfort zone.

## Styles of Shy Social Interaction

Shy teens may not be able to identify why, exactly, they find making friends to be so difficult. There is likely a mix of nature (biological) and nurture (environmental)

### Time for Reflection

Take a friendship inventory. Are you satisfied with the number of friends you have? Do you feel that you have high-quality friends who truly understand you? Or are your relationships less intimate, more on the level of acquaintances? What do you feel is holding you back from befriending more people?

factors coming into play. Some of the biological influences may be attributed to having a slow-to-warm-up temperament. Shy teens may take longer to become acclimated to new people because they're simply wired that way.

But during adolescence, biology, or temperament, becomes less influential than environmental factors. That's because teens use their intellect to overcome their biological responses, whereas babies and young children are less likely to use specific strategies to make them feel more comfortable during difficult social situations. For example, a shy teen like Olivia may know that she gets nervous when speaking to someone new, so she will give herself time to warm up, will learn the small talk formula, and will not judge herself harshly if she makes any flubs. A child simply doesn't have that sort of self-awareness.

According to development psychologist Kenneth Rubin, there are specific types of social interaction—or, in some cases, noninteraction—that children typically favor.[8] The patterns of social interaction or play you develop in childhood can often carry into the next stage of life—adolescence and beyond. This is your dominant response to being with others. But it isn't your only response. If you try out other ways of being with others, you can expand your comfort

We can carry our style of play from childhood into our style of social interaction in adolescence. Kids who play well with others tend to grow up to be teens who welcome social interactions, while kids who prefer solitary play will often gravitate to more independent activities in adolescence.

zone and begin incorporating alternative social styles until you find one that works for you.

Unless we make a deliberate decision to change our behavior, we'll carry our childhood style of play into adolescence and adulthood, where it becomes our social style. This can affect how we spend our time with others, how we interact with friends and strangers, and what sort of social environments we prefer.

## Identify Your Social Style

When making friends, social skills are some of the most important environmental factors that come into play. When analyzed, they can be grouped into specific kinds of social interaction that begin showing up during childhood and can be adapted to adolescent friendships.

To determine your social style, take this quiz. Identify the statement that seems most like you:

- Statement A: I like to be with other people and work on projects, but not necessarily interact with other teens when I'm working. When I was a kid, I'd help others put together intricate Lego projects or play team sports, but I was more focused on the task and my role in getting to the goal. Now, I like team projects or group gatherings where we have a purpose but I don't have to be very social. My ideal job would allow me to work with others but not have to socialize with them too much.
- Statement B: I don't mind being with other teens and I'm very independent. When I was a kid, I'd do the same things as other kids, but I'd be off on my own doing it. For example, if other kids were creating an elaborate Lego village, I'd play with Legos, too, but not join them. I don't like group projects now or being in a group. I much prefer doing my own thing and not bothering with other people.
- Statement C: I've always liked being around other kids although there are times when I'm unsure of myself. When there's a group endeavor, once I decide to join in I'm in the middle of it. If kids were playing games on the playground or building a Lego tower, I was a total team player. I like seeing the results of our joint efforts. Now, I'm happy to get involved in after-school activities, even if it is uncomfortable at first when I don't know anyone and I'm not certain about what I'm doing. I like to be in a study group because the other kids help me to be a better student.
- Statement D: I feel anxious when I'm around other teens. This results in my sort of zoning out and focusing on something so that I don't have to

deal with my social anxiety. When I was a kid, I'd do something over and over just to soothe myself, like banging a toy or bouncing a ball. Now, I try to withdraw from social interactions by playing games on my cell phone, or repeating some action over and over. Other teens make me feel uncomfortable.

- Statement E: I'm very imaginative and have a hard time relating to other teens. I'd rather create my own little world and get lost in it. I even have imaginary friends who keep me company. As a teen, I prefer doing solitary activities that take me out of reality. I like to daydream and imagine what my life would be like if I were a different person or living somewhere else. I wouldn't act these things out in real life, though.

- Statement F: I like being with other teens but I don't always know how to break the ice and actually get involved in what they're doing. When I was a kid, I'd be on the edges of whatever the other kids were doing, and sort of mimic them. That helped me figure out if I really wanted to join in. Eventually, someone would notice me and invite me into the group. Now, I go to parties and games and hang out with other teens. But it takes me a while to move from the edges into the inner circle.

- Statement G: Unpredictable things make me nervous. I'm a good student and I really thrive in the classroom, since I understand the format and the structure makes me feel secure. But I've never liked being called on. I also like any other kind of group activity that is highly structured and doesn't shine a spotlight on me. For example, I like singing in the chorus but I'll never try to be a soloist. I like to blend in. And I don't really hang out with any people from these activities. That's too unpredictable.

- Statement H: I like being with other teens, but we don't really do anything with a goal. When I was a kid, we'd just mess around and move from activity to activity without really thinking too much about it. We'd watch a lot of TV. Now, I still hang out with my friends and watch a lot of TV or waste time on the computer together.

Now that you have identified which statement sounds the most like you, discover your social style.

### Statement A: Parallel Constructive Social Style

This occurs when kids play next to each other, but not necessarily with each other, and they're doing some sort of constructive activity. For example, this may happen when kids play in the sandbox together and build a village with toys or a sand castle. They focus on the project, not each other, although they are coordinating their efforts.

In adolescence this is more likely to look like participating in a team sport or after-school activity, or even working at a part-time job. There's a sense of shared purpose, but not a lot of give-and-take and intimacy. Outgoing, shy, introverted, and successfully shy teens all participate in this type of interaction, since the aim is the group goal, not friendship.

## Statement B: Solitary Constructive Social Style

This style of noninteraction occurs when a child is part of a group and doing the same activity as the other kids, but he does it alone. The child may build his own sand castle, instead of participating with the group's project. This noninteraction teaches a child self-reliance and problem-solving skills, but it doesn't provide him with social opportunities. He may be too immersed in his project to want to join others or to allow them to join him. Or he may want to join the group but not know how to do so. Instead, he mimics their efforts by himself.

Adolescents who rely on this style of social noninteraction tend to remain on the edges of groups of their peers. They may eat in the cafeteria, alone, surrounded by their classmates but immersed in a book; hang out at athletic games but not engage other kids as they focus on the action; or be involved in sports that don't require teamwork, such as long-distance running or weightlifting. These teens are near other kids, but they're not interacting with them. Shy or introverted teens may rely on this social strategy; they're focused on their personal efforts.

## Statement C: Collaborative Constructive Social Style

This style balances the camaraderie of a group endeavor with the participants' desire to achieve their goals. They know that there is strength in numbers even if there is some friction in the group. Children who play in this style favor group or

> "I had and still have a very hard time looking into someone's eyes when they talk to me. It's really only strangers. I am fine once I know someone and feel comfortable with them."—nineteen-year-old groundskeeper[c]

team activities that have a purpose, such as team sports, group crafts, theater, or collaborative projects. The upside of this type of play is that kids are immersed in their project and learning valuable social skills, such as negotiation, problem solving, and taking on a leadership role. The downside is that some shy kids may not always speak up and will take a more passive role.

Adolescent activities look much the same, although shy teens may feel reticent at first about joining in. Teens who prefer the collaborative constructive style are involved in group activities that have a sense of purpose, such as after-school clubs, and seek out socially oriented part-time jobs or volunteer positions, such as working in a restaurant or fast-food place or helping out at a food pantry.

### Statement D: Solitary Functional Social Style

When a child is playing alone and is engaged in repetitive, nonconstructive activities, she's involved in this type of noninteractive play. Imagine a child bouncing a ball over and over, or repeatedly banging a stick against a wall. This activity is fine, occasionally, but shouldn't take up a lot of a child's playtime. It doesn't stretch a child's mind or teach her social skills.

In adolescence, this may become doodling, aimlessly surfing the Internet, or doing any activity repeatedly without having a goal. Shy teens may withdraw into this type of behavior to lessen the anxiety they feel about interacting socially.

### Statement E: Solitary Fantasy Social Style

Children love to play dress up and construct elaborate fantasies they can act out. This is healthy if they're acting out these fantasies with other children or role-playing to stretch their imaginations. However, if they get lost in their fantasies, alone, they will have a difficult time relating to other children and the real world.

Adolescents often withdraw into fantasies either as an escape from the stresses of the real world or to imagine what life would be like under different circumstances. They may imagine themselves as another person to get some validation or to play out a scenario that they couldn't in the real world. But, just like in childhood, too much time spent constructing fantasies can be unhealthy, especially if shy teens miss out on new adventures in the real world. They may spin elaborate fantasies to compensate for their unsatisfying social lives. This may happen alone, or online, where they may get lost in social media, pornography, or games that take them out of their daily lives. A word of caution, though: The purpose of adolescence is to try new activities and expand one's comfort zone. Retreating into a fantasy world will further separate shy teens from their peers and their goals.

"I always feel like I'm on the outside looking in. I see other people having fun but something is keeping me from finding a way to be part of all of that. I feel lonely a lot."—nineteen-year-old barista[d]

## Statement F: Wait-and-Hover Social Style

This style of interacting probably best describes how shy children act on their social interest. When a child waits and hovers, he's on the edge of a group of other children, or perhaps just one child. He notices what the other kids are doing, then mimics them. He doesn't approach the other kids to break the ice because he feels the anxiety of the approach-avoidance conflict. Instead, he hopes that they notice him and welcome him over. The time the reticent child spends waiting and hovering gives him time to slowly warm up to the other kids and cope with his discomfort.

This strategy is often used in adolescence—and beyond. Waiting and hovering can be seen when a teen is dealing with a tough social encounter, but isn't fully involved in it. The stereotypical wallflower behavior is an example of the wait-and-hover style. The teen is at the dance or the party, but is on the edges of the action, hoping someone will ask her to join in. Teens who wait and hover exhibit social interest, but have difficulty overcoming their approach-avoidance conflict until they've warmed up to the new social situation.

## Statement G: Structured Interaction Social Style

This style of social interaction is rigid, governed by rules, and doesn't allow for much creativity or freedom. The rules come from an authority figure and participants understand the role that they play. This can occur in a classroom, where the students know their place and don't interact outside of the rules, or during a highly structured activity, such as a team sport, after-school job, or volunteer position. Shy children can cope with this type of structured social interaction, especially when they see their peers over a period of time—in class, for example. This repeated exposure allows the shy child to warm up to his peers.

In adolescence, this style occurs most often in the classroom. Shy teens may feel comfortable in class, for example, if the rules are predictable and they know what to expect. When that happens, the classroom experience will become part of their comfort zone. The downside of highly structured social activities is that they don't provide shy teens with opportunities to stretch their comfort zone by striking up a conversation or speaking up. Teens tend to allow the rules of the situation to determine their behavior.

### Statement H: Unstructured Interaction Social Style

In contrast to the routine of the classroom, this style of social interaction follows loose rules or no rules at all. In childhood, this often appears on the playground, after school, or when kids are allowed to hang out without supervision or a sense of purpose. Shy kids have difficulty during these encounters, because their unpredictability makes them tense and fearful. They often withdraw, even if they are physically present, because they are anxious about dealing with kids who seem to be a threat.

In adolescence, the experience is much the same as in childhood. Shy teens who have to cope with unstructured social activities feel anxious and fearful about having to participate in an activity with loose parameters or perceived threats. Think about a chaotic cafeteria, hallway, bus stop, or party—these are all examples of unstructured social encounters that heighten a teen's shyness.

Our lives are filled with these styles of social interaction, and how one reacts to them during childhood may predict how they'll be coped with during adolescence if the teen doesn't learn new social skills to change his social behavior. In the rest of the chapter, I'll explore how shy teens can learn new social skills that will allow them to move beyond social isolation to create new friendships as a successfully shy teen.

## Breaking Through

Shy teens often have a handful of very good friends. However, like most people, they would like to have more friends. But they don't know how to break through

### Time for Reflection

Reflect on the patterns of social interaction in your life. Which style of social interaction do you prefer? Why? Is it easy for you? How did that style manifest when you were a child? Did you sit alone at the edge of a group, hoping to be invited in? Or were you so focused on playing that you didn't care what others were doing? Now, as a teen, which styles of social interaction do you avoid? Why? Do you think you can learn new behaviors that will help you cope with social interaction?

and make contact with others. It seems too risky; they may be rejected. They feel nervous and anxious; the other person will think they're weird. They have so much to say that they don't know what to say. Their comfort zone is narrow and rigid and they don't have smart strategies to expand it.

Research has been done on how children approach others, and like one's social style, it can be carried into adolescence and adulthood.[9] There are three ways a child typically approaches another child:

1. Disruptive social approach. When a child breaks up other kids' peaceful playtime and calls attention to himself, even if it's negative attention, he's using a disruptive approach to meeting other kids. This approach works: The disrupter enters the group of kids and grabs the spotlight. He may do it to be funny or to take charge of the situation. But he runs the risk of making the other kids angry. Disrupters are often shunned and avoided in the future because other kids don't want to include someone who is such a contrarian.

2. Wait-and-hover social approach. This is the typical shy child's approach to connecting to other kids, one that balances her temperamental tendency to warm up slowly with her natural social interest and curiosity. Children who use this approach are passive. They hang out near other kids and are interested in what they're doing, but they have a hard time showing their interest. They typically wait for others to notice them and include them in what they're doing. If not, they'll keep hanging out on the edges until they warm up enough to join in the activity. The downside of this approach is that the group of kids sometimes becomes so involved in their play that they don't notice the waiting and hovering child. Or the lone child takes so long to warm up that she misses her opportunity to connect before the group of kids launches into something new.

3. Socially savvy social approach. Children who use this approach offer something of value to others. They notice what another child or children lack and offer to fill that need when the opportunity arises. It may be a team player, a piece of information, a compliment, a snack, a helping hand, or simply another kid to help them build their elaborate racetrack in the sandbox. These kids demonstrate that they can be a good friend and can be trusted.

"I always feel invisible. Everyone remembers my brother, who is really outgoing. But kids in our school didn't even know he has a brother. It's like I don't exist because I'm not as loud or extroverted as he is."

—twenty-year-old carpenter[e]

These three social approaches can be adapted to adolescence and adulthood. Let's take Olivia, for example. She likes to attend concerts, but she feels inhibited and nervous because she looks young. She thinks that everyone notices her and that they think that she doesn't belong.

Concerts are a perfect opportunity for Olivia to try approaching other teens. After all, the audience at the concert shares the same taste in music, which is a big deal for her, so they may have more in common within their personal comfort zones.

Here's how Olivia can use these three social approaches at concerts. Which do you think will be the most successful?

1. Disruptive: Olivia can shove other kids standing around her so she can see better. She can spill their drinks, laugh at others, and generally be obnoxious. She can badmouth the band on the way out of the venue, making others feel bad for actually liking the band.
2. Wait and hover: Olivia can stand at the edge of the crowd, not make eye contact with anyone but her friends, and be totally immersed in the music. When she stands in line to buy a T-shirt, she can remain silent and not talk to anyone about her thoughts about the concert.
3. Socially savvy: Olivia realizes that part of being at a concert is enjoying music among like-minded people. Olivia can hang out with her friends but also notice the people around her. She can smile when others brush past her instead of avoiding eye contact. She can practice making small talk by asking about another kid's T-shirt, offering a compliment to someone, and talking to the other kids in line for T-shirts. She can offer to get her friends sodas or help them if they need anything, which is her way of showing that she is helpful and concerned about their happiness.

Although Olivia is shy, she can use the socially savvy approach without much anxiety. She knows that the people who surround her all share her appreciation for the band that's performing, which means that they're in her comfort zone. And making small talk is the best way to begin making connections with people who are unfamiliar to her but have a common bond. Plus, making herself of use to her friends shows that she really cares about them.

## Attract Friends by Being a Good Friend

After making a connection through a wise social approach, teens must develop the social skills that help them to be a good friend and nurture quality relationships. Fortunately for shy teens, they naturally possess many qualities that make

The key to having friends is being a good friend, especially being an active listener.

them good friends. Shy teens tend to be thoughtful, good listeners, and interesting people, which not only will make them good friends, but will attract more people to them. Here's a list of ways that teens can become better friends to others:

- Be a well-rounded person: The best way to attract friends and have quality relationships is to be a healthy, fully functioning person. That means developing your interests, having a healthy sense of self, being kind and thoughtful, and working toward your dreams and goals with a positive attitude. When you are strong, others will be interested in knowing the secrets of your success. And you will be confident enough to share them.
- Focus on others: The key to becoming successfully shy is moving beyond one's natural self-focus to being other focused. Too often, shy teens become isolated because they are so self-conscious and focused on themselves. Their internal feelings, thoughts, and physical sensations overwhelm them when they're in a social situation. But shy teens can redirect their attention and focus on others, not only to develop their social interest, but to take their minds off of their shy stress reactions. If shy teens are more focused on their friends and not themselves, their discomfort will dissipate.
- Be an empathic listener: Don't just hear what your friends have to say; actually listen to them. This builds on psychologist Carl Rogers's theory

of empathic understanding by engaging in the process of empathic listening or active listening, which is what therapists do with their clients while trying to demonstrate a clear sense of understanding what the client is trying to say.[10] To practice empathic listening, provide your partner with a summary of what he has said and rephrase the conversation to make sure that you understand his concerns. In this way, your friend will know that you truly understand him and are interested in his life.

- Help your friends solve their problems: You can build long-lasting trust if you help your friends with their problems. That doesn't mean that you have to take over and directly solve their problems. But you can provide support and sympathy, help them brainstorm solutions, and be there when they need a true friend.

- Be a social facilitator: People naturally gravitate toward others who are helpful, knowledgeable, and positive. If you have a bit of information or other resource you think others would like to share, do so. Although shy teens may hesitate to extend themselves to another person, it's just another way of stretching one's comfort zone. For example, if you like to play the guitar and you know of someone who'd like to learn how to play it, you can invite him to a jam session at your house. That's one familiar activity (playing the guitar), one familiar place (your house), and one new person (the fledgling guitarist). In this way, you are helping someone reach her goals while you are expanding your comfort zone.

- Become an expert at small talk: As explained in chapter 8, every relationship begins with small talk. To become more adept at it, practice this skill as often as you can, even if it's just quick talk—brief encounters with people you only see casually, and perhaps only in passing, such as the mail carrier, a cashier, someone standing in line with you, or kids you encounter in the school hallway. The more connections you can make with quick talk or small talk, the more friendships you can develop.

- Seek out friends who share your interests and goals: Teens often seek out the friendship of high-status peers because they think they can raise their profile and popularity if they're surrounded by the cool kids. But these friendships are fragile and unequal, and shy teens tend to be the low-status person in these relationships and groups. Instead, choose friends who share your interests—the activity portion of your comfort zone—and will help you to become a better person. If you want to spend your summer at the beach, find people who also want to hang out there and suggest an outing. If you want to study veterinary medicine in college, volunteer at your local Humane Society, where you'll meet like-minded volunteers.

- Remember the rule of reciprocity: When making small talk, it's important to match the level of self-disclosure of your partner, what's known as the rule of reciprocity. You don't want to be too intimate or too distant with someone you're just meeting, so the rule of reciprocity will help you keep up with your partner. In the same vein, remember the rule of reciprocity in your relationships. Don't rush the natural process of getting to know someone by revealing your intimate secrets to someone you barely know. Nor should you keep your cool with someone who is sharing his true self with you. If your new friend is trusting you with his personal information, it's safe to pick up on his cues and let him get to know you better.

- Practice basic social graces: The Golden Rule instructs us to treat others the way in which we'd like to be treated. Good friends act on that directive and treat their pals with respect and caring. They also practice the social graces of compassion, kindness, support, appreciation, and generosity.
- Keep your sense of self: Good friends don't pressure you to do anything, whether it's to take a foolish risk or change your identity. This is what happens in cliques, which can be hazardous to one's sense of self and self-esteem. Rather, good friends help you develop your sense of self and become a better person. If you are feeling pressured to do something, or you feel your friend is becoming reckless, act on your feelings and concern for yourself and your friend. Don't let others make decisions for you that you know are wrong.

## A Successfully Shy Adolescence Is within Reach

Although shy teens may feel a lot of anxiety and pressure to be more outgoing and extroverted, they are absolutely able to navigate the social complexities of adolescence and become successfully shy. As discussed throughout this chapter, shy teens can learn how to make connections with other teens who are worthy of their friendship. What's critical is building one's self-knowledge and understanding how shyness hinders them in expanding their comfort zone and approaching other teens. Armed with this self-awareness, shy teens can give themselves more time to warm up to others, learn socially savvy approaches to make connections with others, and create high-quality relationships. This doesn't happen by magic. It's the result of a conscious decision to take charge of one's shyness and build the life you want to lead.

# DATING

The previous chapter explained how shy people can act on their natural interest in other people and make connections to develop friendships. This chapter will explore how romantic relationships can be built on platonic friendships with someone to whom you are attracted.

Many shy teens feel that they aren't ready to date when their friends are—and, even if they were, they'd be rejected by the one they truly want to be with. This belief, like many beliefs about shyness, is false. Shy teens are every bit as attractive, anxious, loveable, insecure, and curious about dating as their outgoing peers. I've learned from the adults who attend my dating seminars for shy singles, as well as from my own personal experience, that their shyness was intensified during adolescence because dating and talking to an attractive potential romantic partner was so nerve-racking. Fortunately, they were able to overcome their fears and go out on dates. In this chapter, I'll explain how shy teens can, too. I'll also discuss why teens need to date, how gender impacts dating, and how to separate dating fact from fiction.

## Why Teens Need to Date

One of the major tasks of adolescence is learning how to date. Contrary to popular belief, dating and forming an intimate relationship isn't just what teens are driven to do because their hormones are running wild. Rather, dating represents a way of transitioning from a child, with platonic friendships among "pals," to more adult relationships that will eventually lead to long-lasting partnerships, perhaps with children.

According to Erik Erikson, creating an exclusive relationship with another person is one of those tasks of adolescence that teens must try out and master before they can become a fully functioning adult.[1] Just like learning algebra, driving, dealing with a changing body, and developing a life outside of home and school, dating is one of those challenges that teens must cope with and conquer. Among its many functions, dating helps teenagers to practice and prepare for more formal social and intimate relationships in adulthood.[2]

## Omar's Story

A lot of teens can relate to what Omar is going through. Omar responded to my shyness survey about his romantic troubles. He's in love with a girl but can't **seem** to get up the courage to ask her out on a date. Omar is shy with new people and he feels his shyness is more intense and worse than others' shyness—a typical feeling among shy teenagers. He's a high school sophomore who generally gets good grades but is frustrated by his lack of romantic success.

Here's what Omar wrote to me:

My shyness is expressed by being embarrassed and nervous looking into people's eyes (usually girls'), having nervous twitches, sometimes not being able to talk to someone, usually a girl—for example, Petra, who is a beautiful girl from the Czech Republic that I want to ask out and who I love a lot. A lot of times I am too nervous to say hi to her and it drives me crazy because it hurts so much not to be able to talk to someone I love so much. I see people all the time at school with their boyfriends and girlfriends, holding each other, kissing, sometimes just staring into each other's eyes and smiling. I get so depressed when I see them because I think about Petra a lot and what it would be like to be with her, to hold her and kiss her.

But what am I talking about? Who am I fooling? This is a girl I sometimes have trouble saying hi to! I'll bet this is ridiculous for a 16-year-old guy to be so nervous, right? Well, in many ways you might be interested to know that I am not a shy person. For instance, sometimes I will dance to a song when others don't, because when I dance I don't think, I just move to the music.

To overcome my shyness I have talked to people and tried to look girls in the eyes even when I felt nervous to do so. I noticed being more focused on them than me made me feel better and more confident in my social and personal relations.

My shyness seems to be getting better. Now, if I want to ask Petra to sit next to me on a bus trip I do. I never would have done that two months ago. My advice to shy people is to hang in there. Eventually you will realize those girls aren't smiling at you and sitting with you for no reason.[a]

**Time for Reflection**

● What are your feelings toward dating? Do you have a boyfriend or girlfriend? How did that happen? If you don't, how do you feel about that? Are your friends dating? How do you feel about that? Do you think that dating is an important part of being a teenager? Or is it something that doesn't command a lot of your attention?

Because all adolescents must face the prospect of dating, to begin dating when your friends do has many advantages. After all, if you and your friends are all going through the same thing at the same time, you can share experiences, lean on them for advice, and feel a sense of belonging. Perhaps that's why schools hold dances and other social gatherings that have nothing to do with academics. They provide students with opportunities to go on dates at the same time classmates do. When you think of dating in terms of one's psychological and social development, prom and homecoming represent rites of passage into adulthood.

## Why Shy Teens Fear Dating

Most shy teens are just like Omar—they have passionate feelings for someone they find to be attractive, yet they have a hard time taking the risk of revealing their true feelings and asking for a date.

This is perfectly understandable if you think about dating in terms of the dynamics of shyness. Dating is a new, unfamiliar activity that's outside of one's comfort zone and places one's self-worth at risk. The thought of being judged and rejected by a person one admires triggers the approach-avoidance conflict. The shy dater wants to approach another person, but gets caught in the self-consciousness, self-doubt, and anxiety that is triggered by the unfamiliar social encounter. That discomfort makes the shy teen want to withdraw and avoid having to deal with the whole situation. He would rather have a crush on someone from afar, just to lessen his anxiety and fear. This watching-and-waiting period makes the teen slow to warm up to dating. As a result, he begins dating after his friends do. This makes him feel isolated and lonely and less likely to take the risk of dating in the future.

Although Omar can attest to how horrible it feels to have a crush on someone and not feel confident enough to date, what's fortunate is that shyness seems to be a barrier only during the initial phases of the relationship.[3] What is most surprising is that only about 7 percent of shy people said that their shyness caused them

Just 7 percent of shy people say their shyness is a problem for them once they are in a relationship. After the warming up period is over, shy teens can incorporate a romantic partner into their comfort zone and can express themselves fully.

problems once they were in a relationship.[4] That means that once the newness of the relationship wears off, and the shy person warms up to his partner, he is able to reveal his true self with confidence. He feels accepted for who he is and is able to give and receive love and affection easily.

## Being an On-Time and Off-Time Dater

Since dating is something all teens should experience, it's best to do this when your friends are going through the same thing. Being "on time" is when you are encountering and mastering developmental challenges when you are supposed

> ## ❗ Remember This
>
> ● Shyness can be a problem during the initial phases of dating. But once shy people are in a relationship and are able to share their true selves with their partner, their shyness is no longer a barrier to feeling loved and accepted.

to do so.[5] If you are taking on these challenges long before your friends do or a long time after they do—or don't face these challenges at all until much later in life—this is known as being "off time."[6]

Think about Omar. He's in love with Petra from afar, and he wants to ask her out. He's also keenly aware that his peers are dating. He can't help but notice that the kids in his school have paired off; the evidence of that is all around him. Omar wants to be just like them and have his own girlfriend, Petra. But he just hasn't been able to ask her out for a date yet, despite being platonic friends with her. So while Omar is on time in developing feelings for a girl he finds to be attractive, he's a little bit off time in forming a romantic relationship with Petra.

In this Omar is a typical shy teen. All teens begin developing romantic and physical feelings for other boys and girls. This is a natural part of adolescence. But shy teens tend to be off time when actually going out on a date and being in a relationship. Shy teens are typically off time when they have to make big and small life changes because they are slow to warm up to unfamiliar experiences and incorporate them into their comfort zone. These changes can include transitioning to a new classroom or school, getting to know another person, or developing a romantic relationship with another person.

There isn't anything wrong with taking time to warm up to an unfamiliar person or situation. After all, giving yourself enough time to warm up is key to becoming successfully shy. This is how you are able to calm your nerves and think clearly before introducing yourself to someone new, for example, without being blasted by uncomfortable shy symptoms that affect your body, mind, and self.

> "I don't have a boyfriend right now but dating is very difficult for me. I really have to know someone well and trust them a lot in order to date them. And when it gets serious, I have a great difficulty communicating my thoughts and feelings. It has also been my experience that more than once potential relationships have slipped away because I was not secure enough to pursue them."—nineteen-year-old art-supply store clerk[b]

An extended warming-up period does become problematic when it makes a shy teen become off time. In general, it's best to conquer life tasks at about the same time as your peers. You need the social support of your friends to help you out. You need to ask them questions, observe social cues, and not feel left out. It's perfectly all right to be on the slower end of that group change. But you don't want to be the last person to face the group challenge—nor do you want to be totally left behind.

Take, for example, my own experience as a teen dater, which I recounted in the introduction to this book. I wasn't a particularly shy kid, but I developed shyness as a teen when I was faced with the challenge of talking to attractive girls and asking them out. While I definitely was attracted to girls, asking them out was a challenge that made me feel unsure of myself and my attractiveness and therefore made me vulnerable to rejection. Although I was able to talk to girls as friends, I didn't have a lot of confidence in myself as a romantic partner. I thought about it a lot and was interested in dating, but I simply got too nervous and afraid of rejection to actually do it.

All of this was bad enough. But then I had to watch my friends pair off with girls. They made it look so easy, as if they knew some sort of secret that I didn't know and probably would never learn. This made my self-esteem fall for a bit. Even worse, because I had told myself that my guy friends had no problems asking out girls, I felt that they couldn't relate to my insecurity and fears. Therefore, I didn't ask them about what they were experiencing. I didn't want to reveal my fears, and that made me feel more isolated.

I was slow to warm up to dating, but in time I did in fact warm up. Eventually, I began asking out girls and developed a pretty serious relationship with one girl, which lasted for a long time. But I was a little bit off time. My first date happened long after my friends' first dates—at least, that's how it felt to me. I committed to my first girlfriend when my friends were on to girlfriend number two or three. Although I did master the life task of dating, I did so later than my friends. Still, I was able to participate with my girlfriend in double dates with my friends and their girlfriends, prom, homecoming, and other events. I wasn't so slow to warm up that these rites of passage totally passed me by. I was able to incorporate dating into my comfort zone at an age-appropriate time.

If I hadn't warmed up to dating during adolescence, I would have been very off time and this would have caused even more problems in my love life, social life, self-confidence, and self-esteem. For example, if I'd waited until college to ask out a girl, I would have felt even more self-conscious about my lack of dating skills, had a keener awareness of my isolation, and made dating feel far more scary than it really is. I definitely would not have been able to ask my friends about dating, since this would expose me as inexperienced and somewhat not normal. Society expects teenagers to feel awkward and nervous on their

> ### ❗ Remember This
>
> ● Shy teens like Omar and my younger self are commonly slow to warm up to dating. But stalling too long will make a shy teen become off time, deprive him of social support, and make him feel even worse about his lack of romantic success. Remember: Take time to warm up, but don't wait so long that you fail to act on your opportunities.

first dates; it's less understanding of an inexperienced twenty-two-year-old or twenty-eight-year-old adult still feeling overwhelmed by the thought of going on a first date.

Brian Gilmartin at Montana State University studied very off-time men, who he calls "love shy."[7] These men hadn't ever been on a date—ever. It's easy to see why. In general, these love shy men have very narrow comfort zones, with few friends and family ties. They didn't have many connections to females when they were growing up. They typically have no sisters, no platonic female friends, and lack a strong relationship with their mothers. As a result, they have a hard time relating to females. They didn't date during adolescence and that lack of experience hampers their ability to date as an adult. Because they are so off time, they aren't willing to discuss their dating issues with their male friends. As a result, as adults they believe that they will never catch up to their male peers and develop a romantic relationship with a woman. Unfortunately, their lack of belief in themselves and their inexperience will make it very difficult for them to create a long-lasting relationship in adulthood.

## Gender Differences and Dating

When we're children, we notice gender and we often choose to only hang out with boys or girls. That's perfectly natural. But when adolescence hits, the differences between males and females grow.

As explained in chapter 9, teen boys and girls create different types of friendships and social groups. Boys tend to base their relationships around doing things and experiencing the same activities. Status in these groups is raised by how adventurous or risk taking a boy is. Leaders in these groups are boys who display the most bravado or machismo. As a result of their tendency to be more reserved, shy teen boys can find themselves with a lower status in these groups, although they can still find solid friendships with peers who are quieter and less interested in taking risks.

Girls, on the other hand, form relationships that are based on comfort and sympathy, a sense of sharing the same feelings and emotions as their friends. Unlike boys, girls' social status is based on fitting in and having the most social connections. Traditionally, girls aren't expected to be risk takers; they're expected to be caretakers. While boys feel pressured to perform, girls are pressured to fit in and conform. Similarly to others seeking social validation,[8] shy girls with lower peer-group status are likely to be more conforming because they find it easier to blend in than to draw attention by sticking out.

Gender roles and social status become more salient during adolescent dating experiences. Since dating during adolescence also serves as a means of enhancing prestige among one's peers,[9] boys who are at the top of their social group are the ones who are able to break away from their males-only circle and begin dating girls. It seems to be a remnant of evolution. Male animals that were the strongest and dominated the group seemed to be the most attractive to females. Those with a lower status were able to pair off with another female only after the leader of the pack found a mate.[10] In many ways, that hierarchy still exists today, as teen boys seek to be the strongest or most daring member of their circle in order to get the attention of a girl.

That said, we are modern human beings, not animals in the wild. Women aren't only attracted to the top dog—they also find the nice guy, the one who is dependable, kind, and emotionally stable and will stick around and help raise a family, to be the most desirable mate.[11] That should give the shy teen boy some hope. He doesn't need to put on some false bravado just to get the attention of the girl he likes.

What we do know about teen boys is that those who are late bloomers—or off time in terms of physical development—will struggle more with feelings of social inadequacy and inferiority during adolescence.[12] These are the boys who go through their growth spurt later, whose facial hair takes its time coming in, and generally look younger and sometimes weaker than other boys their age.[13] It's easy to see why. When these late-blooming boys use social comparison to size up the competition, they find that boys who are their peers are stronger and buffer than they are. This makes them feel that they are too unattractive and physically immature to go on a date. This can create excessive self-consciousness and shy-

> "I get mad crushes on guys but I don't think they know it. I don't even think they know I exist. I just hang around them and hope that they notice me. But if they did notice me I don't think I'd know what to do. I can't ask them out, either. I'm stuck."—nineteen-year-old waitress[c]

ness and make them off time in dating, too. Fortunately, this can be a passing phase in life, because the teen boy will eventually grow, fill out, and become an adult. However, he will need to catch up socially and romantically to make sure that he isn't very off time in terms of dating.

Some new research from Philip Zimbardo, who was a pioneer in the study of shy people, found that many socially inhibited teen and young adult males turn to online video games and porn instead of dealing with the pressures of dating in the real world.[14] In the virtual world, women are easily attracted to them, so they don't have to face rejection. They don't have to deal with the difficulties of dating; they can take a shortcut to having sex. Unfortunately, their immersion in the online world makes it even harder for them to relate to their peers. They simply don't share the same experiences and they don't form strong social bonds with other teens. This, not surprisingly, leads to more loneliness and isolation, and they withdraw into a virtual fantasy world that doesn't help them achieve their ultimate goal: a real relationship with someone who is attracted to them and accepts them.

Girls have a different experience. While late-blooming boys can develop social inferiority during adolescence, early-blooming girls, due to their early developing bodies, are somewhat less socially outgoing and less popular than their peers and are more likely to report symptoms of anxiety and depression.[15] Appearing very different from their female peers, these early maturing girls are likely to be heavier than many of the boys in their class and exhibit the development of breasts. Such differences in their physical development can make them more likely to be teased by their peers.[16] Another related issue for these early maturing girls is that they may not be as emotionally mature as their full-grown bodies make them seem. Compounding this problem is that these early maturing girls are more likely the ones who are asked on dates before their friends, most likely by older boys.[17] This trailblazing role isn't always an easy fit for them. These older boys have a greater potential to steer them toward more risky social activities, such as smoking, drinking, drug use, and sex.[18] To cope with the attention their bodies generate, these girls might try to become invisible. They sometimes wear baggy clothes; don't join in activities that will reveal their bodies, such as swimming; and become quiet and passive in social settings.

During my time conducting dating workshops for shy singles, shy women have mentioned another problem they face during the dating process. Although they may appear to be quiet and passive during the initial phase of dating, they will likely become more outgoing and bold with their partner once they warm up. That can be a wonderful thing—except if her partner isn't happy that the formerly shy woman is now speaking her mind and challenging her partner. Based on such comments, shy teen girls need to remember that even though their quiet demeanor may have attracted their mate, they shouldn't feel that they have to hide

> **Time for Reflection**
>
> Are you a late-blooming boy or early-blooming girl? If not, do you know of any? Do you understand how his or her physical development can make him or her feel shy? Did you ever consider this before?

their true selves or be pressured into remaining passive with their partners. Shy girls, like all girls, should express themselves when it's important to do so. Don't feel that you have no control over your life or the terms of your relationship.

## Social Expectations and Stereotypes

On top of these biological and social differences, our society has different cultural expectations for boys and girls who want to date. Traditionally, in our society, we expect boys and men to initiate dates and to be sexually assertive. We expect girls to be receptive to dates and not be too overt sexually. Of course, these social norms are constantly upended and contradicted in our modern age—especially in

It's perfectly natural to feel nervous about dating, whether you conform to society's expectations or not. However, nervousness isn't always visible to your partner and will subside as you warm up to her.

---

> ⚠️ **Remember This**
>
> ● Societal expectations shouldn't prevent you from finding romance. Being true to yourself is the best way to develop an honest relationship with the partner of your choice.

---

the media—and women are applauded for being forthright and bold, and many quiet men are very attractive to women. But, for the most part, these stereotyped roles still loom large in our society.

As a result, shy teen boys feel the pressure to ask girls out on dates more acutely than shy girls feel the need to do so. In many ways, shy girls fit into our cultural expectations far more easily than shy teen boys. In girls, the shy traits of quietness, coyness, and passivity are easily accepted, even desirable; for boys, those same traits run counter to societal expectations. So in addition to coping with shyness and dating on a personal level, these shy teen boys must also deal with the messages that society is sending them to be assertive, risk taking, and adventurous with women.

Is this fair? Not at all. Quite frankly, most teens feel nervous and apprehensive about asking someone out on a date, and then actually going on the date and making a good impression. It's perfectly natural to feel that way. So even if you don't conform to society pressure to act a certain way with a romantic partner, don't feel that you are unsuccessful in romance and are doomed to a life without love. Finding the right partner for you, whether you're extroverted or shy, involves a little bit of risk taking, some smart social strategies, and a bit of luck. It has nothing to do with putting on a persona to live up to some sort of arbitrary standard. Rather, developing a romantic relationship is all about expressing your true self.

## Being an LGBTQ Teen

Dating is difficult for most teens. Outgoing teens, shy teens. Great-looking teens and not-so-attractive teens. Popular teens and social outsiders. Straight teens and gay teens, too.

Not much research has been conducted on shy teens who are lesbian, gay, bisexual, transgender, or questioning. Estimates indicate that approximately 9 million adults in the United States, or about 3.5 percent of the population, report being lesbian, gay, bisexual, transgender.[19] But it's likely that being LGBTQ makes them feel shy or self-conscious at times. All teens struggle with their sexuality and attraction to other people. When you're gay, that universal struggle can be even more difficult if you don't feel that you are supported and accepted for your true self. This can make gay teens feel shy about expressing themselves and dating.

Remember that there is absolutely, positively nothing wrong with being gay, although there are some unenlightened people in our society who simply do not understand that fact. The best antidote to their ignorance is surrounding yourself with people who truly understand you and care about you—the people within your comfort zone. And when you feel comfortable doing so, use the tips and strategies within this book to become a successfully shy gay teen.

## Myths and Facts about Dating

I've given a number of workshops about shyness and dating, and no matter where I am or who is in the audience, I frequently hear the same questions and comments from shy people over and over again. I realized that these shy people are clinging to myths about shyness in general and dating in particular. I also realized that many of these myths are believed by outgoing people as well as those who are situationally shy when they are on a date with someone new. While these myths don't hold up to scrutiny, they do have a powerful impact on many people. Here are some of the myths and facts about dating that everyone needs to know:

### Myth: *"I Feel Nervous about Dating, Which Means I'm Not Ready to Do It"*

### Fact: *Feeling Nervous Indicates That You Are Excited about Expanding Your Comfort Zone*

Many teens feel overwhelmed when thinking about going on a date. There are so many things to consider—how to ask for a date (or accept one), what to wear, what to do while on the date, how to seem cool and attractive, how to win your partner's affections. Not surprisingly, all of these unknown variables will produce anxiety and nervousness, whether you're shy or not.

Sound familiar? This anxiety is caused by the desire to expand your comfort zone. It isn't a sign that you're not ready to date or that you'll get rejected by your date. It's simply your body's signal that you are dealing with something unknown and unfamiliar.

In many ways, this is an example of the approach-avoidance conflict. When you feel an attack of nerves when thinking about getting romantic with someone, it means that you are thinking about approaching the person—being on a date with him or her—and also worried about being rejected. There's nothing wrong with the approach-avoidance conflict. In this case, it's a perfectly natural expression of your hopes and fears about finding a romantic partner.

In addition, I'd argue that your nervousness is a good thing. It means that you care about going on a date, that you want to impress your date and succeed. It's a sign that you are expressing social interest in your partner. Think of what would happen if you didn't feel anything about the prospect of dating someone you like, if you only felt blah or bored by the thought of spending time alone with him or her. Wouldn't that be sad?

A good solution to out-of-control nerves is to redefine their cause and relabel them. Instead of assuming that your anxiety means that you aren't ready to date and are destined to fail, view your nervousness as a perfectly natural and positive sign that you are excited by the idea of dating someone you like.

## Myth: *"I Want to Date, but I Don't Know Anyone I Want to Be With"*

## Fact: *Your Comfort Zone Is Full of People Who You Can Date or Who Can Help You Find a Date*

A frequent complaint from shy people is that they want to date but they feel so isolated that they just don't know who to partner up with. There are a few things going on here, and they all center on the shy person's comfort zone.

As explained in chapter 7, shy people tend to have narrow, rigid comfort zones made up of limited people, places, and activities. Because shy people don't like to or don't know how to reach out and broaden their horizons, they stick to routine, tried-and-true activities with the same small circle of people. This works against them when they want to date, since many people find partners who are already friends (and within their comfort zone) or friends of friends (who could be incorporated into their comfort zone fairly easily). In many ways dating is a numbers game, and shy people have a smaller number of people within their comfort zone they can connect to on a romantic level.

That said, shy teens' comfort zones aren't empty. They are full of people, ranging from close friends and relatives to acquaintances they see often even if they don't share a strong bond. (Go back to the inventory of your comfort zone you created in chapter 7 to find the people with whom you are familiar.) All of these people are potential connections for a dating partner, either directly or indirectly.

In fact, the people in your comfort zone are the best matches for you. Studies have shown that familiarity breeds attractiveness.[20] That means that the more you see someone, the more attractive you think she is. As you get to know her, you

A shy teen's comfort zone is the best source of potential romantic partners.

find that you like her more and more; you form a bond with her that's stronger than the one you have with acquaintances. The catch, though, is that the initial encounter has to be positive. That means that you should, in general, smile, have a positive attitude, and have something interesting to say so that you create a positive first impression with those you meet.

How does this work? Well, you can always ask a friend out on a date, or even on a practice date. Or perhaps you are friendly with a cousin who is your age. Why don't you ask your cousin to round up some friends for a group activity? Even if you don't click with one of your cousin's friends, you will have expanded your comfort zone. Or you could go on a platonic practice date with someone in your comfort zone, just to try out some new behaviors and become more accustomed to being with someone one on one.

There's another way to find a date from within your comfort zone. Use the factorial approach to expanding it by keeping two elements the same and adding one new element. For example, if you like to ride your bike around the city, why don't you see if there is a biking group in your town? That way, you will be doing something you love (biking, an activity within your comfort zone) on trails you likely know (a place within your comfort zone) with new bikers (new people, the new element of your comfort zone that will stretch it). Even if you don't want to date anyone in this new group of bicyclists, you will likely have a good time and can tap these new friends for more social activities in the future.

**Try This**

Go back to your comfort zone inventory from chapter 7 and identify the ways in which you can expand your comfort zone to find a potential romantic partner.

## Myth: *"If I Don't Click with Someone Instantly, There's No Point in Pursuing a Relationship"*

## Fact*: Love at First Sight Isn't the Only Way to Start a Relationship*

Many shy people say that they believe the only romantic connection worth developing is one based on instant chemistry. Either it's love at first sight and you click immediately, or it's just not worth it.

There are a number of things wrong with this attitude, but it's easy to see why shy people believe it. They want to take a shortcut to a relationship. They want to meet someone and fall in love in an instant. They want a perfect union made up of soul mates who were destined to be together. They don't want to have to endure the frustration, insecurity, and sense of unease that often is created during the first few weeks or months of dating as you get to know each other.

Another reason why shy people believe in love at first sight is that they are so anxious about making a good first impression. Typically, a shy person is self-conscious, uncomfortable, and worried about how he appears to someone he's meeting for the first time. But if someone will love him in an instant—despite his nerves, blushing, stammering, sweaty palms, and blank mind—then it must be love, right?

In some ways, this is the fantasy that everyone wants. But it happens only rarely in the real world. Real relationships and real love are built on honesty, communication, a sense of shared interests and values, and a lot of time. Building a relationship isn't a chore; it's exciting. In addition, studies have shown that the more you see someone, the more attractive you will find her, so it's in your best interest to continue pursuing a relationship—platonic or romantic—with those you encounter repeatedly.

And while it is true that most of us will have to date a number of people before building a lasting, mature relationship, that doesn't mean that these short-lived relationships are a waste of time. They are a chance to learn more about yourself, your needs, and other people. They are a way to practice how to build a relationship so that when you do find someone who you want to be with forever, you will know what to do. So even if you don't click with someone at first, give him a second chance. You never know. He may be shy like you and need time to warm up to you. Don't reject someone just because it isn't love at first sight.

## Myth: *"Nobody Thinks I'm Attractive; I'll Never Find Love"*

## Fact: *Your Pessimistic Attitude Shouldn't Hold You Back from Finding Romance*

Shy teens and adults—or those who aren't normally shy but feel inhibited about dating—often believe the worst things about themselves. They may feel confident about their academic ability, job performance, and platonic friendships and generally like themselves, but all of those positive attributes just fall away when they think about dating someone they're attracted to. This pessimistic, doomsday attitude holds them back from dating and creating a relationship because they don't believe that they are worthy of love.

Shy people are likely familiar with this pessimistic attitude, since it's part of the "shy mind" that is engaged during a difficult and new social encounter. For example, shy people and those who feel shy about dating use a pessimistic attributional style when thinking about relationships. For example, if they get blown off by someone they want to date, they use negative internal ("I'm not attractive to others"), stable ("I've never been attractive"), and global ("I'll never be attractive and lovable") attributions regarding their attractiveness. They absorb all of the blame for the difficult encounter and let their partner get off scot-free. This self-defeating mind-set, not surprisingly, makes their self-esteem plummet.

Instead, they could use a more compassionate and positive attributional style in which they carry less of the burden for the difficult encounter. Instead of thinking that they turned off their partner because they are unattractive, they could use external ("She isn't interested in having a conversation right now"), unstable ("She's having a bad day"), and specific ("We just aren't clicking right now") attributions that don't allow negativity and pessimism to spiral out of control. In this way, they will have a more balanced and forgiving attitude about themselves and their sense of self-worth that doesn't damage their self-esteem.

Shy daters also use social comparison to reinforce this pessimistic attitude. When they are out in public, they only see happy couples, not those who are single or enjoying a group outing. This makes them feel that they are the only single person in a universe of happy couples—something Omar feels acutely. Obviously,

> **Remember This**
>
> ● Give yourself a break. You are not the only teen who feels apprehensive and awkward about dating. Don't let your nerves hold you back from spending time with someone you admire.

this isn't true. They also compare themselves to the most experienced dater they know—perhaps the golden couple at school or the guy or girl whom everyone wants to date—and the shy person doesn't feel that she measures up. Again, she isn't noticing the other single teens who are just like her, curious about dating but feeling insecure and nervous about it. These shy and hesitant teens outnumber the experienced teens by far.

And, in addition, studies have shown that we generally partner up with someone who shares our level of attractiveness.[21] That means that while the hottest guy or girl in your class may get the most attention, you will likely be happier with someone who is similar to you. The good thing is that there are more people with your level of attractiveness, so you have more potential partners to date. Don't overlook these single peers who may be interested in you. Or, as Omar put it, "My advice to shy people is to hang in there. Eventually you will realize those girls aren't smiling at you and sitting with you for no reason."

## Myth: *"I Need to Be Completely Confident and in Control during a First Date"*

## Fact: *Everybody Feels Nervous and Awkward during a First Date*

The first dates with a potential partner are usually nerve-racking, whether you are shy or outgoing. That's because you want to make a good impression and not be rejected by someone you find to be attractive. So it's perfectly natural to feel self-conscious and a bit nervous while you are getting to know someone else. So the next time you see a new couple out on a date, note that both of the partners are likely feeling awkward and anxious; they certainly aren't feeling confident, no matter how in control they may appear.

Daters often feel heightened anxiety because they are putting pressure on themselves to have a superdate. Superdates are just that: They are meant to wow your partner with a long, overly exciting, action-packed series of activities meant to impress. These are the stereotypical dates that include hot-air balloon rides, a picnic in a remote area, perhaps some horseback riding, a dip in a pool, an expensive dinner, dancing, a movie, and a late-night bite at a hot new restaurant. (You can see examples of fantasy superdates on any dating reality show.)

Superdates should be avoided because they will likely fail. Your date may not have blocked out a whole day and night to spend with you, and superdates are so over-the-top that they don't allow you and your date to get to know each other, which is the whole point of a date anyway. Instead, a better approach is to manage your expectations—and your date's—by suggesting a simple outing together, doing something that allows you to have a conversation. Some examples are studying together in a cafe, going out to lunch, appearing as a couple at an event, or simply hanging out together. In this way, you won't feel that you have to bowl over your date with an incredible series of activities. And you will give yourself and your date an easy way to end the date if it isn't going so well.

There are a few ways to lessen the anxiety created by dating. The first step is to have a plan and do some social reconnaissance, or gather information about your date and what you will be doing on your date. For example, if your date is interested in studying abroad, you may want to get some information on various programs so that you will have something to discuss, or at least have some questions you can ask her about her plans. In addition, you can feel more confident about going on your date if you know something about your destination and your shared activity. If you're going to a new restaurant, download the menu and take a look at what's being offered, and make sure you know how to get there. If you are well prepared, you will be able to incorporate unfamiliar elements into your comfort zone before your date begins.

Another strategy to reduce nervousness during a date is to shift your focus. Shy people, and nervous people in general, tend to focus on their physical discomfort, which makes their thoughts race and fuels their anxiety. A smart way to lessen this is to divert your thoughts. When you begin to feel nervous, focus on your partner. Ask her if she's comfortable and begin using your small talk skills to launch a conversation. Just as the art of conversation is all about your partner, dating is all about your partner. Don't get stuck on your own nervousness and fail to pay attention to your date. That's a sure way to turn off a potential partner.

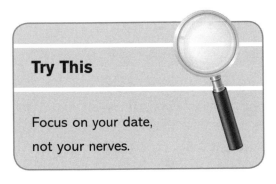

**Try This**

Focus on your date, not your nerves.

Lastly, relax. Make sure that you give yourself enough time to warm up to your date and you will feel more at ease by the minute.

## Myth: *"I Don't Know What to Do on a Date"*

## Fact: *Dates Are Extensions of Friendships*

Many shy teens and adults say that they simply don't know what to do on a date. They are overwhelmed by the idea of spending time alone with someone attractive who may be a potential partner, and they don't know what to do to engage that person.

These folks are overlooking the many items within their comfort zone, as well as the common items in their partner's comfort zone. If both of you enjoy sports, attend a game together or go for a run or bike ride as a couple. If you're good students or have a tough exam on the horizon, study together. If you're into the same kind of music, go to a concert. Dating is nothing more than being friends with someone you are also attracted to.

Once again, small talk skills will help you out in a pinch. If you feel a lull in the conversation, begin offering up observations about your shared environment, offer a compliment, or ask an open-ended question. The awkwardness will lessen in no time.

Another good strategy is to go out on practice dates or group dates with your friends. Just because you aren't romantically interested in your date doesn't mean that you should sit home alone and let life pass you by. Go out with a friend and practice all of the social skills you will need on a romantic date. Then, when you are attracted to someone, you will have critical dating skills in your comfort zone and won't feel that you are in totally uncharted territory.

## Myth: *"I Want to Ask Someone Out, but I'm Sure I'll Be Rejected"*

## Fact: *Rejection Is Nothing More Than Information*

Remember Omar? His story opened this chapter. He's desperately in love with Petra, but he hasn't got the courage to ask her out on a date. What's bothering him, of course, is the fear of rejection. This is a common fear held by just about anyone who has ever asked someone out on a date. He's attracted to someone, and he wants to be attractive to that person, too. A first date is a good indicator that you've got a mutual attraction, but how do you put yourself out there without failing?

I've found that many shy people fear being rejected by a potential partner because they have built up the object of their affection into a god or goddess.

They've created a fantasy world in which they're in love, everything is perfect, and they'll have a storybook ending of happily ever after. Then, when faced with their real lives, they don't want to shatter that illusion by getting turned down and being rejected. So they never ask for a date, and they never get a chance to turn their imagined relationship into a real one.

One way to get over this fear is to simply go for it. Yes, you may be rejected. But what does that really mean? It means that you don't have a date with someone to whom you are attracted. That can be painful and upsetting, of course, but it isn't the end of the world. You are still living, breathing, and pursuing your life goals, even if you didn't get that date.

In fact, rejection may be beneficial for you. It is information that you can use to your advantage. It can end the fantasy you've developed in your mind, which frees you to develop an attraction to someone else who may be more receptive to your advances. And it may help you to develop a different kind of dating strategy. For example, if you're in love with someone from afar and she turns you down for a date, you may want to try dating someone you're more familiar with, such as a study partner or coworker. These matches may be better for you anyway, since you have common links in your comfort zones.

Rejection isn't the end of the world. If it happens, put it in perspective and don't let it affect your attitude toward dating or your self-esteem.

## Myth: *"If I Go on a Date, I'll Have to Have Sex"*

## Fact: *You Get to Decide When You Are Ready for Sex*

Part of what makes dating so daunting is the possibility of being physically intimate with another person. As an adolescent, it's perfectly natural to feel nervous and apprehensive about this, despite your natural curiosity about sex.

But dating does not equal sex. I'll repeat this: Dating does not equal sex.

Do not feel pressured to become physically intimate with someone. If you're not ready for it, or you're simply not attracted to your date in that way, you can minimize the chances you will be pressured to have sex. You can ensure that your dates are in public, so you won't have the opportunity to get intimate. Or you can be honest about it with your partner. You can say, "I'm not ready," "This doesn't feel right to me," or "I just don't think of you this way." Don't worry about being rejected or teased for acting on your true feelings. You have control over your thoughts, feelings, and body. You shouldn't give that power to anyone else. Period.

## Dating Is an Essential Part of Adolescence

Whether you're shy or not, you should go on some dates when you are an adolescent. They don't have to be one-on-one dates with a romantic partner, however. You can go on practice dates or group dates with friends just to try out some new behaviors and develop a robust social life. If you don't seize opportunities to date when you are a teen, you won't develop critical social skills and experiences that you will need to become a fully functioning adult. Shy teens may feel apprehensive about this, but successfully shy teens will use the strategies mentioned in this chapter to be on-time daters who aren't held back by their shyness. Remember: Everyone feels nervous about dating, whether you're a shy teen or an outgoing adult. Don't let your temporary discomfort get in the way of finding love with someone who accepts you just as you are.

# SHYNESS IN SCHOOL

Outside of one's home, school is probably the most important part of an adolescent's life—if not the most important part of it. Shyness, of course, manifests throughout the school day. Teens feel shy when speaking in class, creating friendships with their classmates, and when speaking to authority figures. Fortunately, shy teens can use the fundamental social skills offered throughout this book to help them navigate their challenges in school.

This chapter will explore the purpose of school, where shy teens feel inhibited, and whether homeschooling is a good option for them. Then, I'll apply social skills solutions to the biggest special issues facing shy students, such as speaking in class and making a presentation.

## The Purpose of School

Teens are always told that school is their "job." They have to attend all day, every day, work on their assignments, and do their best to succeed.

That conventional viewpoint is valid to a point. True, students must treat their education seriously, but thinking about school as a job takes any pleasure out of it. School shouldn't be a chore.

Another way of looking at school is to have a more holistic view of it. Not only do teens acquire academic skills at school, but they also acquire many other important problem-solving skills.[1] In this view, school is training for your life. It's how you learn the fundamental tools of your trade—reading, writing, math, science, and more—but it also prepares you for everything you will do in adulthood. It is how you build your identity. Being exposed to and mastering these skills while you're in a relatively protected environment such as school will help you navigate the more complex terrain of adulthood, when you're out on your own. For example, the math skills you learn in school will help you balance your bank account, understand the implications of a mortgage or loan, and if you go into sales, help you calculate your commission or craft the terms of a business deal. And even if you don't pursue a technical career, your science classes will help you talk to your doctor, become a great cook and baker, and make some simple repairs to your home or car.

## Quentin's Story

Quentin is in his final year of high school. Like a lot of shy teens, his shyness affects all aspects of his life. Previously, he felt that his shyness held him back in his social life. Now, as his college-prep classes become more challenging, his shyness is affecting his academic life. Here's what he had to say:

"My shyness is expressed in many ways, such as aloofness, speaking without thinking, incoherent speech, physical escape, making excuses to get out of certain situations," Quentin wrote.

In my personal life, sometimes shyness is seen as selfishness or coolness, a negative thing. In my social life, when I talk before thinking, sometimes it turns people off. In school it's had me think I'm too stupid to do this work, when in reality I've had some of my teachers tell me that if I didn't have so much else to do outside of school, I would be an A student. It's also crippled me in not being able to approach my teachers for assistance with work assignments and such.

I have always been ashamed of my shyness and have negatively labeled myself as too stupid in order to deal with the shyness realistically and in a safe manner. I am harder on myself than anybody else.[a]

These skills aren't just academic skills. They also include social skills that you will need throughout your lifetime. When you go to school, you encounter people who share some things in common with you, but also people who are unlike you. Your classmates come from families that are different than yours, with unique histories, values, and cultures. They possess all different kinds of intelligence. Some kids are smarter than others. And students learn in a variety of ways; some are visual, while others are readers, doers, and listeners. And, of course, your individual classmates have unique personalities. You may not like each and every one, and they may not all hit it off with you, but you must learn how to get along with them within the classroom and school yard. To do so, you'll need to learn how to negotiate, stand up for yourself, defer to others, apologize, introduce yourself, and be loyal to your friends.

In addition to your classmates, you must deal with a wide range of authority figures. When you're in elementary school, you will most likely just need to deal with a few teachers, perhaps some aides, and a far-off principal. In junior high

> **Remember This**
>
> ● School is intended to expose students to new concepts, people, and activities so that they are prepared for adulthood. Instead of viewing school as a job that must be endured, students should embrace its challenges as a way to become well-rounded, fully functioning adults.

and high school, you will encounter more teachers and will have to learn how to live up to their expectations. Some will be strict, some lenient, others welcoming, and only a few, hopefully, who simply are intimidating and unapproachable.

Lastly, an overlooked aspect of school is the emotions of the students. Students are constantly being evaluated on their intellect, skills, and creativity. In this challenging environment, students must learn how to deal with success and disappointment, joy and failure, embarrassment, pride, insecurity, confidence, and, of course, shyness.

Coping with all of these challenges every day isn't always easy, and many teens avoid them because it's simply too much for their shy body, mind, and self. But avoidance would be the wrong path to take, since that will make these students off time in terms of mastering these challenges. This chapter breaks down some of the biggest problems teens—especially shy teens—face during the school day. As you'll see, breaking them down into manageable tasks makes them seem less overwhelming and difficult.

## Shy Students' Challenges

Many shy people have written to me over the years about the challenges they faced in high school. It's easy to see why they felt their shyness was triggered by the many challenges in this environment. Junior high and senior high school involves a host of conditions that can make someone feel shy.

First off, junior and senior high school students are going through all of the physical, emotional, and intellectual changes of adolescence, which makes them feel self-conscious and shy. The combination of their skewed social comparisons, which makes them feel that they are worse off than their peers, and their pessimistic attributional style makes them feel that it is all their own fault and they can't change their fate.

In addition, adolescent students are thrust into larger schools and deal with progressively more demands, such as changing classes each period, dealing with a variety of teachers and authority figures, and fulfilling more difficult academic expectations, such as making more presentations, doing group activities, and undertaking independent studies. Shy students feel an approach-avoidance conflict about learning these new tasks, since they want to excel in school (approach instinct) but also want to shrink from the challenges because they're new and unfamiliar and therefore threatening to their self-concept and self-esteem (avoidance instinct).

The shy body, mind, and self stress reactions kick in when students are in the approach-avoidance conflict. While they may feel comfortable sitting in the back of the classroom and not participating in discussions, when they do have to try something new their shy dominant response comes into play. They feel anxious and overwhelmed by their shy physical symptoms, such as blushing, stammering, sweating, and feeling shaky. Their shy mind focuses on their discomfort and not the academic task at hand. The combination of their physical discomfort and negative self-talk produces dark emotions that lower their self-esteem and self-confidence. It's difficult to listen to the teacher and take in information when you're dealing with these intense shy stress reactions.

Because they're caught in the approach-avoidance conflict, shy teens are slower to warm up to these new academic and social challenges, especially the ones that involve social skills. Their newness and unfamiliarity bring out shy

It can be difficult to focus in class and listen to the teacher when shy stress reactions kick in.

teens' self-consciousness and insecurities. And, like Quentin, many shy students don't know how to ask for help with their studies and feel that they are the only ones in class who are struggling.

Also important to note is that friendships become more complex during adolescence. As schools get larger, students must deal with being surrounded by more people. And, in addition, friendships, social groups, and cliques become more tense. Shy teens may have a tough time dealing with the social politics of school, especially if old friends fall away to pursue new relationships. Plus, being surrounded by so many fellow students makes shy teens feel uncomfortable, as if they are under a microscope and being judged all day—the psychological phenomenon known as objective self-awareness.

Lastly, there's the ever-present comfort zone. Junior high school and senior high school require teens to try new things, both within the classroom and outside of it, and be judged on their performance. This is intended to help students explore new concepts and activities so that they will get a taste of what they will want to focus on after high school, in college, or in a professional career. This exposure to a variety of subjects will help them become well-rounded adults with a wide range of interests. Shy teens may struggle with this because they have narrow and rigid comfort zones. They may feel most at ease when studying their favorite subjects and feel inhibited when trying out new academic interests, especially if they involve new behaviors, such as making a presentation.

Taken together, the many demands in the academic day can bring out an adolescent's shyness and interfere with her ability to learn. But, there's one positive aspect about school that will work in a shy student's favor: the power of repeated exposure. When shy teens go to school every day, their warming-up period will kick in and help to lessen their inhibitions. It may take them longer to warm up to their new challenges than their more outgoing peers, but shy teens will eventually become more comfortable by continuing to be exposed to them—and by utilizing problem-solving and social skills that will make them successfully shy.

## The Absent Shy Student

Since school can trigger a teen's shyness, students typically want to silently fade into the shadows so that they don't have to cope with the discomfort of being around their peers in stressful situations.[2] That's one reason why shy students don't stand out in the classroom: They're trying to flee from the threat to their self-esteem even though they are physically present at school.

Oftentimes, shy students generate a large number of absences because they don't feel comfortable at school and don't want to deal with the stress and anxiety their school day creates. This, of course, is not a positive way to deal with these challenges. In fact, being absent from school makes a teen's shyness even worse

Shy students often have excessive absences or cover up their shyness with other behaviors because they are so uncomfortable in school. But those coping mechanisms aren't as effective as incorporating all of the elements of the school day into one's comfort zone.

because it strengthens her dominant response to avoid school. The best way to redirect her dominant response is to approach school, even though it may take some time and effort to change her behavior.

Another coping mechanism shy students use is to cover up their shyness with other behaviors. Since appearances are very important to teens, they want to seem like they are anything but shy. As discussed in chapter 2, there are many types of shy people, and not all of them are obviously shy on the surface.[3] In school, these shy students may look something like this:

- The Publicly Shy: This is the stereotypical shy student who is quiet, keeps his distance from others, and avoids social contact. He is usually labeled "shy" by his peers and doesn't have a high social status because he lacks social skills and his nervousness makes other people uncomfortable.
- The Chronically Shy: This is a shy individual who has been shy for her entire life and can't imagine being outgoing and relaxed with other people. This is the student who turns up on graduation day and her classmates wonder who she is and where she has been all through the years.
- The Privately Shy: This shy person is difficult to identify in public because although he may feel anxious and self-conscious, he is able to make friends fairly easily. His friends may be surprised to find out that he is shy.

"To me it was easier to fake an illness and stay home than deal with the social part of school. Needless to say it's hard to make friends when you're only in school maybe ten days out of thirty. I would never talk in class."
—twenty-one-year-old medical billing coder[b]

- The Shy Extrovert: This individual feels very anxious and self-conscious, but she masks it in social settings by, quite literally, masking her shyness by being very outgoing. This person is so uncomfortable with her true, shy self that she has to present a false front in public. The class clown is often a shy extrovert.
- The Transitionally Shy: This person feels shy when he is warming up to new phases of life that are outside of his comfort zone, such as starting a new school year. Once his warming up period plays out, he doesn't feel shy anymore.
- The Shy Rebel: This shy teen tries to cope with her shyness by creating a wild exterior and breaking rules. She doesn't want others to know that she feels uncomfortable in social settings so she overcompensates by acting wild and generating negative attention.
- The Situationally Shy: This student feels shy in specific situations, such as being the focus of the class's attention, talking to an authority figure, or finding a new circle of friends at the beginning of a school year.
- The Successfully Shy: This student is self-aware, is in control of his shyness, and has a positive, confident attitude about himself and his abilities even when he is warming up to a new social situation that's outside of his comfort zone.

As you can see, appearances can be deceiving. Even the most outgoing and bold person in the school can feel shy at times, especially during the sometimes-chaotic social environment in school.

### Time for Reflection

Do you understand the school-created factors that can make someone feel shy? Can you relate? Have you ever felt shy, anxious, or nervous about going to school? If so, how did you deal with it? Do you still feel shy at school? Do you think you can change that?

# Should Shy Students Be Homeschooled?

A small but important minority of respondents to my shyness survey say that they opted to be homeschooled during junior high or senior high school. The stress of attending school every day was too overwhelming for them. They typically say that they didn't get along with their classmates, felt bullied or ostracized, or simply never felt comfortable when they began attending the school and never seemed to fit in and feel a sense of belonging. To remove the negative social aspects of attending school, they decided to study at home.

The feedback I've heard in response has been mixed. These students felt their stress and anxiety lessen, but they also missed some of the better parts of the school day, such as seeing their friends and feeling like they were part of something bigger than themselves. While they wanted to be left alone, their isolation made them feel lonely.

Homeschooling can be an option for some teens if they truly are miserable at school. However, homeschooling isn't a silver bullet that will make a teen less shy. School, as tough as it may seem at times, teaches students valuable lessons that aren't always included within the curriculum. The social lessons experienced in school are as important as anything found within a textbook.

If a teen decides not to attend school, there's a good chance that she won't learn these social lessons and will be off time socially when compared to her peers. In addition, because she won't have the same experiences as her friends, she will have less in common with them during her school years. Again, this will intensify her feelings of isolation and loneliness and won't help her become less shy because her dominant response to avoid school will be strengthened.

That said, shy teens can be homeschooled with success if their day includes social experiences in addition to academic challenges. These students can become part of a network of homeschooled students so that they are able to develop friendships and explore social activities that cannot be learned in a book or on the Internet. Overall, homeschooling can help shy teens cope with a particularly bad situation at their school, but it can intensify their shyness and sense of social isolation if they are spending too much time alone.

# Your School Is Your Comfort Zone

Shy students can rethink their school experience by using the factorial approach to expanding their comfort zone, a problem-solving skill covered in chapter 7. This will allow shy students to develop strategies to reduce the amount of unfamiliarity in their world while incorporating new elements into it. This is done by breaking down their comfort zone into familiar people, places, and activities, then changing one factor to make incremental progress in their lives.

Each student, shy or not, can break down his school day into the three comfort zone factors. It may look something like this:

1. People: specific friends, classmates, teachers, aides, certain members of the administration, coaches
2. Places: classrooms, hallways, lockers, library, cafeteria, gym, theater, labs, athletic fields, car or bus
3. Activities: listening in class, doing independent study, focusing on favorite class subjects, eating lunch with friends, after-school clubs

While no two students will have the same comfort zones, they will overlap on the major items because they are in the same environment every day. But some teens will have fuller, bigger comfort zones that are easy to stretch, because they welcome new people, places, and activities into their lives. Shy teens, however, tend to have narrow, rigid comfort zones because they are slow to warm up to new experiences and people. For example, outgoing or successfully shy teens may have dozens of people within their comfort zones. These familiar people will include a lot of classmates from different social groups and teachers and other authority figures. But shy teens will have fewer people within their comfort zone. These familiar faces will be the shy teen's close friends, who are very similar to them, and a few authority figures, if any. And shy students will feel an approach-avoidance conflict when trying to incorporate new people into their comfort zone. This will make their school day seem more nerve-racking, inhibiting their ability to concentrate on their studies and learn their new tasks.

There's nothing wrong, necessarily, with having a narrow comfort zone. There are many people who are satisfied with a few close friends and a tried-and-true pattern to their day. But shy teens want to have a larger, more populated comfort zone. Because they have well-developed social interest, they are sincerely aware of and concerned with other people. They want to make connections with more people, develop new abilities by trying out new behaviors and activities, and feel comfortable in more places, not just their homes and the back row of the classroom.

The problem is that shy teens don't know how to expand their comfort zone in a smart, stress-free manner. They either jump with both feet into a new environment—for example, by showing up to a party with little preparation and no friends to give them social support—or they avoid the challenge and withdraw from new encounters.

As discussed in chapter 7, shy teens can have more success in expanding their comfort zone by using a factorial approach and changing one new element while

**Try This**

Write down the people, places, and activities within your school day's comfort zone. Now, write down the people, places, and activities you'd like to be part of your comfort zone. Can you change one factor to expand your comfort zone with a minimum of stress and anxiety?

keeping two elements the same. Quentin, for example, would like to be able to talk to his teachers about tasks in the classroom, but he doesn't feel confident enough to do so. He can modify one factor to expand his comfort zone in an incremental manner. In his current comfort zone, Quentin's got his teacher (familiar person), the classroom (familiar place), and listening, but not participating, in class (familiar activity). He wants to change the activity from passive listening to actively asking his teacher questions.

Quentin has a number of options. He could e-mail his teacher instead of asking him in person. Or he could ask a friend the question, and if she can't figure out the answer, they could approach the teacher together. Quentin could try any of these approaches to make an initial connection with his teacher to get answers to his questions. If he can remind himself that he's only changing one factor within his comfort zone, and not trying something totally new and unfamiliar, he will feel more confident about speaking to an authority figure and addressing his academic concerns.

There isn't anything magical about expanding one's comfort zone by using a factorial approach. All it takes is a little analysis and a strategy, and shy students will be able to feel more at ease in more environments while making connections with new people.

## Speaking Up in Class

One of the most difficult obstacles for a shy student is speaking in class. Just sitting in the classroom, waiting for the teacher to pick a pupil to speak, can bring on intense anxiety that can block out any information the shy student is trying to take in. Instead of focusing on the day's lesson, the shy student's mind will create a mental loop that goes something like this: "I know she's going to call on someone. I don't want to be that person. Maybe if I look like I know the answer she won't

"I remember as far back as elementary school, the teacher calling on me when my hand was not raised and not knowing the answer to the question. When I answered, I remember classmates laughing at me. As a result, it made me even more fearful to raise my hand in the future and more afraid to speak in front of a group."—twenty-one-year-old administrative assistant[c]

call on me. Maybe if I look like I'm not even here she won't call on me. I can't make eye contact with her. What was she even talking about? Whew! Dodged that bullet. Oh no . . . She needs to call on someone else now. I'm doomed. Why does so much of my grade need to be based on class participation?"

Everyone has had these thoughts, even the most outgoing student, because speaking in class can make a student feel very self-conscious and judged. After all, the entire class's attention will be focused on the lone student, and the teacher and the rest of the class will be evaluating that person's answer. That intense amount of attention will make the phenomenon of objective self-awareness kick in. That occurs when an individual is under scrutiny and feels as if a spotlight is shining on him or as if he is under a microscope or being recorded. When that happens, whatever that individual is focusing on becomes more pronounced. For example, if he feels his voice waver, he will think that it's very screechy and unsteady. If he is trying to hold a pencil, his hand will shake. If he is trying to sit still, he will start to get jittery. This uncomfortable feeling will make that individual feel more self-conscious and feel that the entire room notices his discomfort and is judging him harshly. He will try to clam up and withdraw to cover up his nervousness.

No wonder why speaking in class is a powerful shyness trigger.

That said, there are many things you can do to lessen your anxiety about speaking in class, including the following:

- Change your focus: Instead of concentrating on your nervousness, focus on what the teacher is saying. Too often, a shy student is completely caught up in his own anxiety and cannot hear what anyone else is saying. A good way to cut out the noise is to totally think about what the teacher is saying. Then, if you are called on, you will be prepared to answer.
- Be proactive: Don't wait to be called on, which may happen when you don't know the answer to your teacher's question. Speak up when you aren't forced to do so. Raise your hand if you know the answer, because that will put you in control of the situation and make speaking in class more routine and your new dominant response. And it will lessen the chances that you will be called on when you aren't feeling confident.

Speaking up in class is a common shyness trigger.

- Be an active listener: A good way to make your teacher your ally and to be helpful to your classmates is to be a good listener and become part of the conversation. One tip is to ask questions during a discussion. You can ask a question of clarification, which is an attempt to get more information about the information the teacher is sharing. An example would be, "Could you repeat that step? I didn't quite catch it." Or you can ask a question of extension, which is how you expand the topic of conversation. You can ask, "Could you give an example of that?" Chances are that your classmates also have the same question and you will be doing them a favor by asking the teacher to provide more information.

Overall, the more often you speak in class, the easier it will be. As you become more accustomed to speaking in class, this activity will be incorporated into your comfort zone and you won't feel that you are being scrutinized by your peers.

**Try This**

Write down one way in which you can participate more in class. Do you think you can put it into practice this week?

## Making a Presentation

Another shyness trigger is making a presentation in front of a classroom full of students. Public speaking is a concern of shy adults, so it makes sense that teens feel anxious about public speaking in school, where this skill is first learned. Due to its tendency to intensify feelings of self-consciousness, making a presentation has the power to create a bout of shyness, since, like speaking up in class, it forces the student to step into the spotlight, fear being judged, and step out of his comfort zone with this highly unusual activity.

Many people, not just shy people, feel anxious about speaking in front of others. According to a 2013 report from the National Institute of Mental Health, 74 percent of Americans fear speaking in public, far more than the 40 percent of us who are shy.[4] One reason so many people dread public speaking is because it happens so infrequently. Most of us only make a public presentation once or twice a year, if ever. It's an action that's outside of our comfort zone, no matter how shy or outgoing we are. Therefore, our dominant response will be to feel nervous and threatened by it.

Some people will do everything they can to turn down the invitation to speak in public because it is so scary. Students, however, can't avoid making a presentation since it is typically part of their academic experience. Oftentimes, students will be so unnerved by this task that they will avoid preparing for it. They will procrastinate on it until right before their deadline, and then rush to pull everything together and try to wing it during their presentation. When they're finished, they'll feel that they failed and are not suited to speaking in public. That would be the wrong assumption, however. Public speaking is a social skill that can be learned. What's key is practicing until it feels natural.

To become a better public speaker, try these suggestions:

- Practice: Perhaps the most important part of speaking in public occurs before the presentation takes place, when you are rehearsing your speech. Shy students can become more comfortable with public speaking if they

"I hate the way my voice sounds when I speak up in front of a group. It gets shaky and I rush through whatever it is I have to say. I feel like everyone is laughing at me."—eighteen-year old community college student[d]

warm up to it by rehearsing well in advance of their performance. Instead of waiting until the last minute, begin preparing your speech by writing down notes and then expanding them into your speech. Then, say it out loud and make any revisions you think are necessary. The next step is to gradually increase your audience. Speak into a recorder, webcam, or mirror so that you can witness yourself speaking. Make adjustments. Then, try it in front of a friend or family member so you can get feedback. Try it again. Then keep rehearsing as much as you can. When you finally get your chance to make your speech, you will have conquered your jitters and be so comfortable with your material that you will feel confident and relaxed. (Go back to chapter 4 for Dante's experience trying out for a play, for another example of how to rehearse before a public presentation.)

- Don't avoid opportunities to speak in public: If you are asked to speak in front of a group, take it, even if the group is small or insignificant to you—especially if the stakes are low. The more often you speak in public, the easier it will become for you. The very act of doing it will help you to develop a dominant response and comfort zone that includes public speaking.

- Adjust your expectations: Public speaking is difficult for many people, so it's perfectly natural to feel nervous about it. Instead of feeling that you are the only one who is having difficulty making a speech, remember that the other students in your class are experiencing the same struggles. You may want to ask a fellow classmate to rehearse with you so that you will gain more experience and not feel so alone.

- Listen to feedback: Many people who are learning a new task don't want to be evaluated because they feel too vulnerable to hear feedback on their performance. But it can be helpful to get feedback from those you trust and who have your best interests at heart. When you do get comments from someone you trust, just listen to them. You don't need to defend yourself, nor must you allow it to affect your self-esteem or self-confidence. Remember that feedback is just information that you can use—or not.

Public speaking can be frightening for some people who aren't confident of their ability to appear to be an expert on a topic. But, if you seize opportunities

> ## Remember This
>
> According to National Institute of Mental Health data, 74 percent of people say that they dread making public presentations.[e] However, anyone can become a good public speaker by preparing for their speech and making public speaking seem like a routine activity that's within their comfort zone.

to do so and give yourself time to prepare, you can become a great public speaker who actually enjoys the experience.

## Creating a Support System

Many shy teens have trouble during the school day because they feel alone. They may be new to the school and haven't created any satisfying friendships yet, or they may have a few close friends they don't see often while they're in school. When they look around, they feel surrounded by students who are part of friendships and social circles or cliques that provide them with a sense of belonging. This makes shy teens feel left out and diminishes their academic experience.

Shy teens, of course, do have friends. But they aren't satisfied with their friendships. They want to include more people in their comfort zone and have a wider circle of friends. Shy teens need to act on their social interest and focus on being a good friend, instead of their nerves.

Here's how you can develop more friendships within your school:

- Look at your comfort zone: A good way to find more friends is to take an inventory of your comfort zone. Take a look at your acquaintances; these are people who you can turn into better friends by spending more time with them. Then, look at your activities. Are there any solo activities you can turn into social activities by inviting someone to share them with you? Then look at the places in which you feel comfortable. Can you invite a school friend to any of those places? By changing one factor in your comfort zone you will be able to expand it with little risk.

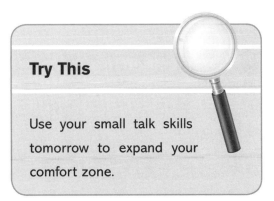

**Try This**

Use your small talk skills tomorrow to expand your comfort zone.

- Practice your small talk skills: As discussed in chapter 8, every friendship begins with small talk. When you are at school, use your small talk skills to make more connections to the people with whom you are spending your day. Remember that small talk isn't about you; it's about the people with whom you are speaking. Focus on them and their interests and you will make a good impression on your future friends.
- Adjust your social comparisons: Just about every student feels unconfident about her place in the social hierarchy of school. So when you look around at the students who surround you and compare yourself to them, remember that they are feeling as vulnerable and lonely as you at times.
- Take control of your social life: Students who take control of their lives tend to deal better with change.[5] So, you don't need to be passive and wait for others to notice you and develop a friendship with you. Instead of spending your time alone, turn your solitary activities into social ones. Your comfort zone inventory can help you develop a strategy. Start a study group, join a club, walk to your classes with someone else, or invite an acquaintance to a social activity.

## You Are in Control of Your School Experience

It's perfectly normal for shy teens to feel anxious or pessimistic about attending school. Not only are their academic challenges increasing, but trying to learn something new in a complex social environment can make shy teens feel less confident in their abilities to succeed in school and manage their relationships. But shy teens don't have to suffer throughout their day. By understanding the fundamental dynamics of shyness, using a factorial approach to expanding their comfort zone, and breaking up overwhelming challenges into manageable pieces, they can conquer their fears and knock down their social obstacles. As they become more successfully shy in school, they will learn how to embrace their challenges and develop skills that will help them mature into independent, well-rounded adults.

> ### ! Remember This
>
> Students who take control of the changes in their lives do better dealing with these transitions. Use the knowledge and practice the strategies you have acquired while reading this book to be the agent of change to take control of your school experiences instead of letting these experiences control you.

# BULLYING AND SOCIAL MEDIA

........................................................................................................

In the previous chapters, we discussed shyness primarily in terms of how it feels within the shy person—the fundamental dynamics of shyness and the shy body, mind, and self—or how shyness manifests in one-on-one situations that are unfamiliar and new, such as dating. In this chapter, we'll explore how shy teens experience encounters that include more than two people—bullying, social media, and cyberbullying.

These issues have come to the fore in recent years. The prevalence and consequences of bullying are now being addressed as the serious issues that they are, especially during the middle school or junior high years. In addition, this generation of teens is the first generation that has grown up in the Internet age. Prior to this generation, kids lived their lives off-line, and their relationships were more or less restricted to face-to-face ones. That limited the self-expression of previous generations of teens. Today's media allow a teen's Tweet to potentially reach more people in an instant than some people will seemingly meet in their entire lives. This has advantages and drawbacks for all teens, but shy teens have unique experiences when using social media and when they're entangled in an experience with a bully. This chapter will cover the many facets of bullying, what shy teens say about their social media use, the pros and cons of online media for shy teens, and how shy teens can protect themselves.

## Teens and Bullying

It's important to listen to Rashida's story (see page 218) because so many teens—shy or not—are victims or targets of bullying. According to data collected by the U.S. Department of Health and Human Services (DHHS), 28 percent of American students in grades 6–12 and 20 percent of high school students have been bullied.[1] Bullying seems to peak in the middle school years and is less common among high school students.

## Rashida's Story

Rashida, a college sophomore, says that she used to be shy all the time, but now she's only shy during very specific situations. You may say that she is successfully shy, because she overcame her shyness and is now in control of it. It's a hard-won success. Back in high school, Rashida had been bullied because she was overweight. But she had some insights about herself, her shyness, and the power she was giving to others, and how her sense of self-awareness helped her to take control of her life. Let's hear what Rashida has to say.

"I was overweight and teased every day," Rashida wrote to me.

I wouldn't talk very much. In fact, I wouldn't do anything to make them notice me. I didn't ask for things that I wanted. I was passive, hoping that people would know my needs.

Once I turned eighteen, I started to feel better about myself. I realized the bullies weren't a real threat to me. I wasn't around them every day, either, which really helped. The weight started coming off as I thought about myself in a different way. I'm trying to lose the last few pounds. But as I go down in sizes, my confidence goes up. Not only because I'm doing something good for myself, but from the attention of men. Actually, I've always gotten attention from men; it's just that it happens more often now.

But, last year, a guy said something nasty about me to one of his friends within my earshot and I went through another bout of shyness. Then I analyzed the situation and realized that I didn't need to feel inferior to him. I haven't felt shy since then, even though I see that guy all the time. I just don't care what he thinks of me. I know who I am and I accept myself as I am.[a]

About 30 percent of adolescents say that they have bullied someone else. But those troubling numbers pale in comparison to the numbers of adolescents who are affected by bullying. A full 70 percent of teens and 70 percent of school staff say that they have witnessed bullying—what researchers call "bystanders."[2] That means that if you haven't been bullied, been the bully, or seen bullying happen, you are in the minority.

Almost a third of teens say they have been bullied and have bullied others. Being systematically ridiculed or excluded from social activities is a form of social bullying.

But what, exactly, are we talking about when we talk about bullying? Many people seem to think that a negative comment here and there, some occasional teasing by a mean girl, not getting along with a "frenemy," or "boys will be boys" roughhousing equals bullying. These situations are negative and can impact a teen's self-esteem and quality of life, but they are not bullying. Although definitions of bullying can be loose, the U.S. DHHS considers bullying to encompass repeated and intentional verbal, social, or physical acts of aggression against someone who has less power than the instigator.[3] When these sorts of attacks are made while using technology, it's called cyberbullying,[4] which will be covered in depth later in this chapter.

Verbal and social bullying are the most common ways young people bully another person. Verbal bullying means using one's words to demean another person. This includes taunting, teasing, name-calling, and threats of violence. The attacks are meant to diminish a target's self-esteem, self-worth, and confidence. They can severely wound a bully's target's emotions and sense of identity.[5]

Social bullying affects a target's friendships. These teens are isolated by the bully and shunned by bystanders. Girls seem to be more likely to use this indirect form of bullying. They manipulate situations to dominate weaker girls, exclude

**Time for Reflection**

Have you, like Rashida, been a victim of bullying? Have you bullied someone else? Have you witnessed bullying? How did that feel? What did you do about it?

and isolate targets from their groups, spread gossip and untrue rumors to damage a target's reputation, and use social media to shame their target.[6]

Physical bullying is exactly what it sounds like. These bullies physically intimidate their target by shoving him into lockers, getting into fights with him, damaging the target's property, spitting on or kicking the target, and pressuring the target to do something he doesn't want to do. Boys are more likely than girls to physically bully their target.[7]

Middle school students who were bullied said that it included being called names, teasing, having rumors or lies spread about them, being pushed or shoved, being hit or otherwise attacked, being left out of a social activity, being threatened, having their belongings stolen, having sexual comments or gestures made, or being the target of offensive e-mails or blog postings.[8]

Bullying typically occurs in schools, on the grounds of the school, or on the school bus, places where kids gather and are loosely supervised. It can take place in all areas of the school, from the classroom to the hallways to the bathroom.[9]

Although bullying is prevalent in middle and high schools, researchers have found that only about 20 percent to 30 percent of those bullied let an adult know about it.[10]

## *Bully*, the Movie

The realities of bullies' targets was the subject of the 2012 documentary film *Bully*, which features the lives of targets, their families, and their experiences in school and in their hometowns.[11] Also portrayed were the families of two teens, Tyler Long and Ty Smalley, who had committed suicide as a result of toxic bullying.

The central target highlighted in the film was Alex, a thirteen-year-old in Des Moines, Iowa, who was repeatedly bullied and shunned by the kids in his school. Alex admitted that the only place where he truly felt free and safe was at home, among his parents and four younger siblings. His mother told the filmmakers that Alex had been born very prematurely and hadn't been expected to live one day. He survived, however, but struggled to make friends as a young man and was held back by his shyness and lack of social skills. At the bus stop, he didn't know how to talk to the other kids waiting with him. On the playground, he'd approach other kids but couldn't talk to them. They'd walk away without really noticing him. (That's classic wait-and-hover behavior used by shy kids, which was discussed in chapter 9 on making friends.)

Alex was terribly bullied. Being ignored at school was bad enough, but his worst experiences seemed to be on the bus. Kids would punch him, choke him, stab him with pencils, call him names, and shove him around. One day, a high school student sat next to Alex. Alex told the older kid that they were now "buddies." Instead of being polite and civil, the high school student told Alex that he was going to bring a gun to school the next day and shoot him and warned Alex never to speak to him again.

All the while, the bus driver ignored the constant taunts and acts of physical aggression against Alex. But the filmmakers were so upset about Alex being attacked on the bus that they showed the film footage to Alex's parents and the school administrators. His parents were concerned but didn't know how to help him. His mother wanted to know why Alex allowed kids to bully him. His father told Alex to punch the bully to show him that he wasn't afraid. His parents went to the school to complain, but little was done about it.

As bleak as Alex's story may seem, it does have a happy ending. After the film *Bully* was made, the kids in his school saw it. They finally understood what Alex was going through. The film humanized him. As a result, those who shunned him— the bystanders in school who knew Alex was bullied but did nothing—suddenly befriended him. That's all it took to turn Alex's life around. He came out of his shell, discovered how to talk to other people, and wasn't bullied again.

*Bully* is a difficult movie to watch whether you're a high school student or an adult, but it contains many hard truths that kids, families, schools, and communities must address. Bullying is so common because we tolerate it. *Bully* demonstrates that we cannot allow such hurtful acts of aggression to occur in our schools and communities.

## Try This

The film *Bully* was so powerful that it inspired the Bully Project, a campaign to educate kids, parents, and educators about the harmful effects of bullying and how it can be stopped. It sponsors showings of *Bully* to groups of kids and adults who want to put an end to bullying in their schools. Its website includes videos, tool kits, and resources for kids and adults. Go to thebullyproject.com to share your story or learn more about bullying.

## Are Shy Teens Always the Targets of Bullies?

The stereotypical victim of bullying is a nerdy, shy, weak kid who cannot stand up for himself or herself. But researchers have found that this stereotype doesn't necessarily conform to reality. Not all targets are shy kids.

Bullies target all kinds of victims, but they tend to cluster in the following way:[12]

- Kids who seem to be "different" than others. They can be different because of their looks, their weight, the way that they dress, their family's income level, their sexual orientation, their ethnic group, or simply being the new kid in class. LGBT (lesbian, gay, bisexual, transgender) teens, teens with special needs, and teens from minority groups are often targeted because they are different. Rashida would fall into this category, because she was teased and bullied because she was overweight.
- Kids who appear to be unable to defend themselves. This could be due to their physical attributes (they may be smaller in size than their peers) or because they don't have a circle of friends who will protect them.
- Kids who seem troubled by depression, anxiety, or low self-esteem. Their personal problems may isolate them from other kids.
- Kids on the low end of the popularity scale or those who don't have many friends. The higher-status kids may tease or bully these less-popular kids to assert their own power over their cliques and their classmates. Alex seems to fall into this group, because he was socially isolated at school.
- Kids who simply don't get along with others, antagonize their peers, or draw negative attention. These kids may not have critical social skills that can help them build friendships, or, at the very least, neutral, civil relationships with their classmates.

If there's any thread that weaves these targets together, it's that they lack friends who can help them deflect negative attention from bullies. Bullies seek out kids who they believe have less power than them. And in middle school and high school, when relationships mean so much, having few friends is a negative attribute, while having many friends—or trying to create new friendships by seeming powerful and intimidating—is a positive attribute. Therefore, teens with a weak social circle or a limited comfort zone can be easy prey for bullies.

Shy teens could fall into any one of the categories of victims. Like Rashida, they may feel self-conscious and not confident about their physical appearance. Or, like Alex, they may simply not have the social skills like small talk that enable them to make contact with other kids. In addition, some of the attributes of shyness may isolate teens from their peers. Shyness often correlates with depression,

Bullies tend to target those who appear to be different and don't have a strong social network.

anxiety, and low self-esteem, which hinders shy teens' relationships. They may have a few very strong friendships, but not many acquaintances, so they have fewer friends to fall back on when a bully wants to single them out for attack. And they may create a false, negative identity to hide their true shy selves, which provokes other teens into bullying them.

Shy teens aren't destined to be victims of bullies. Rashida, for example, realized that those who bullied her over her weight really had no power over her. She could be true to herself and self-confident while shrugging off the taunts of the bullies. This greater sense of self-awareness has led her to become successfully shy and more in control of her life.

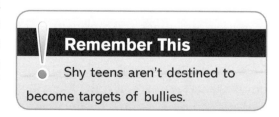

**Remember This**

Shy teens aren't destined to become targets of bullies.

"I believe I developed my shyness as a defense against inconsiderate children who teased me mercilessly during my preadolescent and adolescent years. My elementary school years were wonderful. I had plenty of friends and none of the children at that time shunned me because I was in the class for learning disabled children. When I moved into junior high, however, things changed—even my best friend from elementary school denied we were friends in front of the 'normal' kids. I guess she wanted to protect her reputation. A good number of the other children continually accused me of being stupid. Even though I was no longer enrolled in any 'special' classes as such, my lower social status remained with me throughout my high school years."—nineteen-year-old college student[b]

## Effects of Bullying on Targets

Bullying impacts a targeted teen's social life, but it also has an enormous effect on that teen's psychological and physical health and well-being. Research shows that kids who are bullied tend to have problems with their mental health and emotions. They are more likely to have depression and anxiety, feel sad and lonely, and lose interest in activities they used to enjoy. They also have trouble eating and sleeping normally. This makes perfect sense. If you were being targeted by a bully, you'd feel worried about going to school, feel that your efforts to change your circumstances are futile, have a pessimistic attitude, have trouble maintaining and creating friendships, and not want to participate in activities that will bring you close to other kids, who may be a threat to you. This isn't a temporary issue, either. Researchers have found that these emotional issues can last into adulthood.[13]

The effects of bullying don't stop there. Targeted teens may eat for comfort or lose their appetite because they are anxious about being around the bully. They may have health problems because of the ongoing stress of the bullying. Our bodies aren't meant to experience high levels of stress, with a racing heart and increased hormones and adrenaline. This high level of arousal is meant to protect us when we are faced with an immediate threat, like a bear in the woods or an attacker about to strike. But when we are frequently at that high level of arousal, our nervous system is at risk of burning out. Chronic, long-term stress can lead to anxiety and depression, digestive and sleep problems, heart disease, weight gain, and impaired memory and concentration.[14] So not only does bullying create social and emotional problems, but it takes a toll on a target's health, too.

All of this makes going to school and concentrating in class very difficult. Kids who are bullied seem to have lower academic performance than their peers, don't participate in class, and are more likely to have a higher number of absences or drop out of school.[15] Again, this seems to be a logical response to being bullied and shunned at school. If you are constantly worried about being attacked, you won't enjoy going to school and will find any excuse to be absent. Your health issues may force you to stay home. And if you are consumed with anxiety about being bullied, you won't be able to concentrate when you are in the classroom. It's hard to listen and think clearly if you are constantly on high alert, waiting for the next attack from your tormentor.

Interestingly, researchers have found that bystanders—kids who witness bullying but aren't targeted—also experience some of these negative impacts of bullying. They are more likely to use tobacco, alcohol, or other drugs; have increased emotional problems, such as depression and anxiety; and be absent from school frequently.[16] Having a sense that you do not have control over your environment can lead individuals to feel a sense of helplessness, which has been found to be associated with feelings of depression and other negative emotional and behavioral consequences.[17] It seems that bullying creates a tense, chaotic environment for kids who aren't directly involved in bullying, making school an unsafe place for everyone. And the lack of control over their situation can make bystanders feel pessimistic about themselves and their school situation.

Lastly, the media have reported many examples of teens who committed suicide after being bullied or cyberbullied, and *Bully* showed the pain of those who were left behind after a loved one's suicide. There are far too many cases of targeted teens who took their lives after being bullied. Targets of bullies are at risk of suicidal feelings, but it could also be due to their depression, anxiety, or social isolation—not the bullying itself. However, most targets of bullying don't commit suicide, think about it, or engage in suicidal behaviors. They feel the negative impacts of bullying, but they don't let it spiral out of control.[18]

As you can see, the impact of bullying goes far beyond the immediate moment of an attack. Bullying can create long-lasting health and emotional problems in a teen target. That's why it's so important to address bullying, whether you are a target, a bully, or a bystander.

---

## ❓ Time for Reflection

Would you bully someone if you knew that you were causing your target long-term health and emotional problems?

# Bullies and Bystanders

Now that we know a little bit more about the targets of bullying, what do we know about the two other parties in this triangle—the bullies themselves and the bystanders, those who witness bullying but don't stand up for the victim and put an end to the aggression?

Once again, the stereotypes of bullies and bystanders don't conform to reality.

## *Who Bullies Are*

Bullies aren't simply dumb, mean kids who threaten, tease, and intimidate targets just because they can. Kids engage in bullying behaviors for a number of reasons. Some are trying to become popular and believe that intimidating others will help them fit in the complex social universe of adolescence. This shifting and sorting of relationships is intense during the middle school years, which seems to be why bullying peaks during the same time.[19] Others use bullying behaviors because they are exposed to violence in their home and view it as an acceptable way to solve social problems. Some male bullies believe that their intimidating behavior is merely a way to fulfill our society's stereotype of assertive, masculine behavior. Still others may use bullying to deflect attention from their own perceived short-comings and insecurities.[20]

Bullies seem to be motivated by wanting to find their place in the wide social web of their peers, but don't know how to do so other than by intimidating other kids. They don't seem to have social skills that enable them to make friends in a positive way. They don't feel empathy for their targets and they want to be in control of others. They don't know how to negotiate to get what they want and they get frustrated easily, so they resort to threats or violence to achieve their goals. They can be very intelligent and good at manipulating people and situations so that things go their way.[21]

Bullies tend to fall into three categories:[22]

1. Kids with high social status who want to keep that status. These are the cool kids in school who on the surface don't seem to be bullies. They push other kids around to keep them from rising up in the power structure and threatening them, and to draw other kids to them. They tend to use social bullying to get what they want by manipulating relationships, spreading rumors or gossip, isolating targets they don't like, and exploiting kids' vulnerabilities. Other kids are too fearful of them to fight back.
2. Kids with low social status who use bullying behaviors to gain status. These are kids who want to become popular and hang out with the cool

kids and don't know how to do it in a pro-social manner. They bully other kids as a way to impress the popular kids, feel more secure about their place in the social universe, and push other kids down. They may feel peer pressure to bully others. These bullies are sometimes called bully-victims because they can be targeted by higher-status kids who know that they feel vulnerable.

3. Antisocial kids: These teens are the ones who most closely conform to the stereotype of the thuggish bully. These kids use bullying behavior to get what they want because they don't have social skills, empathy, or respect for rules. They use physical bullying—and the threat of physical bullying—to intimidate and control targets and bystanders. Their friends tend to be as antisocial as they are.

As you can see, kids who use bullying behavior do so because they feel threatened by other kids. They don't view relationships as simple relationships. They are keenly aware of status, power, and control. But even though relationships are so important to them, they don't know how to form and maintain them unless they are always in charge.

Bullies threaten targets, but they also create an atmosphere of intimidation that affects bystanders, too. Research has shown that up to 70 percent of all adolescents have witnessed bullying as bystanders, so this group includes the majority of kids. These bystanders don't always intervene to stop the bullying, however. They prefer to ignore it, enjoy it, or are sidekicks of the bully.

## Who Bystanders Are

Like targets and bullies, there are different types of bystanders:[23]

- Silent witnesses: These kids don't get involved in bullying although they have seen it happen. They may be intimidated by the bully and don't want to become a target, or they may not know what they can do to stop it. They may avoid places where bullying is engaged in or the bullies themselves. They don't want to attract trouble or "drama," so they do their best to mind their own business, even though they may feel some empathy for the target.
- Kids who enjoy it: These bystanders appear to be allies of the bully. They seem to enjoy the spectacle of humiliating another child and may take it further by recording it and showing it to other kids or posting it online. They may participate in verbal bullying, too, by laughing at jokes or spreading rumors or gossip. They may not always enjoy it, but they go along with it because they want to support the bully.

**Try This**

Reach out to one target of bullying tomorrow. You can smile, say hello, offer her help, or strike up a conversation with her. Targets of bullies need to know that they are not alone and need some encouragement to become more confident and socially active.

- Sidekicks: Sidekicks foster an atmosphere of intimidation and spur on the bully. These bystanders don't instigate the bullying, but they sometimes participate in it once it's started. They are followers of the bully. They may join in the physical bullying or be part of the crowd that actively watches it and encourages it. They may be part of the verbal bullying by spreading rumors and forwarding harmful messages and videos online. These sidekicks help to create a culture that tolerates and condones bullying and abuse.

Bullies, targets, and bystanders are caught up in a complex triangular relationship that seems to be permanent. Bullies don't seem to want to change their behavior because they can get what they want by using intimidation, threats, and control. Targets feel powerless to stop the bully's behavior because the bully can come back with renewed attacks. And bystanders don't want to change the dynamic because they don't want to get caught up in the drama, become a target, or feel the bully's wrath. That said, bullying needs to stop. It harms students' health and well-being, interferes with their ability to learn, and stunts their social skills development, which will make them off time in adulthood. Bullying is never an appropriate response to any situation.

## What You Can Do to Stop Bullying

Bullying doesn't exist in a vacuum. It happens when kids are trying to find their place in a social structure that tolerates it. Whether you are a target, an adolescent who uses bullying behavior, or a bystander, the common denominator is that antisocial behavior is being used to create, control, and manage relationships.

Instead of tolerating bullying, all members of the triangle need to stop it in its tracks. This won't happen all at once, but if each person does his or her part, the

"In school, kids could tell that I was timid and shy so they teased me. (Especially when I was new at school, of course.) But when I did form friendships, they tended to be close and confiding where I was usually the listener or empathizer. In some ways, my shyness could become an asset in my chosen career (possibly teaching, counseling, or social work). Being shy and introspective makes me more empathetic and nonjudgmental toward others."—nineteen-year-old college student[c]

contentious, abusive atmosphere created by bullying can become a more tolerant and friendly culture.

Here's what you can do to stop bullying:

- Enhance your small talk skills: Targets of bullies like Alex, as well as bystanders and bullies themselves, seem not to have adequate social skills that will help them make friendships in a positive manner. They can be shy like Rashida and Alex or simply not socially skilled. Small talk is probably the most important skill that can be used to prevent bullying. If you are a target, it will help you make connections to other kids, which will make you less vulnerable to bullying. If you are a bully, small talk will help you develop positive relationships, instead of antagonistic ones. And if you are a bystander, small talk can help you provide support to targets, who are isolated and need a helping hand.
- Go to your strengths: A good way to make friends and feel more confident is to engage in an activity that you really enjoy, and to do so with other kids. Take a look at the activity portion of your comfort zone for clues about your strengths. If you like to read, create a book club or volunteer at the library. If you like to watch vampire movies, invite someone to join you. If you like listening to a specific band, make connections with other fans. In this way, you will find more allies and develop your own talents, which will make you more confident and less vulnerable to bullying.
- Find an ally: Bullies like to target kids who are alone and isolated. It's easier to pick on a kid who doesn't have many friends—including shy ones—than one who is surrounded by pals who will protect him or her. If you are a target, find other kids who are like you by taking an inventory of your comfort zone. Like you, your allies may be targeted by bullies. Or they may share your interests, such as riding bikes or playing soccer. Or your allies may be kids who you see all the time, like the ones who

ride your bus. Joining forces with other kids diminishes a bully's power to control a situation.

• Be an ally: If you are a target or are a bystander, you can be another person's ally. Reach out to kids who are targeted to let them know that they are not alone. If you witness bullying, you can help the target by befriending her or joining forces with other bystanders to protect the target from the bully.

• Build empathy: Alex's life as a target ended when his peers watched his experiences in the film *Bully*. Until then, they hadn't considered what he was going through when he was constantly taunted, teased, and attacked at school and on the bus. The next time you encounter a bully, a target, or another bystander, put yourself in his shoes and think about what he is experiencing. Find a way to let him know that you understand him and want to help him become a better person.

• Become an "upstander": Bystanders witness and seem to condone bullying. In contrast, upstanders actively prevent bullying from happening. They don't participate in it. They help targets by befriending them or helping them talk to an adult, or address the bully directly. This isn't easy, but upstanders can find strength if they work with other bystanders to put an end to bullying.[24]

• Don't condone violence: Violent behavior should never be tolerated. If you see a target get hit, slammed, stabbed, kicked, punched, or otherwise physically attacked, you need to be part of the solution. Contact an adult you trust. That can be a parent, a teacher or school administrator, a safety officer, or a bus driver. If you don't feel able to act on it in the moment out of fear of retaliation, address the matter after it happens. What's important is that an adult is aware of the physical violence.

• Make bullying an action item in your school: Bullying can create a poisonous atmosphere in school that affects all students' ability to learn and feel safe. You can create awareness of the problem by starting an upstander club, getting involved in the Bully Project, or writing about it for your

**Try This**

Write down three things you can do to address bullying. Circle the one thing you will do first to put an end to bullying and change the culture of your school.

school newspaper.[25] One independent voice speaking out can create a ripple effect that positively impacts the entire school.

Bullying affects the majority of middle school and high school students in a negative way. Even if you are shy, you can help to solve the problem and create a better atmosphere at school, one that includes all kids in a positive manner.

## How Teens View Social Media

This current crop of teenagers is the first generation to grow up with social media. Parents, teachers, and academics have had a lot of concerns about the influence of social media and the Internet on adolescents' lives, since this new technology has the power to affect so much of our daily lives.

A team of researchers from Common Sense Media decided to ask teenagers themselves about their views of social media, how they use it, and how it affects their own lives.[26] The researchers surveyed 1,000 thirteen- to seventeen-year-olds across the United States, and found a number of eye-opening insights about teens' use of social media.

Nine out of ten teens have used social media platforms such as texting, social networking (like Facebook), e-mail, instant messaging, video chatting, blogging, Twitter, and online gaming, the Common Sense researchers found.

Even though teens overwhelmingly go online, 49 percent of them said that their favorite way to communicate with their friends is in person, while 33 percent said that they prefer texting and 7 percent said it's through a social networking site. Teens who prefer face-to-face interaction said that it's more fun and that you can better understand what other people mean when you're communicating in person.

Half of teens said that using social media has helped their relationships. Only 4 percent said that it's hurt them.

Social media seems to help teens' social experiences and sense of well-being. Almost a third of the teens surveyed—29 percent—said that social networking has made them feel less shy, and only 3 percent of them said it makes them feel more shy. Similarly, 28 percent said it makes them more outgoing, 20 percent said it makes them feel more confident, and 19 percent said that it makes them more popular.

The downsides of social media use are very rare, the researchers found. Only 4 percent said social networking makes them less outgoing, and only 5 percent said that it makes them more depressed.

Social media seem to make adolescents less inhibited. About 30 percent said they had flirted with someone online they wouldn't have flirted with in real life, and 25 percent said they had said something bad about someone that they wouldn't have said in person.

Almost a third of teens say that social media helps them feel less shy.

Although there are solid minorities of teens who said that using social media enhances their social and emotional well-being—including the 29 percent who said it makes them feel less shy—the vast majority of teens said it has no effect at all on their lives, either positive or negative.

A majority of teens said that they "love" posting photos online. But it can cause some anxiety, especially for girls. Girls are significantly more likely than boys to say that they sometimes feel left out after seeing photos of others, worry about others posting ugly photos of them, and get stressed out about how they look when they post photos of themselves.

For teens who feel rejected, depressed, or isolated in their off-line lives, social media use is a mixed blessing. They're more likely than their happy peers

## ? Time for Reflection

How well do you match up with the findings from the Common Sense Media research? Do you use social media more or less than the national average? Does using social media make you feel more or less shy, confident, or depressed? Why do you think that is? Do you feel any anxiety about posting photos online? What do you think causes that anxiety?

to say that social media makes them more outgoing and popular but also more likely to say that it makes them feel more depressed. They are also more likely to feel stressed about posting photos online. The researchers found that these "less happy" teens are more likely to be older and female.

## Shy Teens and Social Media

As you can see from the Common Sense Media research, most teens feel that their lives are not negatively impacted by their social media usage. They seem to accept social media as part of their lives and feel that there are advantages to using it, especially to cement their relationships. That said, there are pros and cons of using social media when you are a shy teen.

### *Benefits of Using Social Media*

Shy teens may like social media for a number of reasons related to overcoming their shyness.

First, shyness is reduced as they warm up. Shy teens, according to the Common Sense Media study, feel that social media makes them less shy. There does seem to be some logic in this. When you are composing a Tweet or posting on your Facebook wall, you can think about your message for a bit and edit it before it is made public. Or you can merely lurk and read without contributing to an exchange of ideas. In many ways, you can think about that time spent as one's warming-up period. Shy teens don't have to immediately publish their text the way they feel they have to be "on" and sociable as soon as they walk into a room full of other people. They can take a breath and consider the best way to express themselves while they are warming up to the task.

Since they give themselves time to warm up, the shy body isn't bothersome. Shy teens may feel more outgoing online because the physical dimension of shyness—the shy body—isn't a factor. No one can see you get nervous, sweaty, blush, or feel fidgety when you are texting, IMing, or Facebooking. This reduces the acute self-consciousness that's so critical in shyness. Your phone or tablet doesn't care if you are nervous, so you won't care, either.

Social media also puts shy teens in control. When you are online, you are in control of your persona and image. You choose your avatar, screen name, the photos you post, and your messages. They can be as close to the real-world truth as you want. So if you are a shy teen and feel limited by the label "shy," using social media can help you put on a totally different persona, with few immediate consequences. You can also post messages anonymously, which allows everyone—shy or not—to be less inhibited. There's a downside to this, of course,

> "It's easier for me to text or Facebook people than to talk to them in person. I don't check myself as much and I'm not as worried about what others will think."—seventeen-year-old high school student[d]

but the anonymity of the Internet can help shy people break out of their social limitations.

In addition, low-level social contact doesn't produce much anxiety. Social media allows shy teens to stay in contact with friends, but at a level of low involvement. Sending a text, liking someone's Facebook post, or exchanging photos allows a shy teen to be connected to others without having to be physically present or become involved in a high-risk social situation, such as a school dance or making a public presentation. Since the social risk is low, a shy teen won't feel as much anxiety about being judged or living up to the standards other people have set.

Lastly, online relationships seem uncomplicated and easy: In real life, you are surrounded by others who are from diverse walks of life. For example, no matter how much peer pressure there is to conform in your school, you and your classmates look different, act different, have different talents and interests, and form different social circles. Online, those distinctions often disappear. When you are interacting with others through social media, you can choose with whom you associate. You "like" your Facebook friends and accept their contact, visit websites and watch videos that reflect your interests, and chat with those who share your interests, no matter how obscure they may be. As a result, you reduce the number of people who make you feel uncomfortable, whom you don't like, or whom you simply cannot relate to and at the same time allow specific people into your social circle. In many ways, you can think about this in terms of your comfort zone. Your growing number of online friends have overlapping interests or activities with you, at least when you are online.

As you can see, using social media has many advantages for shy teens. They feel that they are in control of their relationships and comments and can be more selective about those that they encounter online. They can make connections with others with more ease than in real life. This can make them feel less shy and more successfully shy—aware of their shyness but not limited by it.

### Drawbacks of Using Social Media

Although social media can have some benefits for shy teens, there are some negative aspects as well.

"Sometimes I look at my friends' Facebook pages and I feel like their lives are more interesting than mine. When I want to post something I don't know what to say that will match them."—eighteen-year-old retail clerk[e]

First, social comparison can be turned into competition. When we're viewing our friends' online profiles, we're seeing the image they want to project—a positive one. That can trigger the phenomenon of social comparison, which we use when we're in new situations as a way to figure out how to fit in. Shy teens typically make social comparisons that are biased against them. So when they look at the smiling faces of their friends in selfies, pictures of a great night out, or someone's boasting about a new achievement, shy teens will likely think that they aren't as attractive or successful as their friends. This can make them feel more anxious about posting a picture or commenting or more negative about their own self-worth.

Another serious drawback is that anonymity breeds extremism. Much online content is generated by anonymous writers, typically commenters on videos, blogs, profiles, and pictures. And it's no secret that these comments are often wildly inappropriate if not downright hostile. These comments would be bad enough if they were just posted and forgotten, but they live on long after the page has been read. Even worse, hostile comments can trigger more hostility, which can be what the hateful online commenter wanted in the first place. Shy teens may feel hesitant to comment online, even when they have something very important to say, or they may have a more difficult time brushing off the hostility coming their way.

In addition, truth and honesty can be rare online. We've all heard stories about people assuming completely different identities when they're online. Commonly, this phenomenon is called "catfishing," which refers to someone who puts on a different persona to dupe another person, typically to begin a romantic relationship with him or her.[27] It's natural to want to believe that the person with whom you are communicating is being honest. But it would be better to remain a bit more cautious when you're in contact with someone you only know online. Shy teens, who tend to be more trusting of people they have befriended, could be more likely to be on the receiving end of a catfishing scheme. And shy teens who are using an invented persona online can feel like "shy extroverts," people who feel they can only shake off their shyness when they hide their true selves. A better strategy is to become successfully shy and retain one's true identity while taking steps to reduce the bothersome aspects of their shyness.

What's more, the traditional rules of small talk go out the window. When we're online and chatting with someone we've just met, it's tempting to skip all

> **Time for Reflection**
>
> Write down all of the positive and negative experiences that you've experienced online. How did you react? Did any of these experiences affect the way you felt about yourself or your real-life friendships? What did you do? Would you do things differently now?

of the preliminary steps of small talk and rush to more intimate activities, such as flirting or sharing secrets. But this could be problematic, if someone uses that information to his advantage or is turned off by too much intimate information, too fast. Shy teens who are eager to make a connection with someone else could risk losing a fledgling relationship because they are not letting the relationship develop naturally.

And, finally, online friends can become more important than a real-life social life: Shy teens tend to become more outgoing online, so it's easy for them to prefer chatting with their Internet friends. But this can become problematic if they are replacing their online friends for their real-world relationships. This is especially true for shy teens who believe their personal fable that they are so unique that no one else truly understands them—except for their online friends. While this can give a shy teen a sense of comfort and camaraderie, it can also further isolate them from their real-world peers.

Overall, shy teens have many of the same challenges as more outgoing teens when they're online, but they could experience more of the downsides if they let their online experiences rule their own lives. Shy teens need to remember to keep their online life in perspective and not let it prevent them from forming relationships in their real lives.

## Cyberbullying: When Social Media Turns Toxic

Just like in real life, bullying can occur online. That's because human behavior doesn't change a whole lot when we are online or off-line. When someone is bullied online, it's called cyberbullying, which is repeated taunts, attacks, shaming, or other acts of aggression online or through texts. According to one study conducted in 2010, about 20 percent of eleven- to eighteen-year-olds said that they had been a target of cyberbullying.[28] Some studies indicate that up to 40 percent of teens have been cyberbullied. It seems that the same kids who are involved in bullying in the real world are involved online. They tend to be the same targets, bullies, and bystanders. However, kids who wouldn't bully someone in person can

Up to 40 percent of teens say they've been cyberbullied, or the victim of repeated aggression online.

become cyberbullies because they can alter or hide their identity and don't have to deal with physical differences, such as being smaller or weaker than the kid they are targeting online.[29]

Cyberbullying shares some common traits with real-world bullying. It involves a bully, target, and in some cases bystanders. But cyberbullying has these unique characteristics:[30]

First, the identity of cyberbullies isn't always known to the target. The cyberbully can hide behind anonymity or alter her own identity so that the target doesn't know who is antagonizing her. It's difficult for a target or upstander to put a stop to cyberbullying if she doesn't know the identity of the perpetrator.

Another unique quality of cyberbullying is its ability to go viral. Cyberbullies can send nasty texts or messages directly to their target. Or they can blast embarrassing videos to others, spread rumors online, or forward personal messages to others. When this happens, the target feels even more victimized, because people they don't know can join in and bully them or engaged bystanders.

Unlike bullying, cyberbullying can occur remotely: The cyberbully won't always witness the reaction of his target. This can make empathy difficult to build, and he will be less likely to feel remorse for his actions.

Shy teens aren't necessarily targeted by cyberbullies, but they may be more susceptible to being a victim. If they don't have a lot of friends at school, they will have fewer defenders in the real world and online. If they spend a lot of time online because it's easier than creating an off-line social life, chances are that they will have more opportunities to be cyberbullied. And they may rebound less quickly from an embarrassing video or Tweet than a more outgoing, socially successful peer. The pain of cyberbullying may be more acute for a shy teen than one who can shrug it off and ignore it.

## What You Can Do about Cyberbullying

It's difficult to put a stop to cyberbullying because technology changes so quickly that a cyberbully can adapt and change his or her ways to attack. However, there are things that we can all do to reduce the amount and negative impact of cyberbullying:

- Strengthen your real-world relationships: Cyberbullies are less likely to attack someone who has a lot of friends and allies. And teens with lots of friends won't be so caught up in their online lives that they will blow one or two attacks out of proportion. In this case, the best defense is a good offense.
- Block your cyberbully: If you are receiving mean texts or messages, simply block that cyberbully. This may not eliminate harassing messages, but it can reduce them at least temporarily.
- Don't give in to pressure: A cyberbully may ask you to do something you don't want to do, such as taking a nude photo, meeting him in person, forwarding a mean e-mail, or documenting some embarrassing behavior that can be posted online. Don't do it, and contact an adult or ally for more help. A cyberbully won't have power over you if you refuse to engage in it.
- Stick up for targets: If someone forwards you a nasty message or video about someone else, you don't have to engage in that behavior. You can

delete it, write a message in support of the target, or tell the cyberbully to stop.
- Tell an adult: You are not alone. If you are being harassed online, tell a trusted adult. In some cases, cyberbullying can be a crime. Create a record of your cyberbullying and get help from an authority figure. You can also contact the host of the site or the Internet provider and ask to have that user blocked.

Cyberbullying is a new behavior that is rooted in age-old antisocial behavior. Teens who spend a lot of time online, including shy teens, need to protect themselves from predatory behavior. They can do so by building their real-world social skills and friendships. Bullies and cyberbullies will be less likely to attack someone they know has many friends and allies who will come to the rescue.

Shy teens, like all teens, have to contend with challenges they face in school and online. But no matter how difficult it may seem at times, shy teens—like Rashida and Alex—can become successfully shy and create solid friendships if they learn how to cope with these challenges, become empowered, and live the lives they want to, free of the negative impacts of shyness and antisocial bullies and cyberbullies.

# THE SUCCESSFULLY SHY YOUNG ADULT

When they act on their interest in others, shy teens can navigate their social world with ease. They will develop a circle of friends who accept them, they'll feel comfortable at school, and they'll learn to develop their talents and skills as they become older and wiser.

However, even the most confident teen feels some trepidation about the challenges she'll face as a young adult, such as moving away from home, going to college or tech school, creating a committed relationship, and developing a career. Shy teens may feel more apprehension about these new tasks since they seem so unfamiliar. But as you'll see throughout this chapter, these more adult challenges may be outside of one's comfort zone, but there are plenty of facets that are within it. Once shy teens learn how to identify these familiar aspects, they can feel more confident about expanding their comfort zone and will transform from shy teens to successfully shy young adults.

This chapter will explore how shy teens can tackle some of these common young adult challenges and the strategies they can take to conquering them. As they build up a series of conquests, they will feel less restricted by their shyness and will become successfully shy and confident individuals. Their confidence in a variety of social situations will help them to become global citizens who are comfortable with others, no matter where they are. The world becomes their comfort zone.

## Shalini's Story

Shalini is a sixteen-year-old high school student who struggled with shyness when she was young. She had a difficult time relating to other kids and feeling comfortable around them. Those feelings persisted during adolescence—to a point, at least. After much soul-searching and the determination to conquer her shyness, she's made great strides in opening up to other people and feeling more confident in social situations. Now, she only feels shy when she's with boys she finds to be attractive, a completely natural reaction to being around someone desirable. Shalini is a great example of a successfully shy teenager. Here's what she has to say about being shy:

"In my particular case, I feel my intelligence caused me to be shy up until recently," Shalini wrote to me.

> When I was in grade school and junior high, and even the beginning of high school, many people rejected me. I didn't fit in with the cliques at school and because of that felt awkward and that I didn't belong. This caused me to be shy and hesitant to express my thoughts and opinions. It was only recently that I began to view my intelligence as an asset rather than a restriction or handicap. Now that I have honestly evaluated myself and my abilities, I am very confident and only become shy in certain circumstances and with certain people. In fact, because of my self-assurance, I tend to make others feel shy around me at times. I view that as simply another obstacle to overcome.
>
> My shyness is usually expressed by being quiet and being hesitant to voice my thoughts and when I do, it is usually accompanied with feelings of inadequateness. I experience a temporary loss of confidence and feel that everyone is watching my actions.
>
> It was very difficult for me to make friends and meet new people when I was younger. That led to feelings of low self-esteem. I told myself that no one liked me. I still get shy at times around people I don't know, usually males, which is only natural since I am a teenage female. That sometimes causes me to be more willing to accept their views and opinions—even if I don't agree with them—because of my reluctance to voice my own. I wouldn't want to offend someone I didn't know very well and risk starting our relationships on a bad note. My shyness hasn't gotten in the way of my job. At work, I become very dominant and I usually take things over. It is very easy for me to meet new people at work because of this.

One of the main factors for taming my shyness was my joining high school forensics. It has helped me to feel comfortable in front of people and with myself in general. You meet many different people and get a chance to talk in a low-pressure atmosphere. Another thing was my summer job. I worked a cash register in a food stand at a water park. Just talking with different customers every day showed me how easy it is to start conversations. I feel I am only 10 percent as shy as I was five years ago.

When I was younger, I thought I was sentenced to be shy for the rest of my life. Now I know it is not true. It took a few years and some work on my part, but I rarely feel as shy as I used to. I feel another contributor to conquering my shyness is all of the people I write to around the world. Things are more natural and relaxed when you write an e-mail to someone and I incorporated that into my daily life.[a]

## What It Means to Be Successfully Shy

Shalini's story is so instructive because she knows what it feels like to be shy and how it feels to be in control of her shyness. She's a great example of what it means to be successfully shy, a concept explored in depth throughout this book.

But what does it mean to be successfully shy? As Shalini's story shows, it means being true to yourself. It means feeling shy and awkward at times, perhaps when

### ! Remember This

All teens have the ability to become successfully shy like Shalini (see page 241). That means that they are still shy but in control of their shyness. Successfully shy teens understand how shyness affects their body, mind, and sense of self and make a few changes in their thoughts and behaviors so that shyness doesn't hold them back from living a full life. They act on their natural sense of social interest instead of dwelling on their shy stress reactions. Successfully shy teens understand which social situations trigger their shyness and create a plan for getting through those situations.

you're in a new situation, perhaps when you are talking to a cute guy you want to impress. But instead of feeling that you are doomed to a life of shyness, awkwardness, and anxiety, being successfully shy like Shalini means taking opportunities to stretch your comfort zone and become more self-aware and empowered. With time, being outgoing, relaxed, and self-expressive in social situations—in other words, being successfully shy—is the result.

The key to being successfully shy is to act on one's natural social interest. Remember, shy teens are not introverts. When they are with other people they can hold their own, but they tend to prefer to be on the outskirts of things. They tend to display great arousal to sources of excessive external stimulation, which might appear as feelings of being drained after spending too much time around lots of people for long stretches during social situations, such as a party.[1]

Shy teens, on the other hand, want to be with other people and take action to do so, such as going to the mall, dances, and the park and trying to talk with others they would like to know.[2] What brings out their shy reactions is their belief that they are being judged by others. That makes shy teens feel excessively self-conscious and produces shy stress reactions—the stammering, awkwardness, and tendency to clam up to reduce their nervous tension—that create the approach-avoidance conflict. They focus on themselves and their discomfort rather than on what their partners are saying and doing. It's difficult, if not nearly impossible, to carry on a natural, free-flowing conversation when you are dwelling on your anxiety and racing thoughts.

Successfully shy teens feel these shy reactions to some degree. However, instead of dwelling on them, they refocus their attention and place it squarely on their partner. Instead of thinking the typical shy thoughts of "I'm nervous and sweaty and shaky and everyone can see that I don't belong here and don't have something interesting to say," a successfully shy teen thinks, "I'm excited about this opportunity to talk to people. I want to introduce myself and chat with them and have a good time."

### Try This

The next time you are in a social situation, act on your social interest. Introduce yourself to someone new, use your small talk skills to strike up a conversation, or offer to do something nice for someone else. The more often you act on your social interest, the closer you will get to becoming successfully shy.

Take Shalini, for example. When she worked as a cashier, she probably felt shy at first. She had to learn how to handle her new job responsibilities and talk to her customers. But as she mastered her job tasks, she probably was able to focus more on the customer service part of her job—talking to customers. She likely felt nervous at first and didn't feel like she could contribute much to any conversation. But she found as the days went by that she was able to talk to the many people who crossed her path at work. That's because she was showing genuine social interest in her customers. And as she did so day after day, she strengthened her dominant response to approach people, not avoid them. She focused on her customers, not her discomfort. In this way, she expanded the "people" portion of her comfort zone, which shy people often have difficulty doing.

Shalini's experience at her job is a good lesson for shy teens who want to become successfully shy: Keep developing your social interest, and your shy stress reactions will appear less often and less intensely.

## Successfully Shy Life Lessons for Teens

Another benefit of striving to become successfully shy is that it helps teens take on more difficult challenges that they must conquer if they want to become fully functioning, well-adjusted adults. In many ways, the lessons of shyness are the lessons for life. What you learn about dealing with shyness and social difficulties helps you deal with life challenges that seemingly have nothing to do with shyness. They may involve your academic career, your job focus, your family life, or your self-awareness. That's because all of these challenges require an individual to expand his comfort zone, develop a strategy to cope with it, and continue evolving as a person throughout his life. You can apply the lessons of shyness to your life lessons to increase your odds of becoming successful.

Just as childhood lessons set the stage for the more complex demands of adolescence, the accomplishments of the teen years pave the way for being an independent adult with a vibrant, healthy identity. Some of the teen challenges include dating, coping with high school classes and a more complicated social environment, developing talents you may want to turn into a field of study or career, and acting on your own code of conduct instead of following the crowd.

Shy teens, like shy adults, are slow to warm up to these challenges, even if they don't completely involve social interaction, because shy teens tend to be slow to adapt to new situations.[3] Think of this in terms of one's comfort zone: Shy teens tend to have narrower, more rigid comfort zones than their more outgoing peers. It's more difficult for them to incorporate new people, places, and activities into these comfort zones. Likewise, it's more difficult to incorporate the new adolescent challenges they face, whether it's finding friends in a larger high school or filling out a job application.

Life tasks build on past achievements and become progressively more difficult as we mature and enter new phases in our lives.

Shy teens' natural tendency to warm up slowly to new challenges is fine if they find ways to take on these goals at roughly the same time as their peers. This will provide them with social support and ensure that they are tackling the tasks of adolescence when they should be doing so. Unfortunately, some shy teens take so long to warm up to these challenges that they fall behind their peers and become off time. Sometimes, shy teens will fall so far behind their peers that they may not catch up until they are well into adulthood. For example, "love-shy" men never dated during their teen years and found that going on their first date as an adult was very difficult.[4] Their friends and potential mates likely wondered if there was something wrong with them, since they had little to no experience on a date when they should have had at least one date or relationship at this point in their lives. Some of these love-shy men probably felt so insecure and embarrassed about their off-time dating lives that they couldn't reveal this information to their friends and potential dates. This further isolated them and made them feel negatively about themselves.

Successfully shy teens may feel hesitant about taking on the challenges of adolescence such as dating. However, they utilize their social interest and develop a strategy to approach each challenge in their own time. For example, if they don't feel that they are ready to date, they can go on group dates, double dates, or platonic practice dates so that they gain social experience. Then, when they are

**Time for Reflection**

What do you think are the most difficult challenges of adolescence for you? Do you feel that your biggest obstacles are social, such as dating or making and maintaining friendships? Or are your biggest barriers more task oriented, such as finding a job or a volunteer position or considering what you want to do after you graduate from high school? Or are your challenges more likely to involve your environment, such as moving to a new city, finding your place in a new school, or learning to be more comfortable and at ease in more places, such as the mall, other people's homes, or new neighborhoods. Once you've identified your biggest challenges, do you think you can develop a strategy to conquer them?

interested in pursuing a romantic relationship with someone, they can draw on that experience and feel more confident about their ability to feel comfortable on a date. That's how successfully shy teens develop a strategy and approach social challenges instead of shrinking from them or going into them without any plans or resources at their disposal. In this way, successfully shy teens decrease the amount of risk they must cope with as they pursue progressively more difficult challenges.

## Building on Your Past Successes to Launch into Young Adulthood

In addition to acting on their sense of social interest, successfully shy teens are constantly building on their past successes and creating a greater sense of accomplishment and self-awareness as they do so. This helps them to become more willing and able to take on challenges in the future.

When you think about it, our lives are full of progressively more difficult challenges and tasks that we must master to transition to the next phase of life, and each task or challenge draws on lessons that we've learned in the past. For example, when you were a very young child, you learned how to identify numbers and count. Then, you learned how to add, subtract, and multiply those numbers. Then you learned how to utilize these numbers in more abstract and complex ways in algebra, trigonometry, and calculus. It goes without saying that you couldn't pass a trig exam in high school if you didn't learn how to count when you were very young.

Life tasks, like math, build on past achievements and become progressively more difficult as we mature and enter new phases in our lives. Let's look at school.

When we're very young, we go to day care, preschool, or kindergarten. All of these opportunities for early education present challenges for children. They have to be away from their parents or caretakers, sometimes for the entire day; they must deal with new authority figures; they must learn how to play with other children; and they must complete some tasks, such as building their vocabulary, learning some letters and numbers, and understanding our world. This seems like child's play to us when we're older, but these are genuine challenges for very young children.

The challenges mastered in the early years are built on and set the stage for middle childhood and adolescence. Instead of staying in one classroom for half a day of preschool, older children must spend a full day in a few classrooms, for example. In high school, instead of sticking with our classmates, we have more individualized schedules and must make our way through a bigger school, changing classrooms each period, alone. Later, in college, we spend our days on a much bigger campus, taking classes in different buildings, with different teachers in larger classrooms.

All of us develop the skills to cope with new life lessons as we grow and mature. But shy people, due to their slow-to-warm-up tendencies, may need more time to adapt to these new challenges. They may be held back because they forget about all of their past successes and feel that each new challenge is utterly new, instead of being built on skills that they've already acquired. They may feel that they have to go from a cozy kindergarten classroom to a huge university lecture hall in one leap. This makes their comfort zone seem rigid and thick, as if it's constructed of cement and will be impossible to expand.

Successfully shy teens, on the other hand, are able to identify the foundation life skills they've acquired that can be used to cope with new challenges. Instead

"I was very shy as a kid—shy and extremely neurotic. Every situation scared me if it required my interacting with others. Luckily, I had my twin sister with me a lot of the time and we fed off each other in order to survive through any interaction. After high school, I became much less shy. I consciously made each interaction an 'exercise' in overcoming my shyness. Just talking to people I didn't (or don't) know, hanging out with people without my sister, getting a part-time job, volunteering at different places. I had always been afraid to sing in front of people I wasn't related to but now I sing all the time everywhere. That was a big deal to me."—twenty-one-year-old editorial assistant[b]

> ! **Remember This**
>
> ● Each life challenge draws on previously acquired skills and successes. We are rarely presented with sink-or-swim situations for which we are totally unprepared. The next time you are faced with an obstacle that seems to be too much for you, think about similar situations you've faced and had the resources to conquer.

of thinking that starting a new high school is an overwhelming obstacle, they think, "I learned how to find all of my classes in middle school. Learning the layout and routine of my new high school schedule isn't that much different." When they are faced with their first day on the job at a fast-food joint, they realize that they know how to follow instructions, work as a team member, and make small talk, just as they have many times in the past.

In this way, successfully shy teens are able to draw on their past achievements and acquired skills to take on new challenges that have the power to stymie them. Their self-awareness and self-confidence help them to navigate the new terrain of adolescence and beyond.

## Your Career Starts with an Entry-Level Job

As teens begin showing more independence, they will want to begin working at a part-time job or volunteering for a worthy cause. This is a positive development in many ways, and not only financially. It shows that teens want to explore their career possibilities, learn new skills, be exposed to people from all walks of life, and expand their comfort zone, sense of mastery, and self-concept.

Shy teens are just as interested in finding a job or a volunteer position as outgoing teens. However, they may be slow to warm up to this new challenge because they dwell on all of the downsides of working and doubt their ability to obtain and maintain a job. This is just the shy mind at work and an expression of the approach-avoidance conflict. These moments of anxiety and reticence have nothing to do with a shy teen's ability to work or volunteer successfully.

It's important for shy teens to explore the world of work during adolescence, when all teens are expected to hold down a part-time, entry-level, low-skill job at the bottom of the ladder—the stereotypical "flipping burgers" job. This is when and how each employee learns the skills it takes to be a paid worker. Expectations are low, as long as each individual develops a strong work ethic and takes pride in the job that he does.

Shy teens shouldn't let their fears hold them back from finding a first job or volunteer position. They have the same potential for success as every other teen, even in jobs that require social interaction, such as waitressing.

Research indicates that shy men are more likely to delay starting a career.[5] It's likely that this is an example of their off-time approach to transitioning into a new life phase. While successfully shy or outgoing young adults are exploring more demanding jobs and developing a career that suits their talents and interests, shy workers may still be casting about in a job that isn't fulfilling. That's why it's important for shy teens to begin working a part-time job or secure a volunteer position when their outgoing peers do. Doing so helps them to be on time and thus avoid being penalized for their slow-to-warm-up tendencies.

That said, shy teens may feel apprehensive about looking for a first job.

Applying for the job could seem to be problematic. Shy teens may prefer to apply online, rather than going to the job site and asking for an application or calling the place of employment to see if they are hiring. It's fine to apply for a job online, and many employers prefer or require it. But shy teens may not want to take the next step and follow up with another e-mail, phone call, or in-person visit. They may assume that someone else has been hired or that they won't make a good impression on the potential employer.

The job interview itself might seem to be too difficult. Job interviews make just about everyone nervous, since they are an evaluative encounter and heighten our self-consciousness. The applicant is being judged by the manager and may be

"My avoidance of situations cost me a great many job opportunities. I would put off placing the phone calls to secure an interview, and eventually, when and if I ever got the courage to call, the response was, 'Sorry. The position has been filled.' I heard this way too many times and I know that I am the only one to blame by letting my shyness and my shyness-induced fear control me."—twenty-one-year-old carpenter[c]

asked difficult questions for which he is unprepared. Everyone wants to make a good impression during the interview so that he can win the job. Since shy teens feel more self-conscious than outgoing teens, and feel that they are being judged critically, the thought of doing well on an interview feels impossible.

Some jobs may not seem like a perfect fit for a shy teen. Shy teens may become anxious about the social demands of a job or volunteer position. Many entry-level jobs require the employee to interact with customers, for example, in retail or fast-food jobs or, like Shalini, as a cashier. This challenge, not surprisingly, may feel insurmountable to someone who is not comfortable with strangers or doesn't have a lot of social skills or experience. The thought of interacting with strangers for a four- or eight-hour shift makes her feel anxious and uncomfortable. She may believe that she will never be happy in a job that forces her to work with the public on a regular basis.

Another common obstacle is a shy teen's comfort zone. Shy teens have more narrow and rigid comfort zones than outgoing or successfully shy teens do. Therefore, adding a job or volunteer position—which includes new people, places, and activities—is difficult for shy adolescents. They aren't as adept at breaking down these components into more manageable pieces that they can handle. Shy teens are more likely to take an all-or-nothing, high-stakes approach to expanding their comfort zone. They believe they have to jump from a rather isolated existence into a high-ranking job for which they are unqualified, without taking intermediate steps to ensure that they make gradual, incremental progress along the way.

Finally, shy teens likely know fewer people who can help them find a job. Many if not most jobs are found through personal connections, not by cold-calling an employer. A sparsely populated comfort zone decreases a shy teen's chances of finding a job through a personal reference.

As you can see, all of these obstacles are created by the shy mind. They aren't grounded in reality. Shy teens can be as successful as outgoing teens in the world of work. They are as intelligent, skilled, and willing to work hard as anyone else.

> **Remember This**
>
> ● Shy teens can be just as successful as outgoing teens in any type of job that interests them. Like Shalini, they can enjoy working with the public, even if they feel shy. In fact, a job that requires a shy teen to interact with others will help her become more comfortable with a wide range of people and she'll expand her comfort zone bit by bit.

Shy teens can succeed in any kind of job, even if it requires a lot of social interaction, as Shalini's job does at the water park.

Shy teens can become successful in the work realm if they analyze this challenge in terms of their comfort zone. Remember, just about everything we do in life is based on tasks and talents that we've already mastered. So finding a job and succeeding in it is just like any other challenge a teen must face. Parts of the solution are already included in their comfort zone.

## Why Volunteering Is a Good Option for Shy Teens

Many shy teens may not be able to look for a part-time job. Perhaps they are too young to work, don't have many opportunities in their area, or lack free time in their busy schedules to commit to a job. That's why it's important for them to consider volunteering. Not only does volunteering help to develop a shy teen's sense of responsibility and work ethic, but in many ways it is less stressful than working a part-time job.

When you volunteer, you are giving something of yourself to another person. You are offering your skills and time for free to an organization you admire. This sense of altruism helps you feel positive about yourself and your generosity; it also helps you foster closer relationships with those you help and your community.[6] After all, even if you are just helping out here and there, you are definitely helping someone in need when you volunteer.

There's another reason why volunteering is helpful for shy teens. Volunteering is typically less stressful than working at a paid job. Since you are offering your services for free, you aren't being asked to perform at a high level. You can make mistakes without fear of losing your job. You won't have to shoulder much responsibility. All you have to do is help with a sincere heart and be willing to do the task at hand, whether it's visiting seniors in a nursing home, cleaning up after animals in a shelter, or tutoring a child who's struggling in class.

Shy teens can benefit from volunteering because these unpaid positions help them to develop their talents, perhaps explore some career options, and allow

Volunteering is a good option for shy teens who seek to offer their talents to others in a low-stress situation.

them to make contact with new people in a friendly environment. An inventory of their comfort zones will help shy teens figure out which volunteer position is right for them.

## Tips for Finding a Job or Volunteer Position

Here are some tips to keep in mind when you seek a job or commit to volunteering:

- An inventory of your comfort zone can help you break down the challenge. When you think about it, a job or a volunteer position is just an

**Try This**

Write down the factors in your comfort zone that you think will enable you to find and maintain a job. Do you think you can draw on these familiar resources when you are ready to look for a job?

extension of the rest of your life. It includes people, places, and activities. Some of these components may already be in your comfort zone, while others may be totally outside of it. That said, there are some elements that may overlap. If, for example, you are applying for a fast-food job that seems totally foreign to you, think again. The job requires you to talk to new people, operate a tablet or computerized register, follow directions, cook, and clean. It's likely that you know how to do some of these things already. Focus on these skills when you feel overwhelmed by the thought of applying for a job.

- Consider your strengths. Work is a lot more rewarding and pleasurable if you actually like it and can develop your talents. Take a look at what you like to do and see if there is a job or volunteer position that allows you to rely on your natural abilities. If you like animals, look for a position at a vet's office, pet store, or animal shelter. If you like kids, then babysitting, day care work, or employment in a store or restaurant that caters to children might be the place for you. If you like to be outside, consider a job or volunteer position in a park, a store that sells equipment for the outdoors, or a camp. The side benefit of this strength building is that shy teens feel more confident when they are focused on a task they love. Their shyness melts away when they are immersed in their favorite activity.

- Job interviews are conversations based on small talk principles. Shy teens can improve their chances of performing well during a job interview if they strengthen their small talk skills. Just like small talk, a job interview includes setting talk, involves an expanded discussion about a topic of substance, and respects the rules of reciprocity. The difference is that shy teens won't be in control of this conversation; they will be the receptive one. The setting talk in the interview may include a brief discussion about how the teen found the job opening, a bit about his education or skills, and why he wants the job. The topic itself is likely the job duties, the workplace culture, and pay. The rules of reciprocity require the teen to reveal just the right amount of personal information. The teen shouldn't get too personal ("I only want this job to get discounts on clothes") or seem too distant and unwilling to fully answer questions. For a review of the small talk formula, go to chapter 8.

- Practice makes perfect. Job interviews are difficult for many people, which is why an entire industry has been launched to coach job applicants on how to present themselves. All first-time job seekers, including shy job seekers, feel nervous about making a good impression on a job interview. The upside is that this nervousness can be diminished by rehearsing and preparing for the interview, then getting feedback from someone you trust. (To review how teens should practice for a similar situation, an academic presentation, go to chapter 11.) Job interviews typically include familiar questions that any applicant should be able to answer. For example, a job seeker may be asked, "Why do you want this job?" "Why are you qualified for this job?" "Why should we hire you?" "Can you work the hours that we require?" "What are your strengths and weaknesses?" and so on. If you have a ready answer for these basic questions, you will feel more prepared and confident when you meet the interviewer.

Shy teens can utilize these tips when they are ready to look for a job or volunteer position. Like most job seekers, they may feel nervous or apprehensive about performing well on a job interview. But with practice and a smart strategy, they can allow themselves to shine and land the job of their dreams.

## Your Life after Graduation

The final year of high school can create much anxiety. Upperclassmen are forced to consider their options after graduation, oftentimes when they don't have a lot of information or support. Some teens embrace this challenge. They talk to academic and career advisers, seek out information about colleges or vocational schools, think about what kind of job they would like, and start preparing for life after graduation. Others, of course, aren't so proactive about their postgraduation lives. The thought of leaving the familiar world and safety of high school fills them with anxiety and dread. They can't imagine themselves in college or working a full-time job. This transition into a new life just doesn't seem to be appealing. It seems to be frightening.

Shy teens are more likely to take the latter route. They have more difficulty making these big life transitions and need more time to warm up to them and encompass them in their comfort zone. As with dating, getting acclimated to a new school, and forming individual friendships, shy teens are more likely to be a little off time when compared to their peers.

Once again, this is the approach-avoidance conflict at work. Shy teens are intrigued by their postgraduation life and want to get started (approach) but they

> "I graduate from college in May and fear entering the real world. I think getting a job is very frightening. I just dread those first few months of awkwardness and not knowing how to behave."—twenty-one-year-old accounting major[d]

feel overwhelmed by having to cope with so much that is unfamiliar (avoidance), whether it's attending a college, living in a dorm, joining the military, or getting serious about a career-launching job. Shy teens may feel that all of these goals are overwhelming and totally out of reach and that they'll fail at what they set out to do. They want to cling to their old, familiar lives and resist change. To relieve their anxiety and dread, they procrastinate and don't seek out information or make plans until the very last minute, when their decision seems like a crisis.

Shy teens can make this transition if they look at their options with a fresh perspective and rely on the assets included in their comfort zone. Instead of thinking about all of the new and potentially threatening aspects of postgraduation life, they should focus on all of the common factors shared by their current lives (their comfort zone) and their new lives. In this way, they will realize that they have already mastered, or at least had some experience with, many of the new tasks that will be asked of them. Remember: As we grow and evolve in life, we are constantly building on talents, skills, and knowledge that we've already mastered in the past. We are very rarely presented with challenges that are wholly unfamiliar to us.

Let's take, for example, a high school graduate's transition to attending college away from home and living in a dorm. Many shy teens may feel overwhelmed by this new life challenge because it seems to be completely outside of their comfort zone. However, when you analyze this new life task, you'll realize that there are many assets and resources within your current comfort zone that your new life will require.

The people within your comfort zone are potential aides in your transition to college. Shy teens may fear being socially isolated when they move away to college because they are leaving behind their old friends and lack the skills they need to make new friends. This is a flawed assumption, however. Shy teens may know some individuals who attend their college. They may be able to introduce themselves to their roommate in the dorm before the semester begins. And they can think back to situations in which they have met new people, such as the first day of the school year, their part-time jobs, extracurricular activities, and so on. They can also think about the social skills they possess, many of which are detailed in this book, such as small talk skills and how to introduce themselves, that enable them to meet new people. Lastly, they can realize that about half of their freshman class—and potentially more—are feeling shy and insecure about starting college, too. These are perfectly natural feelings and aren't a sign that they will hate college or aren't suited for it.

The comfort zone's places also have common traits on which a new college student can rely. Although the college a shy student attends may be located in a different, unfamiliar city, the campus is just a bigger version of a high school. A campus includes classrooms, labs, cafeterias, social areas, theaters, libraries, and athletic facilities. Therefore, shy teens already know how to navigate these types of facilities and feel comfortable in them. They may feel that they will get lost or feel alone and isolated on this expanded campus. But they should realize that as they spend time on campus, they will find places that feel familiar—the library, for example, or their dorm. They can seek out information about the campus by visiting the school beforehand and touring it, viewing maps online, and simply spending time exploring it during the semester. Perhaps they can ask their roommate or a classmate to explore campus with them, which turns a solitary activity into a social one and helps a shy teen build friendships.

The comfort zone's activities will also translate well to college. College courses are usually more difficult than high school classes. But they are built on the foundation laid during the high school years. The difference is that college students are more likely to attend large lecture-type classes and work without close supervision, and they must manage their time during the semester so that they can keep up with their daily assignments and work on research papers or other long-term projects. That said, these academic tasks are reachable goals. College professors generally don't assign students impossible tasks. They genuinely want their students to learn and succeed. With that in mind, shy teens shouldn't fear the academic tasks they face in college. If they were accepted by the college they are now attending, that's a good sign that they can keep up with their coursework. They need to draw on the study skills they learned in high school and act on them. For example, they may want to set up a study schedule, join a study group, meet with their professors and teaching assistants, and ask for help when they need it.

As you can see, the new life challenge of attending college shares many common factors with an individual's high school experience. Shy teens shouldn't feel anxious or daunted by how difficult this new life chapter will be. With some self-awareness and smart strategies, they can become successfully shy college students who fully embrace everything college can offer.

## Tips for Creating a Successfully Shy Postgrad Life

While shy teens make need a little more time to transition into life after high school, they are just as likely as more outgoing teens to find success. Here are some tips to help shy teens warm up to their new life circumstances:

- Use the Four I's to solve problems. As discussed in chapter 7, the Four I's are identification, information, incorporation, and implementation. They are basic problem-solving skills that can help you get a handle on any thorny issue you may face. If you are feeling lonely and want to create

While shy teens may need a little more time to transition into life after high school, they are just as likely as more outgoing teens to find success as young adults.

new friendships, you may want to use the Four I's to help you out. Identification of the problem is wanting to find new friends to hang out with on the weekends. Information is finding out where or how you can meet people who share your interests—perhaps by joining a club, volunteering for a cause you believe in, inviting an acquaintance to spend time together, or turning one of your solitary activities into a social one. Incorporation is creating a strategy to achieve your goal. Implementation is acting on your strategy and continuing to focus on your goal even if it may be difficult at times. In this way, you are minimizing your risk and enhancing your chances for success.

- Go back to your comfort zone, then expand it. It's normal to regress and withdraw a bit when you are faced with a seemingly daunting challenge. But don't let yourself become isolated. Take an inventory of your comfort zone and take a factorial approach to expanding it. (For a refresher, go to chapter 7.) For example, if you don't feel like you are meeting enough new people at college, look at the places and activities that are familiar to you, then add new people to the mix. You may feel comfortable studying at the

> "My advice to shy people is to stop worrying about what other people think of you. Don't worry about making a fool of yourself. Other people will admire your courage if you dare to do something new or unconventional."
>
> —nineteen-year-old salon assistant[e]

library, perhaps. Invite someone from your class to study with you or join a social group that's focused on your interests.

- Don't fear failure. It's tempting to withdraw into your shell if you feel that you are doomed to failure. And it's also tempting to be a shy extrovert who charges into every challenge with no strategy other than a high-risk, sink-or-swim approach. But the chances are that if you take small but significant risks, you will eventually reach your goal. Even if you make mistakes along the way, you can alter your strategy so that you will get to where you want to go. It really is true that the biggest regrets in life are the chances not taken, not those that were acted on.

- Remember that you are in charge of your life. When you're in middle and high school, it's normal to use social comparison to try to figure out where you fit in. The upside is that you will learn how to behave so that you don't draw negative attention to yourself. The downside is that you will feel pressured to conform. When you're older and out on your own, you will still use social comparison to fit in, but you will feel more in charge of your life as you, not the group, determine how you will behave. Be less concerned with fitting in and focus more on blazing your own unique path.

Developing a life beyond high school poses many challenges. But it also provides a shy young adult with many opportunities to succeed. No longer held back by their shyness, anxiety, and inhibition, successfully shy individuals can create the life they were meant to live.

## Try This

Write down a goal you want to achieve. Then write down some ideas you can put into action that will help you reach it.

"Perhaps the way to overcome shyness is to do something one really loves, and little by little the shyness will be diminished by the act itself rather than be overcome by oneself. Sometimes I feel we spend too much time worrying about how we look, how we feel. In some ways I feel shyness is good. It humbles us and forces us to listen to others because we are too shy to speak ourselves."—nineteen-year-old college student[f]

## The Successfully Shy Global Citizen

We live in a world with few borders. With just a tap on a computer, Tweet into the void, or plane ticket to a remote location, we are able to explore far corners of the planet and experience the lives of others who, at least on the surface, seem to have little in common with us. This is the world of a global citizen, one who is curious about the world and confident enough to put her stamp on it.

The key to becoming a global citizen is the same key to becoming successfully shy: well-developed social interest. Global citizens and successfully shy individuals are more focused on the people who surround them, rather than themselves. They reach out to others and introduce themselves to make their acquaintances feel more comfortable. They ask questions, seek out interesting people, and aren't afraid to take a risk and stick out a little bit.

As they continue to focus on approaching others, instead of avoiding them, global citizens learn to feel more comfortable in a wide variety of situations. Initiating social encounters becomes their dominant response. They draw on their varied experiences to help them feel confident when they are in a seemingly unfamiliar situation. They are constantly looking out for others, are willing to help when needed, and give others—and themselves—the benefit of the doubt. Their

### Remember This

As you turn to the last page, remember, this is not the end of *Shyness: The Ultimate Teen Guide*, but merely the beginning of your successfully shy life. Good luck and take care.

Best regards,

Bernardo J. Carducci, PhD

Lisa Kaiser, MA

positive attitude and keen social skills draw others to them, including those who are still feeling held back by their shyness.

Shy teens like Shalini and the others who have shared their stories throughout this book have the capacity to be successfully shy young adults and confident global citizens. They can rely on their enhanced sense of self-awareness and the lessons in this book to help them act on their social interest and expand their comfort zone so that it encompasses the entire planet. This is my hope for them. I'm confident that they will create a bright future for themselves that is free from the negative aspects of shyness.

# Glossary

**anxiety:** feelings of apprehension and distress in response to real or imaginary physical or psychological threats

**approach-avoidance conflict:** emotional discomfort created in a situation where there is a concurrent and equally powerful desire to move toward others and also to avoid them

**attributional style:** a pattern of evaluating and coming to the conclusion for attributing the cause(s) of one's own behavior and the behavior of others

**automatic stress reactions:** biological and psychological responses to real or imagined threats that occur without conscious awareness

**bullying:** the repeated and intentional desire to engage in behavior designed to inflict physical and emotional harm on another individual

**bystander:** an individual who is aware of acts of bullying but chooses not to take action to stop it as it is happening and/or to prevent it from happening in the future

**chronically shy:** a subtype of shyness featuring feelings of shyness in a variety of situations over the course of a lifetime

**comfort zone:** a set of social situations, personal relationships, and behavior patterns that create feelings of easiness because of their familiarity

**conversation termination:** the process of ending a conversation with the intention of creating opportunities for future conversations

**cyberbullying:** the repeated and intentional desire to use electronic devices, such as computers and cell phones, to engage in behavior designed to inflict physical and emotional harm on another individual

**disruptive social approach:** a strategy for gaining entry into a preestablished group of individuals by engaging in a series of negative attention-seeking behaviors

**dominant response:** well-learned, easily performed behaviors typically triggered in reaction to stressful situations

**early bloomers:** teens who experience many of the physical changes to their bodies ahead of their peers

**egocentric:** being intensely self-focused and self-absorbed

**empathic listening:** a technique for demonstrating a sense of understanding of what another person is trying to say by paraphrasing the intended meaning in a response to the individual

**evaluation apprehension:** the real or imagined belief that you are being judged by others

**extroversion:** a personality style featuring a preference for social activities with a heightened level of stimulation

**favorite topic:** a subject an individual feels comfortable talking about that has the potential to be used to dominate a conversation when maintained too long

**fear:** an unpleasant and often strong emotional response in reaction to the anticipated or present awareness of danger that is usually accompanied by automatic stress reactions

**fight-or-flight instinct:** the behavioral tendency to respond to an external threat by either attacking or fleeing from it

**Four I's:** a set of four elements in a process for solving problems: identification, information, incorporation, and implementation

**frustration tolerance:** the ability to accept and withstand setbacks to goals when they are blocked or not achieved

**global citizen:** an individual who is genuinely interested in becoming more involved with people, places, activities, and issues that go beyond his or her own limited experiences and has the courage and confidence in his or her ability to meet these new challenges, and whose actions will inspire others to do the same

**group date:** attending a social event with a number of other teens

**highly reactive temperament:** a biologically based tendency to respond with strong emotional and behavioral reactions to external stimulation

**imaginary audience:** believing that everyone else is looking at you

**inhibited temperament:** a biologically based tendency to display behavioral withdrawal from social situations characterized by newness and uncertainty

**introversion:** a personality style featuring a preference for social activities of a more quiet nature.

**late bloomers:** teens who experience many of the physical changes to their bodies after their peers

**love shy:** the tendency to have little romantic experience relative to one's peers

**narcissism:** a tendency to desire to be the focus of the social attention of others

**nature versus nurture:** the debate over the extent to which heredity versus environmental factors determine mental and physical characteristics of individuals

**negative identity:** an identity that is opposite of what others expect

**negative reinforcement:** any action that has an increased likelihood of being repeated as a result of it serving to reduce or eliminate an unpleasant situation

**objective self-awareness:** an increased awareness of one's thoughts, feelings, and behavior.

**off time:** the tendency for individuals to be behind their peers when achieving various personal and social milestones during the life course

**on time:** the tendency to experience major developmental social milestones in life at about the same time as one's peers

**personal fable:** common belief among adolescents that they are special, unique, and invulnerable

**personal introduction:** information offered early in a conversation by an individual about himself or herself for the purpose of helping to generate possible topics of discussion during the conversation

**personality:** the characteristic style of an individual's unique expression of thoughts, feelings, and behaviors across time in response to a variety of situations

**personality disorder:** a rigid pattern of thinking and behaving learned early in life that tends to cause distress for the person and conflict when interacting with others

**pessimistic attributional style:** the tendency of an individual to consistently blame himself or herself as the principal cause for the negative things that happen in his or her life

**physical bullying:** the repeated and intentional desire to engage in acts of physical behavior, such as hitting, pushing, or kicking, designed to inflict physical and emotional harm on another individual

**platonic friendship:** a close, nonromantic social relationship with another individual

**posttopical elaboration:** the process during a conversation by which an individual attempts to extend the current topic of conversation with other related topics

**practice date:** attending a social event with another individual for the purpose of improving one's social skills

**pretopical exploration:** the process during a conversation when an individual makes statements for the purpose of offering possible topics to be discussed during the conversation

**privately self-conscious:** a heightened tendency to engage in internal self-examination

**privately shy:** the feelings of shyness expressed internally in the form of affective and physiological responses

**publicly self-conscious:** a heightened tendency to engage in external self-examination

**publicly shy:** the feelings of shyness expressed overtly in the form of social avoidance and awkwardness and behavioral inhibition

**purpose of adolescence:** according to psychologist Erik Erikson, adolescents must develop a unique, independent identity

**quick talk:** the process by which an individual engages others in brief conversation

**rule of reciprocity:** the tendency to offer personal information at a similar level of intimacy presented by the other individual during a conversation

**self-consciousness:** the tendency for an individual to focus on a sense of himself or herself

**self-critical feelings:** judging and thinking about yourself in negative terms

**self-esteem:** the general sense or overall view of how you feel about yourself

**semiautomatic stress reactions:** conscious biological and psychological responses to real or imagined threats that are repeated so often that they begin to appear with very little conscious effort and awareness

**setting talk:** a strategy for beginning a conversation by focusing on the features of the surroundings shared by others with whom an individual wishes to start a conversation.

**shy extrovert:** a type of shy person featuring the expression of outgoing and bold social behaviors in an attempt to cope with and cover up feelings of shyness

**shy mind:** the characteristic pattern of thinking by shy individuals

**shy narcissism:** the tendency of shy individuals to believe they are the center of the social attention of others

**shyness:** feelings of excessive self-consciousness and anxiety when someone believes he or she does not know how to perform appropriately in certain social situations

**shy rebel:** a type of shy person featuring the expression of behavior that opposes social expectations in an attempt to hide one's shyness

**shy triggers:** certain situations and specific types of individuals that make someone feel shy.

**situationally shy:** a type of shyness featuring temporary feelings of shyness in certain situations

**slow to warm up:** needing an extended period of time to acclimate to the people, places, and behaviors that are outside of a shy person's comfort zone

**slow-to-warm-up temperament:** a biologically based tendency to take an extended amount of time to adjust to and feel comfortable in situations characterized by newness and uncertainty

**small talk:** the process of engaging others in conversation about a variety of nonthreatening topics

**small talk apprehension:** a sense of uneasiness regarding one's ability to make conversation with others

**small talk formula:** a step-by-step guide describing a series of strategic thought patterns and behavioral responses of engaging others in conversations

**social bullying:** repeatedly and intentionally engaging in negative acts of a social nature, such as spreading rumors or excluding another person, to inflict harm on another individual

**social comparison:** the process by which an individual uses others as a source for evaluating himself or herself

**social saliency:** the process by which people focus their attention on the qualities that are important to them and what they feel they are missing

**strategic stress reactions:** planned and practiced responses designed to deal effectively with real or imagined threats

**stress reactions:** the expression of thoughts, feelings, and behaviors in response to real or imagined threatening situations resulting in, in most cases, the failure to respond appropriately

**successfully shy:** a type of shyness in which people are in control of their shyness

**superdate:** a social event with another person that carries the expectations that everything you say and do has to be perfect

**target:** the intended victim of any form of bullying

**temperament:** a biologically based tendency that predisposes individuals to respond with a characteristic style across time and in response to a variety of situations

**transitionally shy:** a type of shyness featuring feelings of shyness during periods of transition

**uninhibited temperament:** a biologically based tendency to display a weak emotional and avoidant response to social situations characterized by newness and uncertainty

**upstander:** an individual who is aware of acts of bullying and chooses to take action to stop them as they are happening and/or prevent them from happening in the future

**verbal bullying:** the repeated and intentional tendency to say things—for example, through teasing, threatening, and name-calling—designed to inflict physical and emotional harm on another individual

**wait-and-hover approach:** a strategy by which an individual lingers at the fringe of a group of people who are engaging in conversation for an extended period of time for the purpose of finding an appropriate opening for entering into that conversation

**Yerkes-Dodson Law:** a principle of motivation describing the relationship between different levels of arousal and performance effectiveness

# Notes

## Introduction

1. Bernardo J. Carducci, Quentin L. Stubbins, and Michael L. Bryant, "Still Shy after All These (30) Years: 1977 versus 2007" (poster presentation at the meeting of the American Psychological Association, San Francisco, August 2007).

## Chapter 1

1. Bernardo J. Carducci, Quentin L. Stubbins, and Michael L. Bryant, "Still Shy after All These (30) Years: 1977 versus 2007" (poster presentation at the meeting of the American Psychological Association, San Francisco, August 2007).
2. Bernardo J. Carducci and DeAnne L. Clark, "The Personal and Situational Pervasiveness of Shyness: A Replication and Extension of the Major Findings of the Stanford Survey on Shyness 20 Years Later" (technical report, Shyness Enrichment Institute, New Albany, IN, August 1993).
3. Bernardo J. Carducci, "Shyness," in *The Encyclopedia of Cross-Cultural Psychology*, ed. Kenneth D. Keith (Hoboken, NJ: John Wiley & Sons, 2013), 1176–78.
4. Bernardo J. Carducci, *Shyness: A Bold New Approach* (New York: HarperPerennial, 2000), 8.
5. Carducci, *Shyness*, 19–29.
6. Carducci, *Shyness*, 79–149.
7. Carducci et al., "Still Shy after All These (30) Years," 1.
8. Carducci, *Shyness*, 7.
9. Susan T. Fisk and Shelly E. Taylor, *Social Cognition: From Brains to Culture* (New York: McGraw-Hill, 2008), 52–56.
10. Spencer A. Rathus, *Childhood and Adolescence: Voyages in Development*, 2nd ed. (Belmont, CA: Thomson/Wadsworth, 2006), 476.
11. Bernardo J. Carducci, *The Psychology of Personality: Viewpoints, Research, and Applications*, 2nd ed. (Hoboken, NJ; Wiley-Blackwell, 2009), 185–98.
12. Erik H. Erikson, *Identity: Youth and Crisis* (New York: Norton, 1968).
13. Carducci, *The Psychology of Personality*, 191.
14. Carducci, *Shyness*, 64–70.
15. Bernardo J. Carducci, "The Personal and Situational Pervasiveness of Shyness for Shy Teenagers" (technical report, Shyness Enrichment Institute, New Albany, IN, August 2013), 2.
16. Rathus, *Childhood and Adolescence*, 523.
17. Carducci, *Shyness*, 112–13.
18. Bernardo J. Carducci, *The Shyness Workbook: 30 Days to Dealing Effectively with Shyness* (Champaign, IL: Research Press, 2005), 34.

a.  Shyness Enrichment Institute Archival Files. Provided by and used with permission of the Shyness Enrichment Institute, New Albany, IN, 2013.

b.  Interview with the author, 2014.

c.  Shyness Enrichment Institute Archival Files.

d.  Bernardo J. Carducci, *The Shyness Breakthrough: A No-Stress Plan to Help Your Shy Child Warm Up, Open Up, and Join the Fun* (Emmaus, PA: Rodale, 2003), 277–87.

e.  Based on the Shyness Enrichment Institute Shyness Quiz. Provided by and used with permission of the Shyness Enrichment Institute, New Albany, IN, 2013.


## Chapter 2

1.  Bernardo J. Carducci, *The Shyness Workbook: 30 Days to Dealing Effectively with Shyness* (Champaign, IL: Research Press, 2005), 54.

2.  Carducci, *The Shyness Workbook*, 22.

3.  Carducci, *The Shyness Workbook*, 84.

4.  Carducci, *The Shyness Workbook*, 46.

5.  Bernardo J. Carducci, *The Psychology of Personality: Viewpoints, Research, and Applications*, 2nd ed. (Hoboken, NJ: Wiley-Blackwell, 2009), 348–49.

6.  Bernardo J. Carducci, *Shyness: A Bold New Approach* (New York: HarperPerennial, 2000), 36–44, 236–37.

7.  Bernardo J. Carducci, *Shyness*, 113.


a.  Shyness Enrichment Institute Archival Files. Provided by and used with permission of the Shyness Enrichment Institute, New Albany, IN, 2013.

b.  Shyness Enrichment Institute Archival Files.

c.  "Shy Celebrities: 15 Stars Who Have a Hard Time Shining in the Spotlight," *Huffington-Post*, December 6, 2012, http://www.huffingtonpost.com/2012/12/06/shy-celebrities-celebrity-introverts-photos_n_2239122.html; "From Shydom to Stardom," *Glamour*, September 20, 2012, http://www.glamourmagazine.co.uk/celebrity/celebritygalleries/2012/09/shycelebrities.

d.  Shyness Enrichment Institute Archival Files.


## Chapter 3

1.  Bernardo J. Carducci and Kaitlin I. King, "All in the Family: A Frequency Analysis of the Self-Perceived Causal Statements of Shyness," *Journal of the Indiana Academy of the Social Sciences* 12 (2008): 97–109.

2.  Carducci and King, "All in the Family," 100.

3.  Jerome Kagan, J. Steven Reznick, and Nancy Snidman, "Biological Bases of Childhood Shyness," *Science* 240 (April 1988): 167–71.

4.  Jerome Kagan, *Galen's Prophecy: Temperament in Human Nature* (New York: Westview Press, 1994), 210–11.

5.  Steven L. Gortmaker, Jerome Kagan, Avshalom Caspi, and Phil A. Silva, "Daylength during Pregnancy and Shyness in Children: Results from Northern and Southern Hemispheres," *Developmental Psychobiology* 31 (September 1997): 107–14.

6. Bernardo J. Carducci, *The Shyness Breakthrough: A No-Stress Plan to Help Your Shy Child Warm Up, Open Up, and Join the Fun* (Emmaus, PA: Rodale, 2003), 87–88.

7. David R. Schaffer and Katherine Kipp, *Developmental Psychology: Childhood and Adolescence*, 7th ed. (Belmont, CA: Thomson Higher Education, 2007), 163.

8. Kagan et al., "Biological Bases of Childhood Shyness," 167–71.

9. Bernardo J. Carducci, Quentin L. Stubbins, and Michael L. Bryant, "Still Shy after All These (30) Years: 1977 versus 2007" (poster presentation at the meeting of the American Psychological Association, San Francisco, August 2007).

10. Stella Chess and Alexander Thomas, *Temperament in Clinical Practice* (New York: Guilford Press, 1986), 34–36.

11. Bernardo J. Carducci, *The Shyness Breakthrough*, 91–92.

12. Lisabeth Fisher Dilla, Jerome Kagan, and J. Steven Reznick, "Genetic Etiology of Behavioral Inhibition among 2-Year-Old Children," *Infant Behavior and Development* 17 (1994): 405–12.

13. Kagan, *Galen's Prophecy*, 163–65.

14. Doreen Arcus and Jerome Kagan, "Temperament and Craniofacial Variation in the First Two Years," *Child Development* 66 (1995): 1529–40.

15. Kagan, *Galen's Prophecy*, 161.

16. Doreen Arcus, "Vulnerability and Eye Color in Disney Cartoon Characters," in *Perspectives on Behavioral Inhibition*, ed. J. Steven Reznick (Chicago: University of Chicago Press, 1989), 291–97.

17. Kagan, *Galen's Prophecy*, 165.

18. Louis A. Schmidt and Nathan A. Fox, "Patterns of Cortical Electrophysiology and Autonomic Activity in Adults' Shyness and Sociability," *Biological Psychology* 38 (1994): 183–98.

19. Carducci and King, "All in the Family," 102.

20. Carducci and King, "All in the Family," 104.

21. Carducci, *The Shyness Breakthrough*, 52–54.

22. Mark Eastburg and W. Brad Johnson, "Shyness and Perceptions of Parental Behavior," *Psychological Reports* 66 (1990): 915–21.

23. Carducci and King, "All in the Family," 105.

24. Doreen Arcus and Kathleen McCartney, "When Baby Makes Four: Family Influences in the Stability of Behavioral Inhibition," in *Perspectives on Behavioral Inhibition*, ed. J. Steven Reznick (Chicago: University of Chicago Press, 1989), 197–218.

25. Carducci and King, "All in the Family," 100.

26. Avshalom Caspi, Glen H. Elder, and Daryl J. Bem, "Moving Away from the World: Life-Course Patterns of Shy Children," *Developmental Psychology* 24, no. 6 (November 1980): 824–831.

27. Bernardo J. Carducci, "Shyness," in *The Encyclopedia of Cross-Cultural Psychology*, ed. Kenneth D. Keith (Hoboken, NJ: John Wiley & Sons, 2013), 1177–78.

28. Carducci, "Shyness," 178.

a. Shyness Enrichment Institute Archival Files. Provided by and used with permission of the Shyness Enrichment Institute, New Albany, IN, 2013.

b. Shyness Enrichment Institute Archival Files.

c. Shyness Enrichment Institute Archival Files.

d. Shyness Enrichment Institute Archival Files.

# Chapter 4

1. Harry Campbell, "Morbid Shyness," *British Medical Journal* 2 (September 1896): 806–7.
2. Bernardo J. Carducci, *Shyness: A Bold New Approach* (New York: HarperPerennial, 2000), 85–92.
3. Monroe A. Bruch and Lesley Pearl, "Attributional Style and Symptoms of Shyness in a Heterosexual Interaction," *Cognitive Therapy and Research* 19, no. 1 (February 1995): 91–107.
4. Charles G. Morris, Albert A. Maisto, and Wendy L. Dunn, *Psychology: Concepts and Applications* (Upper Saddle River, NJ: Pearson Educational, 2007), 304.
5. Naomi I. Eisenberger, "Broken Hearts and Broken Bones: A Neural Perspective on the Similarities between Social and Physical Pain," *Current Directions in Psychological Science*, 21, no. 1 (February 2012): 42–47.
6. Michael Davis, "The Role of the Amygdala in Fear and Anxiety," *Annual Review of Neuroscience*, 15 (March 1992): 353–75.
7. Mayo Clinic Staff, "Chronic Stress Puts Your Health at Risk," Mayo Clinic, http://www.mayoclinic.org/healthy-living/stress-management/in-depth/stress/art-20046037 (accessed August 20, 2014).
8. Bernardo J. Carducci, *The Psychology of Personality: Viewpoints, Research, and Applications* 2nd ed. (Hoboken, NJ: Wiley-Blackwell, 2009), 548–49.

a. Shyness Enrichment Institute Archival Files. Provided by and used with permission of the Shyness Enrichment Institute, New Albany, IN, 2013.
b. Shyness Enrichment Institute Archival Files.
c. Shyness Enrichment Institute Archival Files.
d. Shyness Enrichment Institute Archival Files.

# Chapter 5

1. Bernardo J. Carducci, *The Psychology of Personality: Viewpoints, Research, and Applications*, 2nd ed. (Hoboken, NJ: Wiley-Blackwell, 2009), 465.
2. Carducci, *The Psychology of Personality*. 466.
3. David R. Shaffer and Katherine Kipp, *Developmental Psychology: Childhood and Adolescence*, 7th ed. (Belmont, CA: Thomson Learning, 2007), 477.
4. Spencer A. Rathus, *Childhood and Adolescence: Voyages in Development*, 2nd ed. (Belmont, CA: Thomson/Wadsworth, 2006), 559.
5. Carducci, *The Psychology of Personality*, 466.
6. Monroe A. Bruch and Debra K. Belkin, "Attributional Style in Shyness and Depression: Shared and Specific Maladaptive Patterns," *Cognitive Therapy and Research* 25, no. 3 (June 2001): 247–59.

a. Shyness Enrichment Institute Archival Files. Provided by and used with permission of the Shyness Enrichment Institute, New Albany, IN, 2013.
b. Shyness Enrichment Institute Archival Files.
c. Shyness Enrichment Institute Archival Files.

# Chapter 6

1. Yorman Kaufmann, "Analytical Psychotherapy," in *Current Psychotherapies*, 4th ed., ed. Raymond J. Corsini and Danny Wedding (Itasca, IL: Peacock Publishers, 1989), 119–52.
2. Bernardo J. Carducci, *The Psychology of Personality: Viewpoints, Research, and Applications*, 2nd ed. (Hoboken, NJ: Wiley-Blackwell, 2009), 458.
3. Carducci, *The Psychology of Personality* (2009), 459.
4. Carducci, *The Psychology of Personality* (2009), 459–60.
5. Carducci, *The Psychology of Personality* (2009), 460.
6. Bernardo J. Carducci, *The Psychology of Personality: Viewpoints, Research, and Applications* (Pacific Grove, CA: Brooks/Cole Publishing, 1998), 394.
7. Carducci, *The Psychology of Personality* (1998), 395.
8. Carducci, *The Psychology of Personality* (1998), 395–96.
9. Carducci, *The Psychology of Personality* (1998), 394–95.
10. Carducci, *The Psychology of Personality* (1998), 395.
11. Carducci, *The Psychology of Personality* (1998), 398.
12. Carducci, *The Psychology of Personality* (1998), 395.
13. Carducci, *The Psychology of Personality* (1998), 396.
14. Carducci, *The Psychology of Personality* (1998), 395.
15. Carducci, *The Psychology of Personality* (1998), 397.
16. Carducci, *The Psychology of Personality* (1998), 396.
17. Carducci, *The Psychology of Personality* (1998), 399–400.

a. Shyness Enrichment Institute Archival Files. Provided by and used with permission of the Shyness Enrichment Institute, New Albany, IN, 2013.
b. Shyness Enrichment Institute Archival Files.
c. Shyness Enrichment Institute Archival Files.
d. Shyness Enrichment Institute Archival Files.
e. Shyness Enrichment Institute Archival Files.
f. Shyness Enrichment Institute Archival Files.

# Chapter 7

1. Bernardo J. Carducci, *Shyness: A Bold New Approach* (New York: HarperPerennial, 2000), 18–19.
2. Carducci, *Shyness*, 15–17.

a. Shyness Enrichment Institute Archival Files. Provided by and used with permission of the Shyness Enrichment Institute, New Albany, IN, 2013.
b. Shyness Enrichment Institute Archival Files.
c. Christopher J. Mruk, *Self-Esteem: Research, Theory, and Practice*, 3rd ed. (New York: Springer Publishing Company, 2006), 12–16.
d. Shyness Enrichment Institute Archival Files.
e. Shyness Enrichment Institute Archival Files.

# Chapter 8

1. Phillip Manning and George Ray, "Shyness, Self-Confidence, and Social Interaction," *Social Psychology Quarterly* 56, no. 3 (September 1993): 178–92.
2. Bernardo J. Carducci, Ariel Fuchs, Marilyn G. Wagner, and Mervil Carmickle, "How Shy Teens Deal with Shyness: Strategic and Gender Differences" (poster presentation at the annual meeting of the American Psychological Association, Toronto, August 2013), 3.
3. Bernardo J. Carducci, *The Pocket Guide to Making Successful Small Talk: How to Talk to Anyone, Anytime, Anywhere, about Anything* (New Albany, IN: Pocket Guide Publishing, 1999), 5.
4. Carducci et al., "How Shy Teens Deal with Shyness," 3.
5. Manning and Ray, "Shyness, Self-Confidence, and Social Interaction," 178–92.
6. Carducci, *The Pocket Guide to Making Successful Small Talk*, 25–40.
7. Carducci, *The Pocket Guide to Making Successful Small Talk*, 41.
8. Carducci, *The Pocket Guide to Making Successful Small Talk*, 49–50.

a. Shyness Enrichment Institute Archival Files. Provided by and used with permission of the Shyness Enrichment Institute, New Albany, IN, 2013.
b. Shyness Enrichment Institute Archival Files.
c. Shyness Enrichment Institute Archival Files.
d. Shyness Enrichment Institute Archival Files.

# Chapter 9

1. Erik H. Erikson, *Identity: Youth and Crisis* (New York: Norton, 1968).
2. Spencer A. Rathus, *Childhood and Adolescence: Voyages in Development*, 2nd ed. (Belmont, CA: Thomson/Wadsworth, 2006), 523.
3. Rathus, *Childhood and Adolescence*, 547–48.
4. David G. Myers, *Social Psychology*, 7th ed. (New York: McGraw-Hill, 2008), 39.
5. Rathus, *Childhood and Adolescence*, 558.
6. Rathus, *Childhood and Adolescence*, 558.
7. Rathus, *Childhood and Adolescence*, 558.
8. Kenneth H. Rubin, "Nonsocial Play in Preschoolers: Necessary Evil?" *Child Development* 53, no. 3 (June 1982): 651–57.
9. Kenneth A. Dodge, David C. Schlundt, Iris Schocken, and Judy D. Delugach, "Social Competence and Children's Sociometric Status: The Role of Peer Group Entry Strategies," *Merrill-Palmer Quarterly* 29, no. 3 (June 1983): 309–36.
10. Bernardo J. Carducci, *The Psychology of Personality: Viewpoints, Research, and Applications* (Pacific Grove, CA: Brooks/Cole Publishing, 1998), 167–68.

a. Shyness Enrichment Institute Archival Files. Provided by and used with permission of the Shyness Enrichment Institute, New Albany, IN, 2013.
b. Shyness Enrichment Institute Archival Files.
c. Shyness Enrichment Institute Archival Files.
d. Shyness Enrichment Institute Archival Files.
e. Shyness Enrichment Institute Archival Files.

# Chapter 10

1. Erik H. Erikson, *Childhood and Society*, 2nd ed. (New York: Norton, 1963).
2. Spencer A. Rathus, *Childhood and Adolescence: Voyages in Development*, 2nd ed. (Belmont, CA: Thomson/Wadsworth, 2006), 559.
3. Bernardo J. Carducci, Kristen D. Ragains, Kathy L. Lee, and Michael R. Johnson, "Identifying the Pains and Problems of Shyness: A Content Analysis" (poster presentation at the Annual Meeting of the American Psychological Association, San Francisco, August 1998), 8.
4. Carducci et al., "Identifying the Pains and Problems of Shyness," 8.
5. Avshalom Caspi, Daryl J. Bem, and Glen H. Elder Jr., "Continuities and Consequences of Interactional Styles across the Life Course," *Journal of Personality* 57, no. 2 (June 1989): 400.
6. Caspi et al., "Continuities and Consequences," 400.
7. Brian G. Gilmartin, "Peer Group Antecedents of Severe Love-Shyness in Males," *Journal of Personality* 55, no. 3 (September 1987): 467.
8. Douglas T. Kendrick, Steven L. Neuberg, and Robert B. Cialdini, *Social Psychology: Unraveling the Mystery*, 3rd ed. (Boston: Pearson Education, 2005), 190.
9. Rathus, *Childhood and Adolescence*, 559.
10. David M. Buss, *Evolutionary Psychology: The New Science of the Mind*, 3rd ed. (Boston: Pearson Education, 2008), 356–60.
11. Buss, *Evolutionary Psychology*, 107–10.
12. David R. Shaffer and Katherine Kipp, *Developmental Psychology: Childhood and Adolescence*, 7th ed. (Belmont, CA: Thomson Learning, 2007), 222.
13. Shaffer and Kipp, *Developmental Psychology*, 214–15.
14. Philip G. Zimbardo, "What Is the Demise of Guys?" in The Demise of Guys (DoGs): What It Is; What We Can Do About It—Teaching Young DoGs New Tricks, chaired by B. J. Carducci (presentation in a symposium conducted at the 2013 meeting of the American Psychological Association, Honolulu, Hawaii, August 2013).
15. Shaffer and Kipp, *Developmental Psychology*, 223.
16. Shaffer and Kipp, *Developmental Psychology*, 223.
17. Shaffer and Kipp, *Developmental Psychology*, 223.
18. Shaffer and Kipp, *Developmental Psychology*, 223.
19. Gary J. Gates, "How Many People Are Lesbian, Gay, Bisexual, and Transgender?" The Williams Institute, April 2011, http://williamsinstitute.law.ucla.edu/research/census-lgbt-demographics -studies/how-many-people-are-lesbian-gay-bisexual-and-transgender/ (accessed September 16, 2014).
20. Rowland S. Miller and Daniel Perlman, *Intimate Relationships*, 5th ed. (New York: McGraw-Hill, 2009), 93–94.
21. Miller and Perlman, *Intimate Relationships*, 89–90.

a. Shyness Enrichment Institute Archival Files. Provided by and used with permission of the Shyness Enrichment Institute, New Albany, IN, 2013.
b. Shyness Enrichment Institute Archival Files.
c. Shyness Enrichment Institute Archival Files.

# Chapter 11

1. David R. Shaffer and Katherine Kipp, *Developmental Psychology: Childhood and Adolescence*, 7th ed. (Belmont, CA: Thomson Learning, 2007), 636.
2. Bernardo J. Carducci, *Shyness: A Bold New Approach* (New York: HarperPerennial, 2000), 232–33.
3. Carducci, *Shyness*, 38–44.
4. National Institute of Mental Health, "Fear of Public Speaking Statistics," Statistic Brain, 2013, http://www.statisticbrain.com/fear-of-public-speaking-statistics/ (accessed September 19, 2014).
5. Spencer A. Rathus, *Childhood and Adolescence: Voyages in Development*, 2nd ed. (Belmont, CA: Thomson/Wadsworth, 2006), 533.

a. Shyness Enrichment Institute Archival Files. Provided by and used with permission of the Shyness Enrichment Institute, New Albany, IN, 2013.
b. Shyness Enrichment Institute Archival Files.
c. Shyness Enrichment Institute Archival Files.
d. Shyness Enrichment Institute Archival Files.
e. National Institute of Mental Health, "Fear of Public Speaking Statistics."


# Chapter 12

1. NoBullying.com, "The Essential Guide to Bullying Statistics 2014 and Recent Bullying Percentages," 2014, http://nobullying.com/bullying-statistics-2014/ (accessed September 20, 2014).
2. U.S. Department of Health and Human Services, "Be More Than a Bystander," Stopbullying.gov, 2014, http://www.stopbullying.gov/respond/be-more-than-a-bystander/index.html (accessed September 20, 2014).
3. U.S. Department of Health and Human Services, "Bullying Definition," Stopbullying.gov, 2014, http://www.stopbullying.gov/what-is-bullying/definition/index.html (accessed September 20, 2014).
4. U.S. Department of Health and Human Services, "Cyberbullying," Stopbullying.gov, 2014, http://www.stopbullying.gov/cyberbullying/index.html (accessed September 20, 2014).
5. Cindy Miller and Cynthia Lowen, *The Essential Guide to Bullying Prevention and Intervention: Protecting Children and Teens from Physical, Emotional, and Online Bullying* (New York: Alpha Books, 2012), 4.
6. Miller and Lowen, *The Essential Guide to Bullying Prevention and Intervention*, 6–7.
7. Miller and Lowen, *The Essential Guide to Bullying Prevention and Intervention*, 5.
8. Catherine P. Bradshaw, Anne L. Sawyer, and Lindsey M. O'Brennan, "Bullying and Peer Victimization at School: Perceptual Differences between Students and School Staff," *School Psychology Review* 36, no. 3 (September 2007): 372–73, cited in U.S. Department of Health and Human Services, "Facts about Bullying," Stopbullying.gov, 2014, http://www.stopbullying.gov/news/media/facts/ (accessed September 21, 2014).
9. Bradshaw et al., "Bullying and Peer Victimization at School," 370–71.
10. Bradshaw et al., "Bullying and Peer Victimization at School," 372.

11. *Bully*, the Weinstein Company, 2012.
12. U.S. Department of Health and Human Services, "Risk Factors," Stopbullying.gov, 2014, http://www.stopbullying.gov/at-risk/factors/index.html (accessed September 25, 2014).
13. U.S. Department of Health and Human Services, "Effects of Bullying," Stopbullying .gov, 2014, http://www.stopbullying.gov/at-risk/effects/index.html (accessed September 25, 2014).
14. Mayo Clinic Staff, "Chronic Stress Puts Your Health at Risk," Mayo Clinic, http://www .mayoclinic.org/healthy-living/stress-management/in-depth/stress/art-20046037 (accessed September 25, 2014).
15. U.S. Department of Health and Human Services, "Effects of Bullying."
16. U.S. Department of Health and Human Services, "Effects of Bullying."
17. Ronald J. Comer, *Abnormal Psychology*, 6th ed. (New York: Woth Publishers, 2007), 236–38.
18. U.S. Department of Health and Human Services, "Effects of Bullying."
19. Miller and Lowen, *The Essential Guide to Bullying Prevention and Intervention*, 28.
20. Mathangi Subramanian, *Bullying: The Ultimate Teen Guide* (Lanham, MD: Rowman & Littlefield, 2014), 11–21.
21. Miller and Lowen, *The Essential Guide to Bullying Prevention and Intervention*, 31.
22. Miller and Lowen, *The Essential Guide to Bullying Prevention and Intervention*, 28–31.
23. Miller and Lowen, *The Essential Guide to Bullying Prevention and Intervention*, 58–61.
24. Miller and Lowen, *The Essential Guide to Bullying Prevention and Intervention*, 189.
25. Miller and Lowen, *The Essential Guide to Bullying Prevention and Intervention*, 189.
26. Common Sense Media, "Social Media, Social Lives: How Teens View Their Digital Lives," 2014, https://www.commonsensemedia.org/research/social-media-social-life-how-teens -view-their-digital-lives (accessed September 25, 2014).
27. Viacom, "Catfish: The TV Show," 2014, http://www.mtv.com/shows/catfish/ (accessed September 25, 2014).
28. Sameer Hinduja and Justin W. Patchin, "Cyberbullying Identification, Prevention, and Response," Cyberbullying Research Center, 2011, http://cyberbullying.us/cyberbullying- prevention-and-response-expert-perspectives-2/ (accessed September 25, 2014).
29. Miller and Lowen, *The Essential Guide to Bullying Prevention and Intervention*, 105.
30. Hinduja and Patchin, "Cyberbullying Identification, Prevention, and Response."

a. Shyness Enrichment Institute Archival Files. Provided by and used with permission of the Shyness Enrichment Institute, New Albany, IN, 2013.
b. Shyness Enrichment Institute Archival Files.
c. Shyness Enrichment Institute Archival Files.
d. Shyness Enrichment Institute Archival Files.
e. Shyness Enrichment Institute Archival Files.

# Chapter 13

1. Bernardo J. Carducci, *The Psychology of Personality: Viewpoints, Research, and Applications*, 2nd ed. (Hoboken, NJ: Wiley-Blackwell, 2009), 348–50.
2. Bernardo J. Carducci, Ariel Fuchs, Marilyn G. Wagner, and Mervil Carmickle, "How Shy Teens Deal with Shyness: Strategic and Gender Differences" (poster presentation at the annual meeting of the American Psychological Association, Toronto, August 2003), 5.

3.  Bernardo J. Carducci, *Shyness: A Bold New Approach* (New York: HarperPerennial, 2000), 64–70.

4.  Brian G. Gilmartin, "Peer Group Antecedents of Severe Love-Shyness in Males," *Journal of Personality* 55, no. 3 (September 1987): 467.

5.  Avshalom Caspi, Glen H. Elder Jr., and Daryl J. Bem, "Moving Away from the World: Life-Course Patterns of Shy Children," *Developmental Psychology* 24, no. 6 (November 1988): 824.

6.  Carducci, *The Psychology of Personality*, 163.

---

a.  Shyness Enrichment Institute Archival Files. Provided by and used with permission of the Shyness Enrichment Institute, New Albany, IN, 2013.

b.  Shyness Enrichment Institute Archival Files.

c.  Shyness Enrichment Institute Archival Files.

d.  Shyness Enrichment Institute Archival Files.

e.  Shyness Enrichment Institute Archival Files.

f.  Shyness Enrichment Institute Archival Files.

# Selected Resources for Teens

## Books

Carducci, Bernardo J. *The Pocket Guide to Making Small Talk: How to Talk to Anyone, Anytime, Anywhere, about Anything*. New Albany, IN: Pocket Guide Publishing, 1999.

Carducci, Bernardo J. *Shyness: A Bold New Approach*. New York: HarperPerennial, 2000.

Carducci, Bernardo J., with Teesue H. Fields. *The Shyness Workbook for Teens*. Champaign, IL: Research Press, 2007.

Miller, Cindy, and Cynthia Lowen. *The Essential Guide to Bullying Prevention and Intervention: Protecting Children and Teens from Physical, Emotional, and Online Bullying*. New York: Alpha Books, 2012.

Subramanian, Mathangi. *Bullying: The Ultimate Teen Guide* (It Happened to Me). Lanham, MD: Rowman & Littlefield, 2014.

## Websites

The Bully Project, thebullyproject.com.

The Shyness Research Institute, www.ius.edu/shyness/index.html.

Stop Bullying, stopbullying.gov.

## Movies

*Bully*, the Weinstein Company, 2012.

# Index

# About the Authors

**Bernardo J. Carducci** (PhD, Kansas State University, 1981) has taught at Indiana University Southeast for the past thirty-four years. Carducci is a full professor of psychology and director of the Shyness Research Institute at Indiana University Southeast and a Fellow of the American Psychological Association. He is the author of *The Pocket Guide to Making Successful Small Talk: How to Talk to Anyone, Anytime, Anywhere, about Anything* (1999), an easy-to-use summary of the techniques for mastering the art of conversation; *Shyness: A Bold New Approach* (2000), a popular-press book offering strategies for controlling shyness in adults and children, which has been translated into eight languages; *The Shyness Breakthrough: A No-Stress Plan to Help Your Shy Child Warm Up, Open Up, and Join the Fun* (2003), a parent-guided program for helping children of all ages to develop critical social skills; *The Shyness Workbook: 30 Days to Dealing Effectively with Shyness* (2005), a concise, self-directed program for helping shy adults help themselves to develop a personalized plan for understanding and managing their shyness; *The Shyness Workbook for Teens* (with Teesue H. Fields, 2007), a self-guided program for teens to help them gain control over their shyness; and *The Psychology of Personality: Viewpoints, Research, and Applications*, third edition (2015), a college-level textbook. In addition to his multiple appearances on ABC's *Good Morning America* and other national and international media services, including the BBC, Professor Carducci's writings and advice have been featured in such diverse sources as *Psychology Today*, *U.S. News and World Report*, *USA Weekend* magazine, *Vogue*, *Allure*, *YM*, *TWA Ambassador* magazine, *Glamour*, *JET*, *Parenting* magazine, WebMD, MSNBC.com, *Walking* magazine, *Good Housekeeping*, *Essence*, *Child* magazine, *Reader's Digest*, *Patents*, *Redbook*, *Real Simple*, *Cosmopolitan*, *First for Women* magazine, the *Futurist*, *Entrepreneur*, *Fitness* magazine, the *Chronicle of Higher Education*, the *Chicago Tribune*, the *Wall Street Journal*, the *Times of London*, the *Los Angeles Times*, and the *New York Times*, to name just a few.

**Lisa Kaiser** earned her BA and MA at the University of Wisconsin, Madison in journalism and political science. She has collaborated with Bernardo J. Carducci on a number of projects, including *Shyness: A Bold New Approach* (2000) and *The Shyness Breakthrough* (2003). She is a journalist in Milwaukee, Wisconsin.